Counting People

a DIY Manual
for Local and Family Historians

John S. Moore

Oxbow Books
Oxford & Oakville

Published by
Oxbow Books, Oxford

© John S. Moore 2013

ISBN 978-1-84217-480-7

This book is available direct from

Oxbow Books, Oxford, UK
(Phone: 01865-241249; Fax: 01865-794449)

and

The David Brown Book Company
PO Box 511, Oakville, CT 06779, USA
(Phone: 860-945-9329; Fax: 860-945-9468

or from our website
www.oxbowbooks.com

A CIP record for this book is available from the British Library

Library of Congress Cataloging-in-Publication Data

Moore, John S. (John Scott), 1937-
  Counting people : a DIY manual for local and family historians / John S. Moore. -- 1st
Edition.
       pages cm
  Includes bibliographical references and index.
  ISBN 978-1-84217-480-7
1. Great Britain--Population--History. 2. Great Britain--Population--History--Sources. 3.
Population--History--Methodology. I. Title.
  HB3583.M66 2013
  304.60941--dc23
                              2013011017

Front cover: Compilation of the Domesday Book by Pat Nicolle
© Look and Learn. Reproduced by permission.

In memory of my father-in-law

David Thomas Jones

A lover of old Bristol

and of my much loved mother-in-law

Florence Rose Jones

Contents

List of figures   vi

Preface   vii

Abbreviations   viii

Introduction   x

Chapter 1. The agenda of local population history   1

Chapter 2. Sources and methods   27

Chapter 3. The study of medieval populations   49

Chapter 4. English population history, 1538–1837   82

Chapter 5. The registration era, 1801–2011   116

Chapter 6. Researching, writing, publishing   135

Appendix: A Case Study: the population of
Frampton Cotterell (Gloucs), 1086–1801   157

Bibliography   163

Index   221

List of Figures

Figure 1   A medieval extent: Frampton Cotterell in 1321

Figure 2   Commonwealth Church Survey of Frampton Cotterell, 1650

Figure 3   An early modern manorial survey: Frampton Cotterell in 1547

Preface

In this book I have tried to show how you can acquire an understanding of local history, and particularly those aspects where some mathematical knowledge is essential. The study of local population is the obvious candidate, but occupational and social structure, agriculture, housing and the standard of living are other topics where an ability to count is essential for a full understanding of the subject. Equally, of course, there are other aspects where counting is unnecessary and misleading. Religion is the obvious topic where, apart from attendance at church or chapel, the historian, like Queen Elizabeth I, can 'make no windows into men's souls'; human characteristics like love and affection are others which cannot be weighed, despite Shakespeare's Cleopatra asking 'If it be love indeed, tell me how much.' I hope very much that you will find this book interesting and helpful in your own investigation of your local history.

As with all my publications, I am grateful to my former colleagues in the department of Historical Studies in the School of Humanities, University of Bristol, for their interest, support and friendship over many years. I must also thank the Inter-Library Loan section of the University Library for all their efforts on my behalf. Special thanks are due to Ann Legg, Supervisor in the Library, for easing my way through difficulties with the Library computer catalogue. Finally, I must thank my family and friends for their help, support and encouragement over many years. It was sad that my father-in-law David Jones died soon after this book was started, followed by his widow Rose as proofs were being read. Special thanks are due to the members of the Frampton Cotterell and District Local History Society over 40 years for inspiring and encouraging my efforts to stimulate local history as a communal activity.

John S. Moore, BA, FSA, FRHistS
(Senior Research Fellow, University of Bristol)
1 June 2012

Abbreviations

Antiq.	Antiquarian
Arch.	Archaeological
C.	Century
c.	*circa* (about)
Comm.	Commissioners
CP	Common Pleas
CUP	Cambridge University Press
DL	Duchy of Lancaster
E	Exchequer
Econ. Hist. Rev.	*Economic History Review*
ed/eds	editor(s)
edn	edition
et al.	and others (authors or editors)
Hist.	Historical
HMSO	Her/His Majesty's Stationary Office
Ibid.	the immediately preceding reference
KB	King's Bench
LPS	*Local Population Studies*
MUP	Manchester University Press
n.	note
n.p.	no place [of publication]
NS	New Series
OS	Old Series
OUP	Oxford University Press
P	Press

p(p)	page(s)
PC	personal computer
PCC	Prerogative Court of Canterbury
PRO	Public Record Office, London
PROB	Prerogative Court of Canterbury records
pt	part
Rec.	Record
Rec. Comm.	Record Commission
rev.	revised
Roy.	Royal
Ser.	Series
Soc.	Society
SP	State Papers
TNA	National Archives, Kew
Trans.	Transactions
UP	University Press
vol.(s)	volume(s)

Introduction

This book is not written for my fellow professional historians (who should know it all anyway), but for undergraduate and postgraduate students wishing to study local populations and for those local people, not professional historians but interested in history, who want to know more about the number of people in a particular area at some time in the past, how and why that number changed over time, what jobs these people had, the structure of their society and its constituent households and families. I have tried to answer the questions put to me over 40 years of academic life by undergraduates writing third-year dissertations, by postgraduates researching theses for higher degrees, by members of Workers' Educational Association classes and extra-mural groups, by members of local history societies like my own at Frampton Cotterell (Gloucs), by 'family historians' who want to know more about the communities and societies in which their ancestors lived, and by anyone who is interested in the past history of England (and Wales) at local level. I say England and Wales advisedly because for most of the period from the 1530s onwards the system of English local administration and the records it generated operated in both countries (though Wales does have some special problems). Scotland before 1707 was an independent country with a different legal and administrative system (which has continued after 1707) and therefore producing different record sources: it would require an entire, different book to cover both its population history and local history. Ireland again is another country, and one in which much of its history is difficult to write because of persistent religious differences since the Reformation and the destruction of most of its central government and church records in 1916–22.

In Chapter 1 I try to outline what are the problems and questions that we need to consider in researching the history of any area, including its population history, from a single parish to a county or town. Chapter 2 looks at the principal approaches to answering these questions, the main methods to be applied and the chief sources to be used. Chapter 3 considers the Middle Ages, 'the dark ages of English population history', from the Domesday Survey of 1086 to the Tudor 'Military Survey' of 1522 and the Lay Subsidies of 1524–45, and Chapter 4 deals with the period from 1538 to 1837 when parish registers are the main source for English population history. Chapter 5 studies the period from 1801 when the official Census every 10 years provides a reliable outline of demographic developments. These can be expanded by means of the birth, marriage and death details collected since 1837 by the Registrar General (now by the Office of Censuses) and by the detailed census returns surviving from 1841 onwards. It is also a time of great change in most localities reflected in more abundant documentation, much of which is in print. Chapter 6 tries to suggest ways of studying the subject, recording the results and circulating them to other interested people. I have put this chapter last because writing and publishing are the end-products of the process, but there is much to be said for reading the last chapter first if you are a beginner.

I have tried not to assume any expertise in my readers apart from a genuine interest in the subject and, preferably, the ability to use a personal computer (PC), though an electric typewriter and an electronic calculator will suffice for many purposes. In particular, as one who struggled to pass 'O' Level mathematics in the 1950s, I have not assumed any arithmetical expertise, though it is obviously impossible to study historical demography or many other aspects of local history without using numbers. I beg you not to be frightened by numbers: they are a useful way of summarising some aspects of the past; equally, do not be conned by claims of spurious statistical precision or the arrogant assumption that only what can be counted is worth knowing. Nor, I hope, have I assumed deep historical knowledge: but the undergraduates and postgraduates among my readers are likely to have a fair knowledge of at least some periods of English history, and it is perfectly possible for the interested learner to find out about his or her place of interest in the past: hence the increasing transformation of 'genealogy' into 'family history' as people want to know more about not just their ancestors but the communities in which these ancestors lived. I have provided details of printed sources, guides to unprinted sources, and useful further reading in the bibliography: shortened titles are used in the notes. The bibliography is *not* a compulsory reading list to be studied with a penalty for failure: it is there to help you when you want to know more, to consider where to go next. I have tried to illustrate topics where possible by using my own researches over the years, locally first in Laughton (Sussex), then in Keele (Staffs) and lastly in Frampton Cotterell (Gloucs), as well as nationally, in a study of influenza in the mid-Tudor period. At least I cannot be accused of preaching what I have not tried to practise! I hope you will enjoy this book and find it useful to you in studying your area in the past. If you do, I shall have succeeded in my task.

CHAPTER I

Agenda for Local History

....

Why count?

First of all, let's consider the question, why count at all? Can one argue, as for example David Crouch has done, that 'calculating numbers of all sorts of things in the Middle Ages has long been an English obsession'?[1] Obviously everyone will deplore obsessive counting as pointless and time-consuming, as indeed is any activity taken to extremes, but counting is nonetheless useful and often vital to researching and writing any branch of history. Why is this so? Why is it so important for historians of every place (whatever its size) to know the size and composition of the local population as precisely as they can? The answer lies partly in the nature of the ordinary language we must use if we want to avoid using numerical indicators of quantity: words such as 'great', 'large' and 'small', 'majority', 'some', 'many', 'most', are all valid words which can nevertheless be understood by different writers and readers in different ways, especially in comparative terms. When we write that this place A is larger than that place B, do we mean 'larger' in terms of area, or of population, or of wealth, or of some other parameter? By contrast, to say that, at a given time, place X has one-tenth the population of London, or that place Y has just over 10,000 people in it at this time, is to convey an accurate idea of the size of both these places without descending to the misleading pseudo-exactitude of final digits or of numbers with multiple decimal places.

The original data, whether these are contemporary figures or modern estimates and calculations, are bound to have some degree of latitude or error, and comparative calculations will merely increase the margins of error. We need to be as precise as possible which means only as precise as the nature of the original data will permit. As E. A. Wrigley pointed-out 45 years ago:

'Other demographic measurements including modern censuses give an impression of accuracy which is spurious. One ought perhaps to replace the last four or five digits of any totals of British population with noughts to underline the wide margins of error of any census figures.'[2]

We therefore always need to ask why contemporaries tried to establish certain facts, how they arrived at their figures, and what these meant to them, before we can then go on to enquire if their efforts are useful to us. We must never forget that exact numbers are likely to convey an impression of precision which is quite misleading.

'Numbering the people' in the past

Although there were no national censuses as such in medieval or early modern England, officials and administrators were nevertheless interested in 'numbering the people'. Such information was relevant to the concerns of both national government and to lords at local levels. On the number of people depended the amount of direct taxes to be obtained by the king's government and the number of men who could be recruited for military service or building services at home or abroad, and the amount of rent and labour services to be received by landlords, both the landed aristocracy and higher clergy, who dominated local rural society for many centuries, and their urban counterparts. In a negative sense, the number of people, if they were poor and hungry, sick or unemployed, posed crucial problems to contemporary governments because such people were a potential or actual threat to public order, as the Peasants' Revolt of 1381 and Jack Cade's rebellion in 1450 both demonstrated.[3] Locally, rates on occupiers had been levied for centuries for the upkeep of the parish church, to which the *Highways Act* of 1555 added rates for the upkeep of roads; county bridges were also maintained by rates; in addition many river basins and coastal areas were subject to the jurisdiction of Commissions of Sewers whose operations were also financed by rates on local occupiers. The number of taxpayers, ratepayers, soldiers and the poor and needy were, therefore, all matters of concern to national and local government, and attempts were therefore made from time to time to discover the requisite data. From the nineteenth century onwards, the area of governmental interest in population and its affairs radically increased: initially, governments were frightened that the influence of the French Revolution would encourage working-class radicalism. Later reformers considered 'improvement' of 'the lower orders' as a major role of government.

The importance of population

Why is it so important for historians of every place (whatever its size) to know the size and composition of local populations as precisely as contemporaries tried to achieve? The reason is that, at any given level of technology (broadly interpreted) at a particular time, a particular area can only maintain an optimum number of people; if this amount is exceeded, some people will suffer under-employment, unemployment and varying degrees of poverty unless they can move elsewhere. In extreme cases, starvation and death may occur, though the number of known 'national' demographic crises in England is small: the mid-1310s, 1348–50, the later 1550s, the 1590s and the later 1640s are the best known. Thereafter, there were no further national crises or declines in national population unless epidemic disease was a major contributory factor, such as the outbreaks of smallpox in the eighteenth century, of cholera in the nineteenth century or the 'Spanish 'flu' pandemic of 1918; poorer areas, however, could still suffer regional crises, for example Cumberland and Westmorland in the 1690s.

We therefore need to consider the effects of changing local land-use on local economy and society. Fairly obviously, an arable area can maintain more people than a pastoral area of the same size because arable farming requires more people to plough, sow, harrow and harvest its crops than does the herding of cattle or sheep (though keeping dairy cattle and the making of butter and cheese need more labour than keeping beef cattle or sheep). An arable area also produces more basic foodstuffs for the majority of the population; meat, except possibly from pigs or poultry, was for most of the past mainly consumed by the more prosperous members of society: bread, cheese and vegetable 'pottage' with ale or cider were the staple foods of the poorer groups of society until the nineteenth century.[4] By the eighteenth century, however, foreign observers noted that English labourers commonly ate white bread, smoked tobacco and used sugar as a sweetener, all things unknown to their continental counterparts. If there is industry in the area or nearby, still more people can be maintained even with a high density of population provided that enough food to feed the labour-force can be produced locally or imported from outside.

All these factors will change over time: an arable area nowadays, with mechanisation, requires far less labour than it would have employed in the past. If the regional transport-system is well-developed, local farming can specialise in the products best suited to its soils, the area's remaining wants being supplied from outside the area, and local industry can also develop. This factor explains the decreasing frequency of food crises, as better roads, river navigations and canals in the eighteenth century, railways and steamships in the nineteenth century and air-transport from the twentieth century have enabled regional and international agricultural surpluses to supply areas of scarcity as well as allowing people to move more easily to where work was available and to enjoy a wider range of consumables. Growing populations, especially if the density of population is high, may also cause additional problems of social control and policing. What began as a welcome development of local housing may become a slum or nowadays a 'sink estate' rather than a prosperous community: look at many council housing estates which were welcomed when they were built but have since horrendously declined.

Towns

Besides changing population-levels and alterations in rural land-use, another possible change in a landscape is urbanisation. Towns, with a much greater density of population than villages, usually arise and grow on the basis of a wide number of crafts and industries and specialised commercial, financial and administrative services serving the surrounding hinterland, which in turn supplies most or all of their food requirements. Some towns of Roman origin, such as London, Gloucester and York, did not survive the economic collapse after the end of Roman Britain though their walled areas were recolonised later in the Saxon period, whilst new towns such as Bristol, apparently founded around AD 1000, had to erect successive sets of walls as the town expanded. As transport systems develop, the supply-area widens: by 1500 London obtained its food supplies from Kent, the Home Counties and East Anglia, and obtained its coal by coastal trade from Newcastle on Tyne; by 1900 most wheat consumed in Britain came from the USA, much beef from the USA or Argentina; by 2000 the market for industrial products was world-wide (most of the components of the PC on which this book was composed were made in Taiwan or S. Korea).

Why towns? Throughout history certain specialised functions have been better performed by groups of professional specialists working in an urban environment, because the demand for such services can be most easily arranged and satisfied in towns which focus and concentrate the demands of their rural hinterland. Hence industries, especially the more technically sophisticated luxury crafts and finishing trades, commercial and administrative services such as banking, money-lending and tax-collecting, the marketing of high-quality goods, often imported, as well as of local agricultural and industrial products, and administrative services generally flourish more easily in towns. The urban environment is often deliberately made more attractive to newcomers by favourable terms of tenure, lower rents and the freedom to organise as collective self-governing units which were offered by many of the royal and noble lords of such towns.⁵ There is of course a down side: growing urban population can lead to overcrowding, unhealthy living conditions and rising mortality; in and after the sixteenth century at the latest, most large English towns could only maintain their size, let alone expand, if their mortality was more than matched by immigration. But successful towns, especially those which acquired rights of self-government in guilds and later town councils, rapidly accumulated their own archive series which, if they survive, throw still further light on urban lives. Some medieval and early modern boroughs, though established in high hopes, later declined to become the 'pocket boroughs' of the eighteenth century which were stripped of municipal status in the nineteenth century.

The area of local history

It is therefore extremely important for the local historian to find out, first, the geographical boundaries and extent of his or her area; second, the level of local population at various times in the past; third, the type of agriculture prevailing at those times; fourth, what industries exist at those times; fifth, how his or her area was integrated into the regional markets and economy at different times; sixth, did the area become partly or totally urbanised; seventh, did normal work take place within or outside the family residence; finally, what other needs are there which cannot be satisfied within the home area. In short, local history cannot be fully understood without an investigation of local and regional history, which, in turn, needs a good understanding of the economy and society of the surrounding region or hinterland.

Local history and local population history are thus linked inextricably to each other. The level of local population at various times has to be established, and the reasons how and why the level changed from time to time understood. The general direction of long-term trends in each period, and the extent to which these long-term trends were affected by short-term fluctuations or even crises, has to be determined, together with the reasons why all these observable developments altered over time, and the effects of all these changes on contemporary economy and society.

In addition to archives, the historian of towns just as much as the historian of villages needs to consider the topographical evidence available in maps[6] and prints and drawings[7] from the sixteenth century onwards, as well as photography in the air and on the ground,[8] in place- and field-names which may date from yesterday or up to 2000 years earlier,[9] and finally the evidence from the present-day landscape which includes and often preserves 'relict features' from past centuries.[10] Unit boundaries can usually be determined from maps after the sixteenth century: the tithe maps of the late 1830s and 1840s and first edition large-scale (6 and 25 inches to 1 mile) Ordnance Survey maps of the mid-Victorian period are the best sources.[11] If your area is fortunate enough to have an Anglo-Saxon or medieval charter, you may be able to establish boundaries nearly a millennium earlier. In default, local place- and field-names will usually provide some local detail linking the periods of mainly archaeological evidence with those mainly with historical evidence. The interpretation of local place-names, especially of the essential earlier forms, is a controversial but essential area which amateurs enter at their peril: a modern name 'As(h)ton', for example, can represent 'the eastern settlement', 'the settlement among the ashtrees' or 'the settlement of Aesc'; only the earlier forms will tell the expert which is most likely to be correct. The best way forward is to try to get the help of an Anglo-Saxon linguist in your local university's Department of English.

The Census

Our forefathers, nearly all of whom spent many hours of Sundays in church or chapel, would have been familiar with the passage in the *Gospel of Luke*, chapter 2, verses 1–2: 'And it came to pass in those days that a decree went out from Caesar Augustus that all the world should be registered. This census took place while Quirinius was governing Syria'. The idea of a census was therefore familiar to medieval and early modern man, but the Roman example, except in a few late medieval and early modern cities in Italy and the Rhineland, was not generally followed until the seventeenth and eighteenth centuries when an increased knowledge of population seemed desirable to both state officials and Enlightenment intellectuals.[12] The practice of taking national censuses at regular intervals gradually spread from Scandinavia across Europe in the eighteenth and nineteenth centuries,[13] but for an official census in Great Britain we have to wait until 1801 when a regular pattern of taking censuses every ten years was established. Over time the census became more detailed, with the names, gender, occupations and marital status of individuals and their ages being regularly recorded from 1841, their birthplaces from 1851, and by the early twentieth century the number of main rooms inhabited by a single household.[14] Copies of the schedules for each household were made from 1841 onwards: these are made available to the public in the National Archives 100 years after they were made; copies are often found in local libraries and are now available on-line for a fee.

The pre-Census period

Nevertheless, we can say that what happened in the history of English and Welsh population from the mid-nineteenth century, at local, regional or national level, is well-established, though historians are still arguing about causes and effects. Before 1841, and even more before 1801, we move into a period where much investigation is still required to establish, at various geographical levels, what happened in the history of population, why it happened, and what were the results for the people in each area. Investigation of local demography in the three centuries (1538–1841) in which parish registers are the main source of information for regional and local historians, both amateur and professional, has already produced much greater knowledge of the both the national and local population history of England and will continue to do so in the future: the available national series produced by Wrigley and Schofield can only summarise the total picture and suggest some causes and results which are often still controversial. But England and Wales down to at least the eighteenth century – some historians have suggested even in the nineteenth century – comprised a collection of regions with differing characteristics and therefore with different demographic experiences which may diverge widely from the national aggregate. The centuries before 1538 have been described as 'the dark ages of English population history',[15] in which there are a few large-scale surveys but very little to cover the intervening periods. In the absence of 'direct' methods, because the necessary data do not exist, we have to rely on 'indirect' methods utilising various substitutes which have to be pressed into service in default.

Occasionally, before 1841, local parsons or overseers made detailed lists in order to compile the required summary totals, especially for 1811, 1821 and 1831, and some parsons in particular had made 'listings' (local censuses) of their parishes in order to get to know their congregations since at least the 1560s.[16] Since 1801 detailed printed *Reports* have summarised the results of the census at national and local levels every ten years (except 1941) which are available in major local libraries. The British census is therefore a good example of one approach to population history, the comparison of levels of population and other population-characteristics at different points in time. But except at the ten year intervals we can only interpolate estimates. From 1837 official registers of births, marriages and deaths were established in England and Wales which are regarded as complete from the 1860s, and the recording of causes of death became more reliable with growing medical knowledge. The results of this system were also summarised in printed *Reports of the Registrar-General* which can also be consulted in major local libraries. The recording of migration in and out of Britain also markedly improved in the nineteenth and twentieth centuries, though recent experience has shown that immigration in times of crisis can be massively under-recorded. But migration whether internal or external, incoming or outgoing, was not a feature which suddenly appeared as Britain began industrialising: historians can demonstrate its occurrence throughout the medieval and early modern periods. Still, the existence of local migration means that trying to update a given census total by adding births (christenings) and subtracting deaths (burials) is a hazardous process, as will often be revealed by the next census total. The local population history of the nineteenth and twentieth centuries is considered in Chapter 4.

Explaining population change

The contemporary demographer in a modern developed society will obtain the desired information on population from a combination of accurate information for individuals, including their occupations, ages, sex and marital status, obtained from censuses which are repeated at regular intervals, with an efficient registration-system which is recording births and deaths and a customs administration at the state's borders recording inward and outward migration. The modern demographer will also be able to utilise expert medical knowledge on the causes of death and factors affecting fertility, and can exploit the skills of a variety of specialist social scientists for knowledge of both popular attitudes and the consequences of demographic change. Even so, it is doubtful whether these modern censuses are entirely accurate, and even more doubtful whether either vital registration or the recording of migration is complete, in all three cases because of either deliberate evasion or omission on the part of the population and of inefficiency or negligence on the part of the state's officials.

The explanation of demographic change and of the effects of such change and, even more, the forecasting of future trends, are still controversial. Highly accurate though modern censuses are, they are not and cannot be 100% complete: there will be an inevitable 'margin of error' of perhaps 1–2%. But in much of the modern world outside Europe, North America, Australasia and Japan, censuses are neither taken regularly nor are they likely to be very accurate; registration-systems are known to be widely evaded and therefore very faulty, and the recording of migration is often rudimentary. In this as in other aspects of life there are some obvious parallels between the modern under-developed 'Third World' and the 'pre-industrial' world of medieval and early modern England. In the absence of official censuses or registration-systems before 1801, we are thus thrown back on a variety of 'indirect' approaches to the problems of the history of local population, which I will consider in later chapters.

The unit of study

What, then, is the appropriate unit of study for local population history? In part, this will obviously depend on the interests of the historian. He or she may be primarily interested in his or her village or town, or a group of settlements either selected on a geographical basis, e.g. a river valley; or a distinctive locality such as the Weald of Kent and Sussex, the South Hams of Devon, the Broads of Norfolk; or an ancient regional grouping, a hundred, wapentake or rural deanery; or, still larger, an old forest such as Dean in Gloucestershire or Sherwood in Nottinghamshire; finally, perhaps, an ancient (pre-1973) shire or county. In the Middle Ages a small market town may be part of a single parish, whereas larger towns may contain several parishes: 100+ in London, 30+ in Norwich, 20+ in Bristol. At the other end of the scale the family historian will mainly be interested in a small number of families that are being studied over a long timespan, though it is becoming increasingly clear that, because of local and regional migration, few families stayed in one place for more than a few generations, and most migrated within a fairly small geographical area. As a result, the families which stayed put in one place for generations were atypical of the whole population, being mostly gentry or farmers with a stake in the land and likely to have better health and therefore longer lives than their poorer neighbours. Nevertheless, there were exceptional migrants: foreign, mainly Protestant, refugees fleeing from the European continent; young men wishing to join the army or navy, both of which were expanding after 1660 as Britain became an Imperial power; clergymen going to Oxford or Cambridge to be trained, and then looking for a parish to serve in England, Wales or Ireland; other young men joining the professions (law, surveying, accounting) or setting up in one of the newer crafts and trades (the making of instruments, clocks and watches, also printing, bookselling, shopkeeping, pottery, etc) as the middle class expanded; finally, of course, the poor looking for work which, after 1750, was more usually found, and better paid, in the industrial Midlands and North. In the last five centuries there have been Jewish refugees, first from Spanish persecution, then from Tsarist oppression and later still from German genocide, immigrants from the Indian sub-continent and the 'new Commonwealth' countries in search of work, and most recently economic immigrants from the European Union and refugees from the Middle East.

Why the parish as the standard unit?

Since the late Anglo-Saxon period, the parish, an area served by a church, has been the lowest standard ecclesiastical unit, although in later centuries some outlying chapelries also became partly independent units, most of which developed into parishes in their own right at various times in different regions between the thirteenth and nineteenth centuries.[17] Many parishes and chapelries were recognised by the Crown as units of lay taxation (tithings) from the thirteenth century onwards and civil parishes have remained as the lowest level of state administration ever since. In addition, in the medieval period and later many manorial boundaries followed some parochial boundaries though the relation between parish and manor was complex and varied from region to region. Even when the names are the same, we cannot assume that manor X and parish X had the same boundaries. If you are interested in a larger area, its history and demography can most easily be approached by combining information from the constituent parishes. But it is usually very difficult to separate data for a smaller unit within a parish before the period after 1841 when copies of the detailed census returns were made every ten years.

Whatever the historian's area of interest, however, he or she will be constrained by the nature of the available and surviving source materials, most of which, even if collected for a county or diocese, have tended to provide information for fairly small basic units, the parish or township and in the north and west the chapelries and townships into which their larger parishes were subdivided, or the manors which co-existed with the parishes from Norman times into at least the early modern period. This of course does not prevent the local historian from amalgamating basic units into larger groupings if he or she so desires by simple addition and aggregation. What, however, it does prevent before 1841, unless local documentation is exceptionally rich in detail, is the comprehensive investigation of areas below parish level or cutting across parish boundaries, such as a suburb or neighbourhood.

Manor and Parish

The evolution of the ecclesiastical parish and its boundaries and the frequent overlap with taxation tithings has already been mentioned. In addition, in the medieval period and later many manorial boundaries followed some parochial boundaries though the geographical relation between parish and manor was complex and varied from region to region. Thus the 14,000 places whose names were recorded in the Domesday survey of 1086–7 were manors, not parishes, which eventually numbered about 9250 in the sixteenth century, although the names were often identical. Even when the names are the same, we must not assume that manor and parish had the same boundaries (see p. 15). Equally, because manors could contain parts of several parishes, many places with names of undoubted Old English origin, sometimes recorded in pre-Norman charters, do not appear in the Domesday Survey: they were included and subsumed within the central place, *caput manerii*, of the manor. If you are interested in a larger area, its history and demography can most easily be approached by combining information from the constituent manors and parishes. But it is usually difficult to separate data for a smaller unit within a parish before the period after 1841, unless parts of the parish were in different hundreds or wapentakes and tithings.

Most local historians have taken the parish alone or in combination with others as the basic unit of study.[18] Fortunately for the family historian, however, many of the historical sources produce data either for households or families within a larger geographical area or which can be related to members of their constituent households (tax-payers, communicants, men fit for military service). Many of the sources yield information on individuals in central judicial and fiscal records and in manorial court-rolls and surveys from the thirteenth century onwards, in parish registers from 1538 onwards, in poor-law records and military musters from the sixteenth century onwards, in estate records in all periods, and increasingly in the seventeenth and later centuries in private correspondence, and from the nineteenth century onwards in evidence given in Parliamentary reports ('Blue Books') and local newspapers. Constantly moving forward in time are oral memories as a first-hand and perhaps reliable source.[19]

Historically, division into manors and parishes can explain why subordinate settlements are frequently found near or straddling such boundaries: often, the founders of such settlements were trying to avoid supervision and control by either the secular lords of manors or the ecclesiastical authority represented by the parish church, an avoidance of authority often clear from the surviving manorial and parochial records. In the past, in most English villages, church and manor house were adjacent: many parish churches were founded in the late Anglo-Saxon, Norman or Angevin periods by manorial lords who tended to regard the new parish church as 'their' church (not unreasonably, given that they or their ancestors and predecessors had built it), to be sited near the manor house to avoid long trips to church, and often to be served by a younger son or other relative of theirs, a tradition which persisted into the twentieth century.

The manor: history and boundaries

There is, however, one further problem, since the boundaries of manors and parishes of the same name do not necessarily coincide; they may do so in perhaps half of England, but there are wide variations. A parish may be split between several manors, especially in the East Midlands and East Anglia, whilst in the north and west and in parts of the south of England, a manor may extend into several parishes. The Domesday manors of Laughton and Stockingham (Sussex), for example, comprised the whole of Laughton parish as well as substantial parts of the neighbouring parishes of Beddingham, Chiddingly, Compton Berwick, Heathfield, East Hoathly, Ripe and Waldron. To further complicate matters, Beddingham, Chiddingly and Ripe had manors named after their parishes, and Ripe parish also contained the manor of Eckington. Nor is the relationship between parish and manor unchanged over time: a manor may be divided between female co-heiresses or diminished by some of its freeholds becoming 'reputed' manors; it may become part of a larger unit if its owners acquire adjacent holdings. If the difference between manor and parish is understood, it is unlikely to create confusion, but it will involve the local historian in careful definition of the area of study and the extent to which his or her figures can be adjusted for different areas. If the quality and quantity of documentation vary across an area, it may be necessary to take the better-quality figures on their own to demonstrate likely rather than definite trends for the whole area. Fortunately for the family historian, however, many of the historical sources produce data either for households or families within a larger geographical area or which can be related to their households (tax-payers, communicants, men fit for military service); many of the sources yield information on individuals in national government taxation records and manorial court-rolls and surveys from the thirteenth century onwards, in parish registers from 1538 onwards, in poor-law records and military musters from the sixteenth century onwards, increasingly in the seventeenth and later centuries in estate records and private correspondence, and from the nineteenth century onwards in evidence given in censuses, Parliamentary reports ('Blue Books') and local newspapers.

Tracing the 'descent of a manor' can be tedious but it cannot be skipped: for the ownership and occupation of land over time (which is what the 'descent of the manor' involves) is of prime importance to the local historian. It is simply utterly contradictory to dismiss the descent of the manor as 'old hat' while at the same time proclaiming the importance of economic factors in local history.[20] What could be more relevant to local economic history than the history of the largest, if not only, estate, usually the largest farm and the greatest local employer, and the centre of local government and justice for much of the past?

Approaches to local population history

The sources and methods for the study of local population will be examined in detail in later chapters, but the methods can broadly be classified as fitting into two categories: the 'direct' and the 'indirect'. The 'direct' approach considers sources which can yield data on the level and composition of population in a given area at any one time: if one is fortunate enough to find several such estimates for the same unit over time, the result will be an outline of the development of local population over a long period, from which broad trends can be inferred but not the reasons for these trends. The 'indirect' approach focuses instead on the direction of population-change over a reasonably long period, from which the reasons for changing trends can often be suggested with considerable success, though the absolute levels at the beginning and end of the period and the degree of change between the absolute levels will remain elusive without independent evidence for total population.

A new approach to population history is 'family reconstitution', which rebuilds families generation by generation primarily from parish register entries but incorporating any information from other sources. This gets round the problem of calculating 'vital rates' for births, marriages and deaths from an outside, independent source most elegantly: the 'total population' at any one time is the number of individuals alive in all the families being reconstituted. Although 'family reconstitution' is most commonly used on data from parish registers, it can also be used where manorial and/or hundredal records or wills survive in reasonably continuous 'runs', and when estate-records exist in long series.[21] Whatever unit is chosen for study, you must always be aware of what is happening in neighbouring units, which will affect and reflect migration and regional specialisation in particular. No parish or manor was an isolated unit: the parish was a subordinate part of a deanery and a diocese; the manor was usually part of a larger landed estate. The economy of the area reflected both the geographical potential of the region and its previous adaption to both circumstances (geology and geography) and history.

Parish and region

This is especially true when you broaden your approach from local population history to local history. You should also be aware that, unless your place is on the edge of a geographical region, its conditions will be typical of a wider area. As I used to tell some of my local history extra-mural groups, 'one parish pump is very like another', which may be heretical but can be advantageous: your place may have few or no surviving manorial, estate or civil parish records, where a nearby place may have them in plenty. These will give you at least some guidance on what is happening in the place you are trying to study. Local records are still being discovered and made available in local record offices: since the *Parish Registers and Records Measure* of 1972, most parsons have deposited the Anglican parish registers and other records in the local record office for their diocese; many nonconformist churches have followed suit. Ever since county record offices began to appear in the 1930s, local landowners have been depositing their family archives in the local record office and allowing genuine students to consult them: given the dominant role played by the aristocracy and gentry in localities near the 'great house', 'manor' or 'hall' down to at least 1914, these will throw much light on local farming, housing, local government and local employment, sometimes also on local industry and trade. A few great houses still keep their own archives but normally have an archivist or librarian looking after them: most have been listed by the National Register of Archives, and their owners are usually willing to allow access to interested people.

In default it is worth considering approaching older libraries (Cambridge University Library, Bodleian Library, Oxford, municipal libraries such as Birmingham and, above all, the British Library, London), which have been receiving manuscripts long before local record offices were established. All these libraries have printed catalogues, nowadays supplemented by online additions; most, though not all, local record office catalogues are also available on line at the A2A website maintained by English and Welsh record offices. In default, an enquiry by letter or email to your local record office will usually receive a helpful response though pressure of work may mean some delay in replying. You may, of course, be fortunate enough to discover family records still *in situ* in a local attic: if so, you have a duty not to alter their arrangement more than absolutely necessary and not to annoy the owner: the records are his or her private property and it is a privilege for you to be allowed to consult them. Finally, the National Archives (TNA) has its own website giving online access to most though not all of its catalogues: virtually everywhere in England and Wales will have multiple references to be followed-up from the thirteenth century onwards if not from the eleventh century or earlier. But beware: the TNA online index is not infallible: I have found entries in indexes in the printed *Calendars* which are not in the online index. Most of the TNA holdings, as opposed to their catalogues, are still only available in the original, though copies (photographic or electronic) can be ordered on-line.

What is to be counted?

Having defined our unit of study, you need to ask what should be counted, given the availability of the appropriate sources for that locality. First, obviously, is the total population at various times. Secondly, the composition of that population, which can expressed in a variety of ways: the sex-ratio (the number of men per 100 females), which normally will be approximately equal; if there is a surplus of women, we may suspect either the emigration of men in search of work elsewhere or an above-average previous death-rate among men, probably due to war. Another measure of the composition of population is the age-structure: in the period before the industrial revolution began, infants under 5 years old constituted 11–12% of the population, which rose during the industrial revolution to 13–14%; children between 5 and 14 years old comprised 19–20% of the population before 1750, thereafter 22–24%; the working population from 15–59 years of age represented about 56–60% between 1541 and 1871, and the over '60s formed 8–10% of the population before 1750 and 6–7% afterwards, figures which did not markedly change before the twentieth century.[22] If the sex-ratio or age-structure for your parish is clearly different from those just given, something odd is happening which needs to be investigated.

Occupational structure

The final component is the occupational and social structure of the local population. Generally speaking, in a normal rural village agriculture (farmers and agricultural labourers) would account for roughly 60–80% of the male population, in the Middle Ages mostly peasant farmers but from the sixteenth century onwards arable farming, being labour-intensive, would have fewer farmers employing an increasing number of labourers who, at most, would only have a cottage and garden. Pastoral farms had fewer labourers who would tend to be more skilled shepherds, sheep shearers and herdsmen. If rural industry was present, this tended to stimulate commercial farmers to produce more food while the workers concentrated on their particular industrial skills, with any agricultural involvement becoming a by-occupation concentrating mainly on pig-keeping, orcharding and growing fruit and vegetables in cottage gardens. The transition to full-scale industrialisation often meant the workers giving up even cottage gardening, especially in towns, where the rising density of population usually also implied giving up gardens altogether – see the back yards in *Coronation Street* – and often living in urban slums. In all periods before the twentieth century, every village had a number of shopkeepers, craftsmen such as carpenters, blacksmiths, millers and millwrights, tailors and shoemakers, possibly a private school teacher, the population being headed by the squire (if resident) and the parson or his curate. The upper class did not usually comprise more than 3% at most of the population and the middle class was small compared to the post-industrial period, though it was increasing quite rapidly in industrial villages and even more in towns. The twentieth century saw the decline of heavy industry, and the rise of 'tertiary' service industries, leading to an expanded middle class as the skilled working class rose in status. This of course explains Mrs Thatcher's popularity in selling-off council houses in the 1980s. The inter-war period saw an expansion of council housing in town and country and a growth in private housing, aided by the rise of 'new towns', as Britain became a 'house-owning democracy'. Correspondingly the upper class either declined or disappeared from sight in order to survive, the breakup of many large estates during and after the first World War producing the greatest transfer of land in Britain since the sixteenth century: the power once exercised by the squire now being controlled by democratic county councils from 1889 and district councils from 1894, including secular parish councils which replaced the Anglican vestries.

Literacy and education

The introduction and growth of new industries and the rise of the 'middling sort' are linked to another factor which can be measured: the rise of literacy. Literacy facilitates the spreading of new information and techniques through newspapers, printed notices and books of instructions. The classic measurement of literacy was the ability to sign one's name instead of putting a mark on various documents, especially the post-1754 marriage registers which enable mass-coverage of a community (see Chapter 4).

Quality of life and standard of living

Two final important factors determining the welfare of the local population are the level of prices and wages and the quality of housing. There is usually plenty of raw material available such as farm and household accounts, probate inventories and accounts and, in the modern period, Parliamentary reports and local newspapers. If money wages are compared with prices, the real value of wages will become apparent. Prices and money wages can be tabulated and graphed over long periods to show the general picture of local welfare. Apart from the 1540s and 1550s, there was no devaluation of the currency before the twentieth century, but money wage-rates can only be used as a substitute for money income if there is full employment locally. Poor Law records, correspondence of landlords and farmers, reports in local newspapers from the nineteenth century onwards and Parliamentary papers are the best guides to the state of the employment market. Generally, also, the quality of housing was important, the more so in the past when the home was also a workshop or mini-factory, and houses below the 'middling sort' were invariably over-crowded as the family grew during the life-cycle. Only when working hours declined after the mid-nineteenth century, when most employment was no longer undertaken or based in the home, when the average family size fell towards the proverbial married couple with 2.4 children or fewer, and when replacement of much housing was achieved by both private developers and councils, did the quality of life for most ordinary people greatly improve. Again, a wide variety of sources from local government reports to newspaper advertisements bear witness to this improvement of housing standards. After World War I the three bedroom house became the norm in both private and council housing; after World War II indoor toilets, 'hot-water circulation', locally available provision of mains drainage and oil, gas and electricity supplies became standard, followed more recently by gas or electric central heating as coal fires were restricted by smoke-free zoning.

From local population history to local history

The ability to look over one's shoulder is especially valuable when you broaden your approach from local population history to local history. As I have already shown, local records are still being discovered and made available in local record offices.

Finally, once we have outlined the broad trends in local population and explained them as far as the records will allow, how can we put further flesh on the bones? Most human societies have had a hierarchical structure, which until the last two centuries was assumed to have divine approval, hence the third verse in the Victorian hymn:

> 'The rich man in his castle,
> The poor man at his gate,
> God made them high or lowly,
> And ordered their estate.'

George Orwell in a splendid piece of sociological satire in his *1984* expressed the same basic insight:

> 'Throughout recorded time ... there have been three kinds of people in the world, the High, the Middle and the Low. They have been subdivided in many ways, they have borne countless different names, and their relative numbers, as well as their attitude towards one another, have varied from age to age: but the essential structure of society has never altered.'[23]

If your area has adequate manorial or estate records, you should be able to learn a lot about the upper groups of society: what proportion of the total population were they, and how much power and influence did they exercise over the rest of the locality. Even if such detailed records do not survive, central taxation records will provide snapshots of the taxpayers at various points from the thirteenth century onwards, followed in and after the sixteenth century by Quarter Sessions archives and records of musters for military service, in the seventeenth century by the Hearth Taxes, in the eighteenth century by militia records and in the nineteenth and twentieth centuries from Census records. In short, we can count the 'people who count'. If there was massive agrarian change at any time from the twelfth century onwards, it is likely to be reflected in official records: inquisitions and their associated 'extents' from the 1230s to the 1640s will record most secular estates; the dissolution of the monasteries in the 1530s and of the chantries in the 1540s produced more useful documentation as well as transferring many records of ecclesiastical estates to the Crown which are now in TNA. Chancery records from the fifteenth century onwards may preserve settlements of changed agrarian layout and customs which may also be preserved in local manorial records: such 'enclosure by agreement' developed into enclosure by Act of Parliament between the seventeenth and the nineteenth century, resulting in awards and usually large-scale maps of which there should be three copies: one in the parish records, one in Quarter Sessions records in the county town, and one in the House of Lords Record Office, now the Parliamentary Archives.

For the nineteenth century the Tithe Awards and Maps will provide detailed information on the ownership, occupation and use of land in the years around 1840 for most parishes. Again, three copies were made, one for the parish, one for the diocese and one for the Tithe Redemption Committee which is now in TNA.[24] For the recent past, the Valuation Office records include maps and surveys of all local farms on the eve of the First World War as a result of Lloyd George's 'people's budget' of 1911, further information coming from Land Utilisation Surveys and annual Crop Returns for each parish since the 1860s, all mostly in TNA. From 1413 onwards, a statute required all men appearing in any law court to state their 'addition' (status or occupation) as well as their place of residence, which meant that most men and many women would have this information attached to their names in legal records. Besides the secular royal and manorial courts, the country was also divided into dioceses and archdeaconries with their own courts, which were by no means confined to what we would think now are 'church' affairs: in the later middle ages debt, and throughout the period before 1858 defamation and slander, and above all marital, family and probate matters, came within their jurisdiction (Tithe-disputes, however, could be pursued either in the church courts or the equity and common-law courts).

Two of the most useful records for local and regional historians, wills and probate inventories, were, therefore, regulated by the church courts until 1857. Both sorts of document will normally yield the occupation or status of the dead person; the inventory will give a description of his or her estate, excluding only freehold land, but including growing crops and livestock, and very often a room-by-room description of the house with their furniture and belongings, including for craftsmen, their working tools and raw materials. For farmers there will be details of land-use as well as livestock and the making of processed foods such as ham, bacon, butter, cheese, cider and beer. Although the numbers of inventories which survive decline after about 1750, they were still made, but were no longer preserved as probate registries became overcrowded. Wills may also provide essentially the same information in the form of bequests, as well as throwing light on links between family members and between the family and other members of the local community.[25] More rarely farm, shop and factory records may yield information on locally produced goods, their manufacture and marketing, and local employment, and the census schedules from 1841 onwards usually the total number of employees in farms, factories and workshops.

Local communities in action

Moreover, both manorial and parochial non-register material may show the community in collective action, whether in manorial courts or in the parish vestry: until 1834 looking after the poor was left almost entirely to the parish overseers of the poor and to the inhabitants 'in vestry assembled'; the local highways also were under the supervision of parish surveyors unless they were of sufficient regional or national importance to be maintained by one of the growing number of Turnpike Trusts (whose minutes, accounts and other records may also survive). All the above are, in the main, manuscript records or, in the case of poor law records, often written answers and information on printed forms; but no local historian should overlook the enormous amount of material available in print: contemporary gazetteers and atlases, law reports, local and national newspapers and magazines, specialist professional journals, and the serried volumes emanating from Parliament, the 'Blue Books' reporting the evidence collected and the conclusions drawn from detailed investigation of witnesses whose words were recorded verbatim. My postgraduate supervisor, Professor Robin Du Boulay, used to smile at his postgraduate students as we presented him with our latest findings culled from manuscripts in what were then the Public Record Office and the British Museum, and then teased us by saying 'you won't forget, will you, that a source does not cease to be a source because it's in print'. A wise warning from one of England's greatest historians.

In conclusion, the local historian must beware of inverted snobbery. It is only too easy to despise what some would have us believe was the 'effete' gentry of the past 'grinding the faces of the poor'. But caution is needed if ideology is not to blind us to past reality. The 'aristocracy' and 'gentry' of the past who survived as rulers of their localities for several centuries did not do so either by being effete or by stimulating class-hatred. They rarely comprised more than 3% of the total population and, apart from the century or so after the Norman Conquest, usually had little military force at their command. They survived because of their recognised utility in local society as governors and employers, in a position generally thought to have divine approval. As such, their records, where they survive, are a valuable window into the local community and its activities. Having outlined the possible ways of approaching the local history and demography of England, we can now turn to consider the available source-materials and methods for exploiting them in the following chapter.

Notes

1   D. Crouch, *The Image of Aristocracy in Britain, 1000–1300* (London, Routledge, 1992), 145.

2   E. A. Wrigley (ed.), *Introduction to English Historical Demography* (London, Weidenfeld & Nicolson, 1966), 109. Unfortunately Sir Tony Wrigley had forgotten his own words by the 1980s!

3   See Bibliography, section 5(ii) 10.

4   See Bibliography, section 5 (v).

5   See Bibliography, sections 5 (iii), 6 (iii), 7 (iii).

6   See Bibliography, section 6 (v) 2.

7   M. W. Barley, *A Guide to British Topographical Collections* (London, Council for British Archaeology, 1974).

8   For all photographs, see Bibliography, section 3 (i) 3–4.

9   See Bibliography, section 3 (i) 5.

10   See Bibliography, section 3 (i) 6.

11   See *TNA Research Guide*, Domestic Ser. 41, and Bibliography, section 6 (v) 2.

12   A fine example of an early city census is D. Herlihy and C. Klapisch-Zuber (eds), *Tuscans and their Families: a study of the Florentine catasto of 1427* (New Haven (USA), Yale UP, 1985).

13   See, for example, M. Drake *Population and Society in Norway, 1735–1865* (Cambridge, CUP, 1969).

14   See Bibliography, section 7 (iv) 1.

15   Wrigley (ed.), *Introduction to English Historical Demography*, xi.

16   See Bibliography, section 6 (iv) 2.

17   See Bibliography, section 4 (v).

18   See the classic introduction of R. B. Pugh, *How to Write a Parish History* (London, Allen & Unwin, 6th edn, 1955).

19   See Bibliography, section 7 (v) 24.

20   This is precisely the position repeatedly taken by the contributors to C. R. J. Currie and C. P. Lewis (eds), *A Guide to English County Histories* (Stroud, Sutton, 1997).

21   For a good example, see Z. Razi, *Life, Marriage and Death in a Medieval Parish: Halesowen, 1270–1400* (Cambridge, CUP, 1980).

22   E. A. Wrigley and R. S. Schofield, *The Population History of England, 1541–1871* (London, Arnold, 1981, repr. Cambridge, CUP, 1989), 528–9 (table A3.1). The figures obtained from generalised inverse projection are similar but not identical (E. A. Wrigley *et al. English Population History from Family Reconstitution, 1580–1837* (Cambridge, CUP, 1997), 615 (table A9.1)).

23   G. Orwell, *Nineteen Eighty-Four* (London, Secker & Warburg, 1949), 189, 206–7.

24   See references cited in Bibliography, section 6 (v) 2.

25   See Bibliography, section 6 (iv) 8.

CHAPTER 2

Sources and Methods

....

Approaches to population history

As we have seen in Chapter 1 (see p. 16 above), there are basically two approaches to studying population in the past. The first is termed 'comparative static analysis', which compares estimated populations of an area at any points in time when sufficient evidence exists to make such estimates possible. But there are some obvious problems with this approach. Population estimates before the nineteenth century rarely derive from direct counts of the population, e.g. the censuses of Great Britain, 1801–2011 and, therefore, usually result from using a series of 'multipliers' to convert figures of taxpayers (mostly adult males), of men mustered for military service (usually aged 15–60), of communicants (men and women over the age of first communion, an age which alters as the brand of religion changes), and of householders. While historians have calculated the size of different 'multipliers' with considerable ingenuity, there will still be margins of error in such calculations because we do not know for certain, and in most cases never will, how many of the poor evaded taxes, how many men, either unfit or simply 'workshy', escaped the muster-masters, and precisely how many men and women received communion, particularly in the period from *c.* 1535–40 to 1603 and later, during which the age of first communion is generally thought to have risen from about 7 in 1535 to 16 in 1603 and later. As the age of communion rose, the proportion of communicants in the total population declined, thus raising the factor needed to convert such communicants into estimates of total population.

The age-distribution of past populations has been based on the statistics on age-structure calculated by Wrigley and Schofield using the process of 'back projection', later refined as 'general inverse projection', a technology that has been called in question,[1] so that the accuracy of its results is far from certain, especially in the period before 1640, whilst the average size of families and households are also open to dispute, since most of the statistics on their size come from the 1690s or later and may well not apply to the sixteenth and seventeenth centuries.[2] An alternative approach to age-distribution would use the populations calculated by model life-tables, notably the Princeton 'North' and 'West' Tables at Level 7. These are believed to represent the general population of pre-industrial western Europe but they cannot be more than, at best, approximately correct.[3] Since there are very few direct sources giving us population totals for large areas, i.e. above the level of parish, chapelry or tithing, before 1801, we must therefore first consider the availability and quality of the available indirect sources for population history at local level.

Indirect sources

These indirect sources fall into two main kinds: the first comprise lists of individuals in an identifiable place with known boundaries (normally a parish or tithing but often a manor in the Middle Ages) which can perhaps yield a total population by using an appropriate 'multiplier'; the second attempts to calculate total population from series of annual data, especially christenings), by using ratios between christenings and population, and by comparing christenings and burials. In order to utilise data in the first category above, one needs to ascertain what information is available, if it is of good quality, and to calculate appropriate 'multipliers' to convert numbers of heads of household, communicants, taxpayers or adult males into total population. To use the second category requires the estimation of a ratio between births and total population, the 'crude birth rate', and therefore also needs to enquire how many infants escaped baptism for any reason. So long as christenings took place on the day of birth, the usual situation in Catholic Europe including the England of Henry VIII, very few births would escape baptism except still births; once the interval between birth and baptism rose above a few days, increasing numbers of babies would be buried before being baptised, and the burial rate of infants would misleadingly appear to be increasing. In some areas by the nineteenth century poorer families often brought all their living children to be christened together, and any who had died before then would not appear in the christening register though they would appear in the burial register at death. Such a practice would, therefore, artificially raise burial rates while the corresponding christening rates would be artificially lowered.

Household data

There is fairly general agreement amongst demographic historians that the average English household in villages and small towns in the past was usually four to five people, and Peter Laslett argued strongly for 4.75 as the mean household size.[4] In larger towns, however, the average household was more likely to be above five people because townsmen were more likely to have servants, apprentices and employees living in. It has also been argued more recently that outside towns a 'multiplier' of 4.2 may be more appropriate.[5] Apart from local 'listings', however, there is only one official source before the household schedules of the national census from 1841 onwards which provide comprehensive lists of heads of household, namely the Hearth Taxes of the 1660s and 1670s. Some have been in print since the late nineteenth century, and the best sets for each county are being edited by the British Record Society; in default it is necessary to consult the original documents in TNA.[6] Although these records have a good reputation for completeness, you must ensure that the holders of 'exempt' hearths are included in the same roll as the assessed hearths: in some counties, such as Gloucestershire in 1672, the 'exempt' hearths are listed in a separate 'exemption certificate' which must be re-united with the main roll.

The 'lordly' household

Although the average household size is the criterion most needed by historians, there are also times when we need to consider the atypical as well as the average. In general the household of the resident lord of a manor at any time before the twentieth century was so much larger than the average household of his mainly peasant tenantry that to ignore this difference would unduly reduce the calculated size of the community. There are, therefore, two problems to overcome: first, is the household of the lord of the manor resident in any particular manor? If it is, his household will almost certainly be much larger than the average peasant household, usually having both male and female domestics, possibly also cultivators of the lord's demesne or home farm. If the lord is a major medieval baron, he will probably have knights and men-at-arms in his retinue to protect him, and his chief residence certainly will be a castle; equally, a major baron will usually have more than one administrative centre in addition to his main residence, the *caput honorii*, on his estate and many of his household will generally accompany him from one residence to another. This factor will also apply if the lord is a major ecclesiastic, an archbishop, bishop or in the medieval period a richer 'mitred' abbot. Whether the greater lords are secular or ecclesiastic, their household will also include stewards, scribes or secretaries to deal with the administration of the estate.[7] In the three centuries after the Reformation many new country houses were built by new gentry as well as established aristocrats, and many more were rebuilt, so that a minority of larger households persisted in England down to 1914. Though such households after the Civil War lost any remaining military members, domestic servants in various grades proliferated, from stewards, butlers and housekeepers to footmen, cooks, maids and outdoor servants. If it is clear that there were, say, 50 households in a village plus the lord's household, the total population, if calculated as 51 × 4.75, is 242.25, rounded to 240; if calculated as (50 × 4.75) = 237.5, + ?15, the total becomes 252.5, rounded to 250. But 15 is at the lower end of lordly household sizes: medieval lordly households could number over 100 people, and aristocratic households in the early modern period were usually between 50 and 100 people even after the garrison or bodyguard element was abandoned following the Civil War.[8]

Communicants

Until the *Act of Toleration* in 1689, it was obligatory for all English people over a certain age to receive communion at least once a year in their parish church, an obligation that was enforced by the church authorities and, after Henry VIII's rejection of papal authority, also by the state. Given the enforcement of this obligation, it seemed entirely reasonable to inquire into the numbers of communicants, first required by the state in 1546 and 1548 in connection with the dissolution of the chantries: thereafter the local church authorities recorded numbers of communicants, often after a further request for numbers from the state as in 1603 and 1676. The proportion of communicants in the population was determined by the average age of first communion which was most likely about 7 years before the Reformation, but probably rose to about 10 in 1546–48, to 14 in 1563 and certainly to 16 in 1603 and later.[9] Allowing for the age-structure of early modern England, this meant that the communicants ('houseling people') in the chantry certificates of 1546–48 constituted about 75% of the total population, and that numbers of 'houseling people' should therefore be multiplied by 100/75, i.e. 1.33, to yield an estimate of total population. By 1603 the age of first communion had risen to 16, communicants then comprised about 63% of the population, and their number should be multiplied by 100/63, i.e. 1.6, to calculate a final population estimate. But the results of a comparison of the 'Compton Census' of 1676 with the *Hearth Tax* totals of 1672 suggests that dissenters were probably under-counted in 1676.[10] Moreover, a comparison of estimated total populations from 'houseling people' with those from household data in the only two places where both sets of data exist in 1546–48 are so close that they suggest both 'multipliers' are correct, at least for the first half of the sixteenth century (See 'Comparing Multipliers' below, pp. 35–6).

Taxpayers

Calculating a 'multiplier' for taxpayers is much more problematic, since, with the exception of the *Hearth Taxes* of Charles II's reign, there was no clear demographic definition of either taxpayers or muster men, though in both cases there was an obvious motive for omission. In 1524–5 the taxpayers were nearly all male, probably including all heads of household, and mostly married, with a few widows. W. G. Hoskins, who made an extensive study of Tudor subsidy rolls and was one of the few historians to discuss the ratio of taxpayers to total population, suggested that the 66–7 taxpayers in the village of Wigston (Leics) in 1524–5 represented a population of 60–70 [heads of] households, i.e. roughly one taxpayer per household and an implied 'multiplier' of 4.75 to yield an estimate of total population.[11] In 1524–5, moreover, all men earning over £1 per annum were taxed, so that most places would have many more recorded taxpayers in 1524–5 than in the next Tudor subsidy 20 years later. Further support for this 'multiplier' comes from Simon Fish's *A supplicacyon for the Beggars* of 1529 which stated that there were 520,000 households in England,[12] a figure probably derived from an official summary of the 1524–5 subsidy: if we multiply 520,000 by a 'multiplier' of 4.5 we obtain a population estimate of 2.34 millions, whilst the multiplier of 4.75 yields a total of 2.47 millions, figures very close to Julian Cornwall's national estimate of 2.35 millions.[13] When considering the provincial town of Norwich, however, W. G. Hoskins used a 'multiplier' of 9.0 to convert taxpayers to total population without providing any supporting evidence for this conclusion.[14] Evading the tax-collector was, however, much easier in a large town than a smaller community, poverty was probably more widespread and the average household size was probably over five. Julian Cornwall, the best-known expert on the 1522 muster survey and the 1524–5 lay subsidy, believed that these three records contain 'in theory ... virtually the entire male population aged 16 and upwards' but because of migration, death and deliberate omission by royal officials 'the composition of lists cannot be taken at face value'; he argued that a correction factor of 3/2 should be applied to nominal lists to allow for omissions.[15]

But uncertainties abound: our figures on the age-distribution in the 1520s come from Wrigley and Schofield's computer-generated statistics for the 1540s: the distribution in the 1520s may not have been the same. Our statistics on the size of households and the composition of their holders derive from Laslett's analysis of 'listings' mainly from the seventeenth and eighteenth centuries; again, these figures perhaps may not reflect the situation in the 1520s. A further problem is that some localities were exempt from payment of the lay subsidy in the sixteenth century – Cumberland, Durham, Northumberland, Westmorland and the Cinque Ports of south-east England. In 1524–5 the subsidy was known to be badly assessed and collected in Lancashire and Yorkshire in the north and Derbyshire, Shropshire, Worcestershire and probably Staffordshire in the Midlands. Many returns are partly or completely missing: those for the City of London in both 1524 and 1525 are missing; Bedfordshire, Hertfordshire and Kent have extremely poor coverage; many Derbyshire returns are in a poor condition; in all other counties some returns for hundreds or wapentakes are missing or incomplete. By way of compensation, a Canadian scholar has recently uncovered a set of London subsidy valuations for 1535–6.[16]

Indeed, the reliability of records of direct taxation can vary considerably: they are generally thought to be fairly reliable from the 1290s to the 1330s, from the 1520s to the mid-1540s and in the 1660s and 1670s. At other times the subsidies were very unreliable; as Sir Walter Raleigh told the House of Commons in 1601, 'our estates that be thirty pound or forty pound in the Queen's books are not the hundredth part of our wealth';[17] the difference was doubtless an exaggeration but certainly the returns did not keep pace with rising land-values.[18] The records of the 1544–5 subsidy have not survived so well as those of 1524–5, and since the former excludes the labourers taxed on wages of £1 or over per year in 1524–5, we cannot use the same 'multiplier' for 1544–5 as in 1524–5. Even in the period before

1334, it is doubtful whether the number of taxpayers is a safe basis for estimating the size of local populations.[19]

Where the 1544–5 subsidy and the 1546–8 chantry certificates survive for the same place, it might be worthwhile comparing the two sets of figures to ascertain if there is any apparently constant ratio between them: the two sets of estimates ought to be fairly close. If parish registers with a usable series of christenings exist for the period 1538–50, we could also investigate if the estimated total populations in 1544–5 have plausible birth-rates, i.e in the range 31–40 per 1000 population. Apart from the lay subsidies, which were increasingly unrepresentative after 1545, the only other direct taxes in the early modern period were the *Hearth Taxes* of the 1660s and 1670s, for which Laslett's 'multiplier' of 4.75 can be used with confidence for rural areas, though in towns, especially large towns, a larger 'multiplier' of 5.5 should be utilised. The land-tax of 1695–6 was not updated and in any case full returns rarely survive before the 1770s.[20] There was no further direct taxation until the Victorian income tax was introduced.

Muster men

As with the taxpayers, defining muster men in demographic terms is difficult, apart from gender. The normal age-range for the Tudor and Stuart musters as for their successors, the militia and 'yeomanry' in the eighteenth century, was between the ages of 15 and 60. For the musters, it could be thought that we can base an estimate on the half of the population aged between 15 and 60, the usual age-group liable for military service, which formed about 30% of the whole population.[21] But in reality figures for muster men varied widely from year to year, depending on the urgency of the state's need for manpower and the ability of the muster masters to track down shirkers and absentees.[22] If good quality parish registers exist, it might again be worthwhile comparing the christenings over a long period with the totals of men mustered to ascertain if the latter were a fairly constant proportion of the former, but the wide variations in men mustered year by year because of the changing need for their services and possible local migration will probably eliminate any constant 'multiplier'.

A final problem with 'multipliers' is that any chosen figure is at best a compromise covering a wider range of figures at a particular place. For this reason, the local historian and demographer should not be afraid to experiment by applying values above or below the norms given above, especially if s/he is fortunate to have a range of estimates from different sources to compare in the same period. There is also another reason why 'multipliers' devised at national level may not be necessarily appropriate locally. This is that England and Wales down to at least the eighteenth century – some historians have suggested even in the nineteenth century – were a collection of regions with differing characteristics and therefore with different demographic experiences which may diverge widely from the national aggregate.

Comparing multipliers

It is fairly rare for us to be able to compare estimates for the same period and place using different sources and therefore different multipliers, but where this is possible and produces very similar results, our confidence in the 'multipliers' used is strengthened. In 1546 the Suffolk chantry commissioners generally omitted to give the number of 'houseling people' (communicants) but in Botesdale, which was being absorbed into Redgrave, they noted '46 householders in the street, by estimation 160 houseling people'.[23] Using the usual multipliers for communicants in 1546–48 of 1.33,[24] and for households of 4.75,[25] the resulting population estimates are 213 from the houseling people and 219 from the households, a close match which confirms the reliability of both the original data and the multipliers used to produce population estimates. A similar conclusion follows from a reference in 1548 to Dogdyke in Billinghay (Lincs) as containing 'certen housholds to the noumbre of 18 ... ther being 70 houseling people': the resulting population estimates are 93 from the 'houseling people' and 86 from the households, again a close equivalence.[26] In Canterbury diocese between 1557 and 1569, a series of vigorous archdeacons secured many figures for both householders and communicants in the same parishes, and here again there is a fairly close correlation between the two sets of population estimates.[27]

Comparing totals at two or more dates

A further difficulty in comparing estimated populations at two or more points in time is that, while such comparison will show the population-trend over the period between these dates, it will not show how long before and after the period that trend prevailed, nor will it show whether the observed trend is realistic. Where the available figures permit, it is always desirable to compare population-estimates across a group of similar parishes, even if we are only interested in one or two of them: such a comparison will show whether any set of figures are atypical of the rest and should perhaps be discarded. But it is by no means impossible for a demographic disaster such as the outbreak of epidemic disease in 1556–60 to affect one parish followed by another 10 miles away, while the intervening parishes show no signs of disaster or crisis. Such phenomena have been observed in the early modern period and probably occurred in earlier times too. Most parts of England can show areas where the demographic experience is reasonably well documented and yet the experience of some parishes is radically different from others in the same region. Although not all English parishes are equally well represented at every date for which numerical data on taxpayers, soldiers and communicants are recorded – the chantry certificates of Cumberland and Westmorland, for example, have no recorded 'houseling people' (communicants) in either 1546 or 1548,[28] and many dioceses have no returns to the diocesan censuses of 1563 and 1603[29] – there is usually enough data for some general trends to emerge in the early modern period.

Elucidating population trends in the medieval period is much more difficult since the main national data consists of numbers of taxpayers before 1334, usually collected on a parish or tithing basis, whilst at local level the main source of data is manorial surveys or 'extents' including the numbers of different kinds of tenant (the Domesday Survey of 1086 is a nationwide summary manorial extent). Since most tenants were heads of household, such figures should yield good estimates of total manorial population so long as we remember that the household of a resident manorial lord will be much larger than the average peasant household (see above, pp. 30–1).

Manor and parish

The major problem is that all the figures from Domesday Book, the 1279 Hundred Rolls, the 'extents' and accounts or court rolls refer to the manor, not the parish; manors and parishes even with the same name are not necessarily identical units with common boundaries, although in many cases they are. Even if the areas of the manors and their parish are known, a simple numerical adjustment will not be sufficient unless the population-density of both manors is identical (which is usually roughly true); otherwise, you are dependent on there being enough data for any other manors in the parish to calculate its total population. Even so, whether the estimates for manor B will be near enough in date to those of manor A is doubtful.

Only when we reach the decennial censuses in 1801 and subsequent years can you be reasonably certain that the data on local population is of acceptable accuracy. Even so, one source of possible inaccuracy needs to be considered. This is that one of the local frameworks used in the early censuses, 1801–31, alongside the parish was the still surviving Anglo-Saxon unit known as the hundred (or wapentake in the former Danish East Midlands). If a parish is divided between two or more hundreds, the totals for all these sections or tithings need to be added together to obtain parochial totals comparable to those of 1841 onwards.

Protestation Returns, 1641–2

Another possible source for population totals are the Protestation Returns of 1641–2, which were nominal lists of (mostly) adult males who had signed or attested the 'Protestation' against the Laudian changes in the Church of England. In two counties, Gloucestershire and Herefordshire, Royalists apparently prevented the 'Protestation' from being circulated and, in others, Royalists refused to sign what they saw as a move towards Puritanism. In many parishes, it seems that most of the signers or attestors were either adult males or heads of households. Where such parish lists exist it would be worthwhile comparing the resulting estimated totals with totals derived both from the *Hearth Taxes* of the 1660s and 1670s, the 'Compton Census' of 1676 and, where they exist, from the Commonwealth Parish Returns of 1650.[30]

Ecclesiastical visitation returns

A final source of parish population returns, one not recognised by historians of population, consists of visitation returns. These had existed since the Middle Ages as a means of inspecting local parishes, clergy and churches, but only in the mid-sixteenth century did they begin to record parish population totals (Gloucester diocese: 1551; Canterbury diocese: 1556). The inclusion of these totals did not become common until the early eighteenth century, perhaps stimulated by the 'Compton Census' of 1676 and fears both of growing nonconformity following the *Toleration Act* of 1689 and of Catholicism after the Jacobite invasions of 1715 and 1745. It is clear from those returns in print that total parish population was a usual item of enquiry together with numbers of nonconformists and 'Papists', and that local as well as national historians need to consider this source seriously.[31]

Unless you are unfortunate enough to be dealing with a parish with no population-data before the national census of 1801 onwards (usually a parish that was an ecclesiastical 'peculiar', exempt from diocesan control), you will now have some data, often separated from the rest by decades if not centuries. How can you fill in the gaps? For most of the Middle Ages, as we shall see in Chapter 3, there is very little direct evidence for long-term population trends, apart from one series for hundred-penny payments at Taunton (Somerset) from 1208 to 1330 discovered in the 1950s.[32] Intensive searching since has only uncovered a few short hundredal series for parts of Wiltshire in the thirteenth century, for parts of Leicestershire in the fourteenth and earlier fifteenth centuries and in parts of Essex in the fifteenth and earlier sixteenth centuries; a similar series for the borough of Shrewsbury (Salop) enables the urban population to be estimated throughout the sixteenth and seventeenth centuries.[33] However, it may well prove possible to reconstruct the continuous population history of a manor if it has a long and continuous run of court rolls: such runs, however, are rarely found.

From about 1350, however, when diocesan registrars start copying wills that have gone through probate into volumes, such series of wills become increasingly common in the fifteenth and sixteenth centuries and can be considered as a proxy for burial or death series. Most parts of England have some regional probate series by 1500, which can be augmented by the national series of the Prerogative Court of Canterbury and the Exchequer and Chancery series at York. Several historians have noted that numbers of wills appear to be reliable indicators of excess burials caused by epidemic disease; if this is so, despite the dislocation caused by epidemics, they should be even more reliable for tracing normal movements of population.[34] Where will-counts can be compared with burial statistics in parish registers from 1538 onwards, both series are moving in the same direction at approximately the same pace.[35]

Manorial records

In rural areas the chief source for medieval local history is manorial records, which include rentals (also known as surveys and, if made by royal officials called escheators, 'extents'); court-rolls and accounts.[36] The surveys, whether made by the lord's servants or by the royal escheators, should provide a complete list of tenants of the manor in addition to a summary survey of the lord's 'demesne' (home farm), which is often still identifiable today as 'Home Farm', 'Manor Farm', 'Court Farm' or 'Hall Farm'. Such surveys can usually be taken as accurate, given the interest of both Crown and manorial lords in the income to be derived from the estates in question, and the tenants can safely be assumed to be heads of household. Nevertheless, they may not be complete lists of local heads of household, for three main reasons. First, there may be tenants holding land in the unit area from another manor, which will only be shown in that manor's records; second, there may be independent freeholders who may be difficult to track down; third, some tenants may have sublet part of their holdings to under-tenants who rarely appear in the surveys. If you can show that the manorial surveys do mention all tenants and there is no indication of either subletting or other manors and freeholds in the vicinity, then the manorial tenants are indeed probably the local heads of household. But court-rolls may reveal the existence of a landless group of inhabitants, perhaps squatters on the waste, especially in areas of royal 'forest', who in some places may be a large proportion of the local population; at Halesowen (Worcs), for example, it has been shown that whereas the tenants tripled in number between 1086 and 1315, the total number of households rose nearly seven times in the same period.[37]

Such manorial surveys, whether made by the lord's servants or by the royal escheators, can usually be taken as accurate, and the tenants can safely be assumed to be heads of household. Nevertheless, they may not be complete lists of local heads of household, for three main reasons, as we have just seen. If you can show that the manorial records do mention all tenants and there is no indication of either subletting or other manors and freeholds, then the manorial tenants are indeed probably the local heads of household. But court-rolls, if they survive, may reveal the existence of a landless group of inhabitants, perhaps squatters on the waste, who in some places, especially in wooded areas, may be a large proportion of the local population; Halesowen (Worcs) is one example noted above.

Estate maps and surveys

From the sixteenth century onwards, the rentals or surveys are often accompanied by, or made in conjunction with, an estate map or series of maps resulting from a topographical survey.[38] Estate maps have continued to be made down to the present day, though after the 1860s they increasingly used the large-scale Ordnance Survey maps as a base. Most plans attached to 'Sale Particulars' produced by estate agents and auctioneers since the 1840s have also been based either on the Tithe maps of the 1830s and 1840s or the large-scale 6 or 25 inches to the mile Ordnance Survey maps. Finally, the Crown occasionally conducted national enquiries into landholding using essentially the same manorial framework and approximately the same layout as the extents: two obvious examples are the Domesday Survey of 1086 and the Hundred Rolls enquiry of 1279, which will be studied in detail in Chapter 3.

Court Rolls

Manorial court rolls, if they survive – many, alas, have disappeared – will also reveal the range of local occupations, often as occupational surnames (weaver, tailor, tanner, shoemaker, she(a)rman, carpenter, mason, wright, miller, baker, butcher, etc).[39] They will also contain much useful topographical information, such as the names and areas of fields, roads, streams and hamlets, and will usually show if the manor's land was being cultivated under any form of 'common field' routine (e.g. in two or three open fields). If the court rolls are continuous for long periods, it may be possible to reconstitute some tenant families, and many deaths in any short period are likely to indicate a demographic crisis caused by either epidemic disease or starvation after bad harvests. A large number of land transactions will reveal an active land-market and reveal which families are prospering and which are not. In addition, tenants could be fined for various offences such as encroaching on 'the king's highway', moving boundary marks, trespass on the lands of the lord or other peasants, assault and other minor crimes. The manorial court was also the forum for settling disputes or recording agreements between neighbours, which can yield much valuable topographical data.

Account Rolls

The manorial account rolls are principally concerned with the lord's income from, and expenditure on, the 'demesne' but again will often reveal much of the local topography in field-names as well as the existence of field-systems, in so far as these affected the lord's demesne. They are also a prime source for local prices and wages which have a large bearing on the welfare of the tenants as well as the lord's prosperity. Rapidly rising prices, especially of cereal foods, invariably indicate the approach of crisis conditions which may lead to increased deaths from malnutrition or even starvation. In contrast, stable prices are generally beneficial to both lords and tenants. In contrast, stable prices are generally beneficial to both lords and tenants. In the earlier 'High' Middle Ages, *c.* 1100–*c.* 1400, you may be able to determine whether the lord relies on forced labour, 'servile work', to cultivate the demesne or whether the villain 'works' are being supplemented or replaced by wage-labour.

The potential utility of manorial records is greatly increased if the manor has a hundred attached to it, '*manerium cum hundredo*'.[40] In the medieval period, local boys became adult at the age of 12 when they formally 'came into the hundred', an event recorded in the hundred court rolls. Thereafter each male paid a 'hundred penny' every year, the payment being recorded in any surviving hundred account rolls. Such payments, though confined to males of 12 or over, are by far the best guide to total local population trends in medieval England, but they are apparently rare in the extreme. As we have seen above, one long series exists for Taunton hundred in Somerset from 1208 to 1325, Wiltshire has a series for landless men in the thirteenth century, and hundred-penny payments still reflected demographic changes in various parts of England in the fourteenth, fifteenth and sixteenth centuries.[41] Finally, local historians should be aware that, apart from the years 1649–60, all manorial account- and court-rolls will be written in latin down to 1733, as will inquisitions post mortem and 'extents', and often also the surveys, and down to the introduction of italic writing after *c.* 1600 generally use a stylised form known as 'court hand'; quantities will usually be expressed in roman numerals before the mid-seventeenth century. None of these obstacles is insuperable: there are good guides to both medieval and early modern handwriting and to medieval Latin.[42] The only real divergence between classical roman numerals as given in most encyclopedias and the roman numerals used in the medieval and early modern periods is that 'iv' is normally written as 'iiii' and that where numerals end with a roman 'i', this is usually written 'j'; hence 4 is usually 'iiij' rather than 'iv', 6 is 'vj', 7 is 'vij', 8 is 'viij' and 9 is often 'viiij' rather than 'ix'; also, a superscript roman number is a multiplier: vj^{xx} is therefore 6 x 20 = 120. All of these obstacles can be overcome: as we have seen, there are good guides to both medieval and early modern handwriting and to medieval Latin. Even if your manorial records are sparse, it should normally be possible to show how the local population changed over time, even if the records do not tell you why the changes occurred, and to say something about the lives of the local people.

Parish clergy

In addition to secular tenants of a manor, the local population will generally include at least one parish priest occupying the parsonage house and glebe land who generally will not occur in manorial surveys unless he holds additional land from the lord of the manor or another lord as a 'lay fee'. If during the Middle Ages the church was given to a monastery, nunnery or other religious institution (including hospitals and Oxbridge colleges), the institution became the rector. The diocesan bishop then usually 'ordained a vicarage', allowing the impropriator (as the institution would be called) possession of most of the glebe land and normally the 'great tithes' of arable crops, while the vicar would have part of the glebe, part of the rectory house or a newly built vicarage in lieu, and the 'small tithes' (of livestock and its products, also timber and minerals).

Following the dissolution of the monasteries between 1536 and 1540, the 'appropriated rectories' passed to the Crown and were mostly sold to laymen who became the owners of rectorial tithes and usually also of the 'advowson', the right to present a new man as rector or vicar on the death or departure of the previous incumbent. If the church was not given to an institution, the parish priest remained a rector having full possession of the parsonage, all the glebe land and the tithes; the advowson, however, unless given to an institution, normally was the property of the manorial lord, again reflecting the historical fact that parish churches had normally been built by one of the lord's predecessors.

Even if the medieval parson was celibate (as he was supposed to be), he would often have an assistant priest and a housekeeper living with him; if he was a married man (very common before about 1250 despite numerous purges by bishops, and again almost ubiquitous after the Reformation), the village priest must therefore be counted as an additional head of household. Before the Reformation, there would often also be a chantry chapel, either attached to the parish church or in a separate building, dedicated to saying masses for the souls of particular people, usually revealed in the diocesan bishop's registers,[43] in royal licences to give land in mortmain,[44] often in wills, such as that of Robert Poyntz, d. 1471, setting up the Poyntz chantry in the 'Gastelin chapel' in Frampton Cotterell church.[45] This chantry was clearly in existence as late as 1522 when the 'Military Survey' recorded it as holding land in the adjoining parish of Winterbourne,[46] but it is not mentioned in the *Valor Ecclesiasticus* of 1535[47] nor in the Gloucestershire chantry certificates of 1546 and 1548.[48] Evidently it had ceased to exist between 1522 and 1535, probably because it never received the full endowment intended by Robert Poyntz. We must not therefore assume that all chantries still existed at the final dissolution in 1546–48 to be recorded in the chantry certificates, covering much of England and Wales, which frequently contain estimates of the number of 'houseling people' (communicants) in the parish.[49]

Until the *Hearth Taxes* of the 1660s and 1670s, clergyman would not appear in lay subsidies or as manorial tenants unless, in addition to their glebe land (the 'parson's freehold'), they also held a 'lay fee'; otherwise they were taxed in separate clerical subsidies. From the sixteenth to the nineteenth centuries, the church, the glebe land, together with the churchyard and other income such as tithes and fees, were itemised for the diocesan bishop or one of his archdeacons, normally in detail, at intervals in documents called 'glebe terriers' which can be useful guides to local topography, field systems and natural resources, especially if manorial records are sparse. Thus the Frampton Cotterell glebe terriers reveal that coal and stone roof-tiles both paid tithes to the rector in the early seventeenth century and also record that the glebe land was scattered in different parts of the parish recalling the open fields that had disappeared from Frampton before the 1390s.[50]

Notes

1   J. Hatcher 'Understanding the population history of England, 1450–1750', *Past and Present* 180 (2003), 83–130, questions much of Wrigley and Schofield's methodology and their underlying assumptions. For earlier criticisms see D. Reher and R. S. Schofield (eds), *Old and New Methods in Historical Demography* (Oxford, OUP, 1993), chaps 1–5. The newer 'inverse-projection' program is claimed to be more robust, but the calculated age-distribution is not markedly different from that obtained by 'back-projection' (E. A. Wrigley *et al.*, *English Population History from Family Reconstitution, 1580–1837* (Cambridge, CUP, 1997), 615).

2   P. Laslett and R. Wall (eds), *Household and Family in Past Time* (Cambridge, CUP, 1972), 130–1 (table 4.1), 174–90 (table 5.1).

3   A. J. Coale and P. Demeny, *Regional Model Life-Tables and Stable Populations* (Princeton (USA), New York (USA), Academic Press, rev. edn 1983).

4   Laslett and Wall, *Household and Family*, chaps 4–5.

5   T. Arkell 'Multiplying Factors for estimating population totals from the Hearth Tax', *LPS* 28 (1982), 51–7.

6   See Bibliography, section 6 (iv) 5.

7   Thus the archbishop of Canterbury's household numbered between 50 and 70 people in the medieval period (F. R. H. Du Boulay, *The Lordship of Canterbury* (London, Nelson, 1966), 251–64). The Lateran Council of 1179 restricted the number of retainers accompanying archbishops and bishops to 70 for

archbishops and 40–50 for bishops (N. P. Tanner (ed.), *Decrees of the Ecumenical Councils* (London, Sheed and Ward, 1990), vol. I, 213).

8 K. Mertes, *The English Noble Household, 1250–1600* (Oxford, Blackwell, 1988); C. M. Woolgar (ed.), *Household Accounts from Medieval England* (Oxford, OUP, 2 vols, 1992–3).

9 E. A. Wrigley and R. S. Schofield, *The Population History of England, 1541–1871* (London, Arnold, 1981, repr. Cambridge, CUP, 1989), 529, 565–6, 569.

10 A. Whiteman (ed.), *The Compton Census of 1676: a critical edition* (Oxford, OUP, 1986), lviii–xxix.

11 W. G. Hoskins, *Provincial England* (London, Macmillan, 1963), 186.

12 S. Fish 'A supplicacyon for Beggars' [1529], *STC*, item no. 10883, repr. in F. J. Furnivall (ed.) 'Four supplications, 1529–1553 AD' (*Early English Text Society*, Extra ser. 13 (1871), 1–15), and J. W. Hebel *et al.* (eds), *Tudor Poetry and Prose* (New York (USA), Appleton-Century-Crofts (1953), 566.

13 J. Cornwall 'English population in the early sixteenth century', *Econ. Hist. Rev.* 2nd ser. 23 (1970), 41.

14 Hoskins, *Provincial England*, 72, n.3.

15 Cornwall 'English Population', 33, 35–6.

16 TNA, E 36/94; SP 1/25, 33; J. Oldland 'The allocation of mercantile capital in early Tudor London', *Econ. Hist. Rev.* 63 (2010), 1058–80, at pp. 1058, 1060.

17 A. L. Rowse, *The England of Elizabeth. The Structure of Society* (London, Macmillan, 1951), 335.

18 R. S. Schofield 'Taxation and the political limits of the Tudor State', in C. Cross *et al.* (eds), *Law and Government under the Tudors* (Cambridge, CUP, 1988), 227–55; R. S. Schofield, *Taxation under the Early Tudors, 1485–1547* (Oxford, Blackwell, 2004).

19 P. Franklin 'Gloucestershire medieval taxpayers', *LPS* 54 (1995), 16–27. There is one possible exception to the general rule that later medieval taxation records were unreliable and useless as sources for population. This comprises the records of the poll taxes in 1377, 1379 and 1381 originally covering the whole of England and so rigorously assessed that they provoked the Peasants' Revolt in 1381. The tax was levied on all adults over the age of 14 and in many places appears to be a complete record of adult males. Fortunately for local historians and demographers, there is an excellent modern edition of the surviving records which do not cover the entire country: in some areas the 1381 poll tax was probably not collected due to popular opposition, and in other areas in all years the records have been lost subsequently. see C. C. Fenwick (ed.), *The Poll Taxes of 1377, 1379 and 1381* (Oxford, OUP, 3 vols, 1998–2005)

20 See Bibliography, section 6 (iv) 10.

21 Wrigley and Schofield, *Population History of England*, 528–9 (table A3.1).

22 E. Rich 'The population of Elizabethan England', *Econ. Hist. Rev.* 2nd ser. 3 (1950), 247–65, esp. pp. 250–5. Rich was a pioneer in recognising the importance of local migration.

23 V. B. Redstone (ed.) 'Chapels, chantries and gilds in Suffolk' *Proceedings of the Suffolk Institute of Archaeology and Natural History* 12 (1906), 31–4, 36, 40.

24 Wrigley and Schofield, *The Population History of England*, 565–6.

25 Laslett and Wall, *Household and Family*, chaps 4–5.

26 C. W. Foster and A. Hamilton-Thompson (eds) 'The Chantry Certificates for Lincoln and Lincolnshire', *Reports and Proceedings of the Associated Architectural Societies* 37 (1925), 89.

27 J. S. Moore 'Canterbury Visitations and the demography of Mid-Tudor Kent', *Southern History* 15 (1993), 36–85, studies the original data in L. E. Whatmore (ed.) 'Archdeacon Harpsfield's Visitation, 1557', *Catholic Rec. Soc.* 45–6, 1950–1, and other Canterbury visitations.

28 R. L. Storey (ed.) 'The Chantries of Cumberland and Westmorland', *Trans. Cumberland and Westmorland Antiq. and Arch. Soc.* NS 60 (1960), 66–96; 62 (1962), 145–70.

29 A. D. Dyer and D. M. Palliser (eds), *The Diocesan Population Returns for 1563 and 1603* (Oxford, OUP, 2005), print all the returns known to survive.

30 See Bibliography, section 6 (iv) 5.

31 See Bibliography, section 6 (iv) 7.

32 J. Z. Titow 'Some evidence of the thirteenth-century population increase', *Econ. Hist. Rev.* 2nd ser. 14 (1961), 231–51.

33 See Bibliography, section 5 (iv).

34 S. L. Thrupp 'The problem of replacement-rates in late medieval England', *Econ. Hist. Rev.* 2nd ser. 18 (1965), 101–19; F. J. Fisher 'Influenza and inflation in Tudor England', *Econ. Hist. Rev.* 2nd ser 18 (1965), 120–9; R. S. Gottfried, *Epidemic Disease in Fifteenth-Century England* (New Brunswick (USA), Rutgers UP, 1978); J. S. Moore '"Jack Fisher's 'flu": a visitation revisited', *Econ. Hist. Rev.* 46 (1993), 280–307.

35 J. S. Moore, *Disease, Disaster and Death in Mid-Tudor England* (forthcoming).

36 See Bibliography, section 5 (ii) 2–3.

37 Z. Razi, *Life, Marriage and Death in a Medieval Parish: Halesowen, 1270–1400* (Cambridge, CUP, 1980), 28, 31.

38 See references cited in Chapter 1, note 3.

39 G. Fransson, *Middle English Surnames of Occupation, 1100–1350* (Lund (Sweden), Gleerup, 1935). More general information on English surnames will be found in B. Cottle, *Penguin Dictionary of Surnames* (Harmondsworth, Penguin, 2nd edn, 1978); P. Hanks and F. Hodges, *A Dictionary of Surnames* (Oxford, OUP, 1988); R. McKinley, *A Dictionary of British Surnames* (London, Longman, 1990); P. H. Reaney, *A Dictionary of English Surnames* (London, Routledge, 3rd edn, 1991).

40 H. M. Cam '*Manerium cum hundred*: the hundred and the hundredal manor', in her *Liberties and Communities in Medieval England* (Cambridge, CUP, 1944), chap. 5. As Dr Cam points out (*ibid.*, 90), in the Danelaw the corresponding unit is the soke rather than the wapentake.

41   See note 29 above.

42   See Bibliography, section 2 (b) – (c).

43   For a detailed list for every diocese see D. M. Smith, *Guide to Bishops' Registers of England and Wales* (London, Roy. Hist. Soc. 1981).

44   See Bibliography, section 5 (i) (Patent Rolls) and S. Raban, *Mortmain Legislation and the English Church, 1279–1500* (Cambridge, CUP, 1982).

45   TNA PROB 11/6 (old reference PCC Wattys), fols 2v–3v.

46   R. W. Hoyle (ed.) 'The military survey of Gloucestershire, 1522', *Gloucestershire Rec. Ser.* 6, 1993, 20.

47   J. Caley and J. Hunter (eds), *Valor Ecclesiasticus temp. Henrici VIII auctoritate regis instituta* (London, Rec. Comm., 7 vols, 1834).

48   TNA E 301/21-2; J. Maclean (ed.), 'Chantry Certificates, Gloucestershire (Roll 22)', *Trans. Bristol and Gloucestershire Archaeological Soc.* 8 (1884), 229–308).

49   See Bibliography, section 6 (iv) 5.

50   Gloucestershire Archives, Gloucester, GDR/EP/136T/1–5.

CHAPTER 3

Population and Local History, 1066–1525

The dark ages of population history

The centuries before 1538 have been described as 'the dark ages of English population history',[1] in which there are a few large-scale surveys but very little to cover the intervening periods. In the absence of 'direct' methods, because the necessary data do not exist, we have to rely on 'indirect' methods utilising various substitutes which have to be pressed into service in default.

Comparing manorial populations

As we have seen in Chapter 2, there are very few medieval sources that provide us with direct evidence of changing population trends, and for the most part we have to try to extract data on population-levels at particular times when suitable records exist, compare these levels at different times and then estimate total populations by using appropriate 'multipliers' where necessary. A full study of the structure of medieval local populations will elude us unless we are exceptionally fortunate in the survival of detailed local records: the explanation of such population trends that we can perhaps deduce may well prove impossible or at best tentative.

But there is no doubt that the period saw important demographic developments: nationally, English population is now thought to have grown from around 2–2.25 millions in 1086 to perhaps 3 millions in 1200 and to between 6 and 7 millions in the earlier fourteenth century. Population then began to fall as a result of the 'great European famine' of 1315–17, a decline greatly accelerated by the 'Black Death' of 1348–50 and later outbreaks of plague, as well as other diseases, until in the mid-fifteenth century the population was again around 2 millions.[2] Growth began to resume in many areas after about 1480 and became general after about 1510, perhaps reaching 2.35 millions by 1525 and growing more rapidly to about 3.5–4 millions by 1555. Source-material for trends in medieval population is even scarcer, rarely rising above the level of the hundred or manor.

The Crown as landlord and feudal superior

The Crown's interests as sovereign, landlord and ultimate feudal superior lay behind the Domesday survey of 1086, the *Rotuli de Dominabus* of 1185, the incomplete Hundred Rolls of 1279–80 and the series of inquisitions *post mortem* and miscellaneous inquisitions from the 1230s onwards. Military and, especially, manpower needs produced the recruitment of foot-soldiers, archers and building craftsmen, especially in the reigns of Edward I and Edward III. Fiscal needs led to lay subsidies (tax assessments) from the 1220s to 1332; these were replaced by town and village quotas in 1334 which become increasingly unrealistic as a result of later exemptions. The 1522 'military survey' quickly developed into the new Tudor Lay Subsidy tax of 1524–5: both the subsidy rolls and the muster rolls, produced at local level from the 1520s onwards, comprised nominal lists which are of potential demographic significance.

There are, therefore, in the period 1086–1524 numerous 'surveys' (often called 'custumals', 'extents' or rentals) which potentially should provide data on the number of manorial tenants at various times: these can be compared with each other so long as we can show that they are presenting data for the same unit-area, essentially the names of their lords and the holders of manorial tenements, which are comparable at both dates, 1086 and the date of the survey (see Fig. 1). This comparison, moreover, does not depend on the correctness of any 'multiplier' since we are comparing two sets of 'raw data'; only if we apply different 'multipliers' at either or both dates do we need to discuss the exact 'multiplier' to be used on each occasion. The medieval lay subsidy taxes, however, are certainly less comparable with either Domesday Book or the 'extents': they are concerned with the assessment of 'moveable' wealth (goods and chattels but not land). Nevertheless, locally as nationally, the hierarchy of moneyed wealth is not identical with the hierarchy of landed wealth: many cottagers may occupy a cottage and garden, even a few acres of land, but have little disposable property. Consequently, historians have not been able to agree on a suitable 'multiplier' to convert numbers of medieval taxpayers into numbers of inhabitants. W. G. Hoskins suggested that the 1327 lay subsidy in Leicestershire recorded between a quarter and a third of the taxable population, but considered that the subsidy payers of 1524–5 were heads of household.[3]

The Domesday Survey, 1086

Before we can use the Domesday Survey preserved in the two volumes of 'Great (or 'Exchequer') Domesday Book' and 'Little Domesday Book' (hereafter *DB* I and II) and in so-called 'satellites' (copies of the 'original returns' to King William's commissioners made by some bishops and abbots), we need to understand what the Domesday Survey was and why it was compiled. The nickname Domesday originated in the 'day of doom', the 'final judgement' of mankind by God, and expressed contemporaries' belief in the survey's authority: it was the 'survey of the whole of England' (*descriptio totius Angliae* in Latin), made by order of William the Conqueror 20 years after the Norman Conquest of England. Why then? The previous year, 1085, had seen an 'invasion scare' when a Danish invasion had seemed likely: the king brought a large mercenary army to England which had to be billeted on the barons. The urgent need to billet and maintain foreign mercenaries for much of 1085 must have highlighted deficiencies in the official knowledge of England's resources and their division between King, the Church and the barons, especially given the considerable changes in the higher ranks of society since 1066, with 'English' earls, bishops, abbots and thegns being replaced by 'Norman' barons, bishops, abbots and knights. Although local assessments to the land-tax (*geld*) were perfectly well known, they were often centuries old, had been lowered in many cases as a result of privileged reduction and thus no longer corresponded to agrarian or fiscal reality.

There can be no doubt of the thoroughness of the Domesday Survey: according to the *Anglo-Saxon Chronicle*:

> 'The King had much thought and deep discussion with his Council about this country, how it was occupied and with what sort of people ... So narrowly did he have it investigated that there was not a single hide or yardland, nor indeed ... an ox nor a cow nor a pig was left out and not entered in his record.'[4]

This thoroughness was also emphasised by two other contemporary eye-witnesses, Robert of Losinga, bishop of Hereford from 1079 to 1095, and the chronicler John of Worcester.

Despite its claims to completeness, in fact the Domesday Survey did not cover the modern counties of Durham and Northumberland (which were certainly in Norman hands by 1070 at the latest), for reasons which are not known, and its coverage of England north of Cheshire and west of the Pennines is sketchy (Cumberland and Westmorland remained part of Scotland until conquered by William Rufus in 1092). Further south, there are some gaps in the coverage of Derbyshire, Staffordshire and Yorkshire resulting from the 'harrying of the North' in 1067–70, and occasional blanks for missing information occur throughout the rest of England. Nevertheless it is clear from the 'terms of reference' prefixed to the 'Cambridgeshire Inquest' (*ICC*) that an enumeration of rural heads of household was one of its intents:

> [6] How many villagers, how many cottagers, how many slaves?
> [7] How many freemen, how many sokemen?[5]

Although the terms of reference specified that 'All this is to be given three times, that is, in the time of King Edward [1066], when King William gave it, and now [1086]', in fact few population data were recorded for the intermediate date and *DB* I rarely recorded the numbers of people in 1066, though 1066 figures as well as 1086 figures are commonly found in *DB* II. But population-details are usually given in both volumes for each manor in 1086. It will, however, be seen that the 'terms of reference' failed completely to mentioned boroughs and burgesses, and as a result major towns like London, Winchester and Bristol were not fully recorded, and other towns were awkwardly inserted at the beginning of each county section. Other omissions result because Domesday Book was not designed as a modern census, consequently certain groups of the local population were not included: these comprise the members of royal and baronial households, the garrisons of castles and monks or nuns in convents. Most of the recorded lay individuals were probably heads of households, though the position of slaves is less clear; probably most male slaves were heads of households, but female slaves may well have been unmarried household servants or dairymaids.[6]

The enumeration of the different groups of rural population inevitably invites calculation of the size and distribution of that population. There is, however, a major problem, namely that the main unit for which Domesday recorded local information of all kinds, agrarian details as well as population, was the manor, a unit which charters show was already present in Anglo-Saxon England, and which remained significant in many parts of England until the early twentieth century.[7] There is no necessary equivalence between the manor and other units such as the tithing or township and above all the parish, even if manor, tithing and parish had the same name. In some areas, notably the south-west, the west Midlands and Yorkshire but also on old royal and ecclesiastical estates in the south, a manor could spread over more than one parish, and in such cases only the central place, the *caput manerii*, will be named in Domesday. In the northern Danelaw the centre was often called a 'soke' (the soke of Peterborough survived into the twentieth century) with its outlying portions styled 'berewicks'. This explains why many villages with undoubtedly Old English names, and therefore in existence well before 1066, sometimes being recorded in Anglo-Saxon charters, are not mentioned by name in the Domesday Survey.[8]

But manorial lords and their officials, stewards or lessees where the lord is non-resident will be clearly visible: they will be at the head of lists of taxpayers to the subsidy from the 1220s to 1332 and again after 1522 as well as in sources like the Hundred Rolls of both 1254–5 and 1279–80 and the *Quo Warranto* proceedings of the 1270s–90s. They and any of the substantial freemen may well appear in the central *Curia Regis* rolls and in the local court-hearings held by itinerant justices and later assize judges, both as parties and as jurymen.[9] Those below them in the social scale will mainly appear in the manorial court rolls, if these survive, as jurymen, as parties in disputes and as offenders against the communal agricultural regime for blocking ditches, diverting streams, abusing common rights, and as buyers and sellers in the 'peasant land market'.[10]

Calculating the total population of the manor should not be difficult, given that the average medieval peasant household was around 4.7 people;[11] the principal problem is deciding if the lord and his household were resident. This is subject to a proviso: it is probable that Domesday under-estimated the number of tenants, in particular by excluding under-tenants and demesne lessees who appear only in a few counties, notably Cheshire and Shropshire: perhaps 10% should be added to the totals of manorial lords in the other counties to allow for them. In some counties, notably in the East Midlands, slaves were not included for some unknown reason, though they are found in 'satellites' such as the Cambridgeshire and Ely inquests, and total population in these counties should also be increased by about 10%.[12] As we shall see, information on monastic population is sparse;[13] the other major demographic omission is the garrisons of castles which were likely to be fully manned during an 'invasion scare'.[14] Local castles can be studied in a variety of sources, both archaeological and historical; a manor which is the centre of either a barony or a substantial sub-tenancy is likely to have a castle there.[15] Of course, not every castle was in existence in 1086, but it has been estimated that approaching 500 had been built in William I's reign, though Domesday Book mentions under 50.

Manorial surveys

Since the basic territorial unit of the Domesday Survey was the manor, it is obviously appropriate to look to later manorial records to obtain comparable data on population. The most relevant documents to be consulted are manorial surveys which describe the lord's demesne land and list individual tenants and their holdings with the rents and services due from them. Since there is no agreed terminology for describing such documents, surveys may also be called 'custumals' (because 'customary' rents and services were often described in detail), rentals or even rent-rolls; when they were compiled and valued ('extended') by royal escheators or other officials as part of compiling an inquisition post mortem or as part of an action for debt, they were known as 'extents' (see Fig. 1. A medieval extent: Frampton Cotterell in 1321).[16] Whatever the name, the information was the same in all these records: a description of the lord's demesne and an enumeration of various categories of tenants.[17] However, you must check that your extent does not include non-residents who must be excluded from your count: thus you will see that both in 1321–2 and 1547 (Figs 1 and 3) the freeholders in Frampton Cotterell are headed by the lord of the neighbouring manor of Iron Acton (John de Acton in 1321–2, Sir Nicholas Poyntz in 1547) who must be excluded from the Frampton totals.

As we have already seen, the church was a notable landholder in medieval England: its share of English land in 1086 comprised one-fifth of all landed estates which had risen by 1535 to one-third.[18] Nevertheless, some of the documentation is less plentiful for ecclesiastical estates, while surveys are much more plentiful for secular than for ecclesiastical manors: the reason was that most secular manors after *c.* 1235 were likely to be surveyed every generation or so, say roughly every 30 years, in 'extents' created by the royal escheators

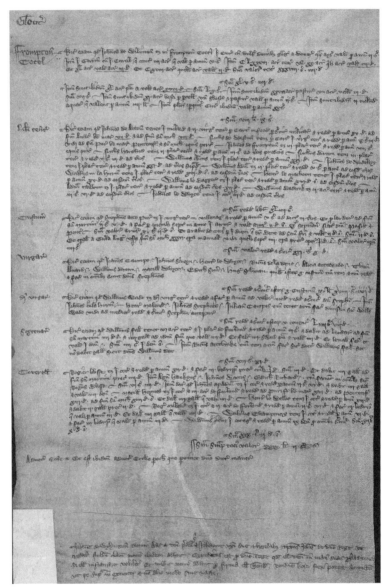

Figure 1 Survey of the manor of Frampton Cotterell, 1321–22 (TNA E 124/24, m.8v). Original MS. Crown (C) Copyright.

Translation:

(m.8v) Gloucestershire

Frampton Cotele — They [the jurors] say also that Sir John de Wilintone holds in Frampton Cotele one court with various buildings, barns and cattle-sheds worth yearly 2s. Also 1 garden and curtilage which contains 4 acres and is worth 5s. yearly. Also 178 acres of arable land, each worth 4d. yearly, and 40 acres each worth 3d. yearly, and 118 acres each worth 2d. yearly.
Total 45s. 4d.

There are 40 acres of meadow, each worth 18d yearly, total 60s. Also 28 acres of pasture, each worth 3d. yearly, total 7s. Also 11 acres of wood with underwood and pasture worth 2s. yearly. Also 2 watermills worth £4 yearly. Pleas and perquisites of court worth 20s.	Total £8 9s. 0d.

Free tenants — They say also that John de Acton holds a mill and 2 yardlands of arable land by charter for knight-service in fee and pays yearly 15d, at Lady Day 7d and at Michaelmas 8d. Nicholas de Weston holds by charter a yardland of arable land and pays yearly 9s 3d. at Lady Day, Pentecost and Michaelmas by equal portions. John de Frampton holds 3 plots of arable land and pays yearly 8s. by equal portions. Nicholas Harshed holds 2 plots of arable land and pays yearly 3s. at the aforesaid terms. Nicholas Broun holds 3 plots of arable land and pays yearly 5s 3d at the [aforesaid] terms. William Clark [or the clerk] holds a plot of arable land and pays yearly 21d. John de Wodeleye holds a plot of arable land and pays yearly 21d. at the said terms. William Adams holds 2 plots of arable land and pays yearly 5s. at the said terms. Walter in la Hurne holds a plot of arable land and pays yearly 16d at the said terms. Henry le Machom holds a plot of arable land and pays yearly 15d. at the said terms. William le Daggere holds a plot of arable land and pays yearly 16d. at the said terms. Adam Taillour holds a plot of arable land and pays yearly 12d. at the said terms.

acting on the assumption that these estates were held directly from the Crown, 'in chief', by knight service. (For reasons that are not entirely clear, 'extents' became less frequent after the mid-fourteenth century, though private estate surveys made for lords continued to be made.) Although estates not held from the Crown in chief were exempt from being 'extended' on their own, if the holder was also a tenant-in-chief for other land, however small in area that was, all his estates would be included in the 'extent'. In practice, therefore, as estates grew in size and fell in number, more and more secular manors were liable to be surveyed in an escheator's extent down to at least the later fourteenth century.

By contrast, although ecclesiastical estates were temporarily controlled by the Crown under its 'regalian right' on the death of a bishop or abbot,[19] very few royal surveys of monastic estates were made before *Valor Ecclesiasticus* in the 1530s.[20] Similarly with bishopric estates, the royal keepers rarely made an extent of the episcopal possessions.[21] Effectively, ecclesiastical estates were only surveyed when their owners decided to do so in order to ensure good estate-management. As a result, some ecclesiastical estates have good surveys generally at rather infrequent intervals, but many have not survived once they became outdated, and series of surveys of ecclesiastical estates are rather rare.[22] Much more common are the rentals and surveys of secular estates, often linked to royal extents of these estates on the death of their holders: although the extents were, regrettably, not printed in the *Calendar of Inquisitions Post Mortem* before 1422, they have often been printed by local societies as well as in some *Index Library* volumes.[23]

Three other useful series of extents in TNA are only partly listed: Chancery Extents for Debts, Series I (C 131) cover the period 1316–1669, and have recently been listed together with allied documents in C 241 (Certificates of Statute Merchant and Statute Staple) for the period 1284–*c.* 1530; miscellaneous Extents and Inquisitions (E 143) covering the period *c.* 1216–*c.* 1830 and extents for debts (Series II), *c.* 1530–*c.* 1650, remain unlisted, as do Extents and Inquisitions relating to Crown Debtors (E 144). Two good volumes of extents for debts for London, Middlesex and Wiltshire have been printed.[24] Moreover, many extents are mentioned (but not printed) in the *Calendar of Miscellaneous Inquisitions* covering the period *c.* 1216–1485.[25]

The 1279–80 Hundred Rolls

Finally, a good number of manorial surveys of both secular and ecclesiastical manors are found in the returns to the Hundred Rolls enquiry of 1279–80, often considered to be a 'second Domesday', though the survival of these returns is patchy, mainly for the East Midlands and parts of East Anglia, but also including north-west Shropshire. Although most have been printed, there are still unprinted returns for parts of Cambridgeshire, Huntingdonshire, London, Norfolk, Oxfordshire, Rutland and Shropshire.[26] To conclude, finding figures of manorial tenants in 'extents', rentals or surveys of secular estates between *c.* 1230 and *c.* 1400 is quite a high probability; records for ecclesiastical estates are less frequent but some go back to the twelfth century.

Both in 1086 and later, a manorial lord's household should only be included in addition to the manorial tenants if you can show that the manor in question was his chief residence at that time, his *caput honorii*; if you do decide to include it, remember that a manorial lord's household will be well above the average of 4.75 or thereabouts (see Chapter 2, pp. 30–1).[27] A final caution is necessary regarding manors or sub-manors which contained an abbey or priory. Neither Domesday Book nor any of the secular sources mentioned above included the inmates of these institutions, whose populations have to be found from any surviving records of the monastery, any episcopal visitations or clerical subsidies which survive and occasional mentions in chronicles. Since the monastic population was, by definition, separate from the laity, and since monastic populations are much less well evidenced than the local lay population, it is probably safest to disregard the former when comparing changes in population over time.[28] The position of the secular parish clergy is more complex. The Domesday Survey sometimes mentioned churches, sometimes priests, and occasionally both in the same manor; but very often in 1086 the village priest was silently included among the villagers and, as explicitly stated for Norfolk, 'the churches are appraised with the manors'.[29] The variations in the mention and description of clergy in *DB* I and II is probably the result of different commissioners' understanding of the original instructions given to them for their circuit.

Identifying manors and their lords

The chief problem in comparing Domesday statistics on population with numbers of tenants in later surveys (or between one survey and a later one) is ensuring that like is being compared with like as units. One cannot simply assume that the manor of Bloggston named in 1086 is the same unit as the manor with that same name two or three centuries later. (In this matter, of course, as local historians you may be far better equipped and more knowledgeable than the professional from outside the area.) The identification may be true, it often is true, but it need not be. If you are fortunate, your manor will already have had its 'descent' (succession of owners) worked out in the relevant volume of the *Victoria County History* of your county or in a good earlier history. This was a matter on which the local gentry of the seventeenth–nineteenth centuries, who were both lords of manors themselves and subscribers to local histories, took very seriously: to be a manorial lord then gave one secure status in the local community and in county society. Obviously earlier writers did not have at their finger tips the serried ranks of *Calendars* produced by the Public Record Office between the 1890s and the 1960s or all the other research aids to be found in record offices today. Nevertheless the authors of such county histories were in general hardworking and well-informed: they may have made mistakes, but they also preserved, by copying, earlier records that have since been lost. Thus the seventeenth-century antiquary William Burton copied two returns of the 1279–80 Hundred Rolls enquiry for Gartree and Guthlaxton hundreds in Leicestershire, which are now the only surviving records of the enquiry for that county; these copies were given to the Bodleian Library, Oxford, and partly printed in Nichols' *History and Antiquities of the County of Leicester.*[30]

It is, therefore, very unfortunate that the reference value of the *Victoria County History* (*VCH*) series has been weakened by modern distaste for 'manorial descents' which allegedly pander to the snobbery of antiquated and effete gentlefolk, and the latest volumes of the *VCH Yorkshire (East Riding)* entirely omits them. The situation is not helped by silly demands for 'more economic history' instead of manorial descents.[31] What, you may well ask, could be more relevant to local economic history than the history of the largest local estate, the largest local farm, usually the largest local employer, probably at the head of local government? Fortunately, much manorial history will be found in the relevant county historical society's proceedings, which are always worth inspection, also any county bibliographies, as well as any older county histories.

In default of a ready-made manorial descent, you must construct your own for the period from Domesday until the last usable manorial survey in the fifteenth or sixteenth century. It may well be that your manor was owned in the medieval period by a lord whose other manors' histories have been investigated elsewhere; if he was a tenant-in-chief *per baroniam*, his family should appear in Sanders' *English Baronies*;[32] if the manorial lord or his successors achieved a peerage in or after the fourteenth century, the history of the ancestral family will be found in the appropriate volume of the *Complete Peerage*.[33] For a lord from a large landowning family, it is worth looking at the *VCH* volumes for other counties, in which his descent has already been written-up. If none of these authorities help you and there is nothing in the secondary historical literature (books and articles), you must construct your own manorial descent for most of the medieval period: for the twelfth and earlier thirteenth centuries, you may be able to trace the lord as either a tenant-in-chief or a sub-tenant in the *Cartae baronum* (feudal returns) of '1166' (correctly 1165) or in lists of fees held from tenants-in-chief in the Pipe Rolls (Exchequer Accounts) at various times after 1155.[34]

The inquisitions post mortem will contribute much after the earlier thirteenth century, together with the *Book of Fees* and *Feudal Aids* which provide information on manorial lordship at various dates between 1212 and 1431;[35] these books, unlike the inquisitions and their allied 'extents', also include ecclesiastical estates. The Hundred Rolls of 1254–5[36] and the *Quo Warranto* enquiries later in Edward I's reign also often preserve knowledge of changes in manorial lordship at much earlier times.[37] Unlike the monastic estates, which were dispersed to lay owners at the Dissolution of the Monasteries (1536–40), most bishops' and cathedral estates remained with their owners, and monastic cathedrals were secularised; sales of bishops' and cathedrals' estates by the Commonwealth regime (1649–60) were abruptly reversed in 1660. Thereafter these lands remained with their owners until the mid-nineteenth century when most were transferred to the Ecclesiastical Commissioners; nearly all their estate records are now in local diocesan record offices.

Manorial fragmentation

The three most obvious ways in which a medieval manor's area and boundaries would alter after 1086 are, first, by subinfeudation, second, by grants to a religious institution, and third, by division among co-heiresses and their descendants. Subinfeudation was effectively ended by the statute *Quia Emptores* in 1290: it consisted of a lord granting part of his land to another person who would then hold it from him for defined services. If, for example, a feodary informs you that at a later date Sir X.Y. holds the manor of Bloggston in chief or from another lord, and A.B. holds land in (or adjacent to) Bloggston from Sir X.Y. for defined services, assuming there is no separate Domesday entry for this smaller manor, it is almost certain that the subinfeudated land was part of the Domesday manor of Bloggston.[38] Consequently, unless you can get demographic information on both manors (Bloggston and the part subinfeudated) at more or less the same time, no comparison is possible with the population of the Domesday manor of Bloggston in 1086.

Another source of attrition of manors after 1086 is the very common medieval habit of giving land to a religious institution for the spiritual benefit of the lord, his ancestors and his family, usually in the form of prayers for their souls. There are various ways in which such gifts can be identified and located. One hint, not invariably true but usually so, is that ex-monastic land after the Dissolution of the Monasteries is often recorded in documents such as glebe terriers, estate surveys and especially the Tithe Awards and Maps of *c.* 1840 as 'tithe-free'. A very useful *Supplementary List and Index* of 'Lands of Dissolved Religious Houses', arranged by county and well indexed, has been supplemented by Nigel Ramsay's *English Monastic Estates, 1066–1540* which, with the *Valor Ecclesiasticus* of 1535 should tell you if any land was held by a religious body (and which body) in or adjoining your manor.[39] Once you have identified the relevant body, normally a monastery but possibly a military order (Knights Templars (until 1308) and Knights Hospitallers (until 1540), a hospital or an Oxbridge college (though the latter were not affected by the Dissolution of the Monasteries), you can pursue their surviving records. Hospital records may be difficult to trace unless the hospital continued until the National Health Service or became a recognised charity. If your manor came into the hands of an Oxbridge College, you are very fortunate, for most colleges kept their estate records and nowadays have archivists looking after them. Records of ancient royal estates are to be found in many series at TNA and are mostly listed. The Duchy of Cornwall records are kept at a separate Duchy office in London and for the records of private royal estates (e.g. Sandringham) you must contact the Comptroller of the Royal Household. Finally, estates split between co-heiresses can normally be traced quite easily, since the division was authorised by the Crown as part of the 'extending' the lands in question; such extents are often followed by informative entries in the Close and Fine Rolls.[40]

Identifying and locating manors

If you are able to define precisely the lands granted either to a lesser secular owner or to an ecclesiastical body, you may be able to determine if it achieved an identity of its own as a manor or tithing; you can then check if any surveys of that manor or tithing were made by its owners, and if these were near in date to surveys of the main manor of Bloggston. If, of course, the records tell you that the monastic land was either waste or woodland with no evidence of later manorial settlement, you can then discount its existence for demographic purposes. But you must check first. You may of course find evidence in either the manor of Bloggston or an ecclesiastical sub-manor, of declining population or even depopulation. Falling population before about 1300 is most improbable as a general rule: the most likely exception in that period is that land which was given to the Cistercian order was meant to be free of any lay tenantry, agricultural work thereafter being performed by the monks and lay brothers (*conversi*), so that existing lay tenants would be encouraged to leave or be resettled.[41] Some medieval towns and villages especially on the east coast disappeared under the waves: Ravenserodd (Yorks) is the classic example. As a general rule, however, most ecclesiastical landlords endeavoured to develop their estates as far as this was possible, and their records at the Dissolution either went to the Crown and will now be found in TNA, or were passed to the new secular owners who were more likely to preserve estate records, of practical value to the new owners, than purely religious records such as service books.

Feet of Fines

Some central government records greatly help to trace the 'descent' of manors at this point from one body or person to another. The first is the series of Feet of Fines or Final Concords (TNA CP 25). A foot of fine was the official record ending a legal suit for land in the Court of Common Pleas; by the later thirteenth century the suits were entirely fictitious, being agreed by both parties, who thus secured a royal court's judgement to support the change of ownership. Three identical copies of each fine were made, one for the seller or grantor (usually the 'tenant'), one for the buyer or grantee (generally the 'demandant'), the third, the 'foot of fine', being retained by the Court of Common Pleas from 1195 to 1833. This is therefore a useful though not complete guide to landed transactions in this period and later, arranged under counties and 'Divers Counties', many of which have been calendared and indexed by local county historical societies.[42] Feet of fines generally follow a standard layout from which perhaps land-use can be obtained (see below).[43]

Deeds and enrolments

The second useful category of documents in TNA consists of the various collections of private deeds which accumulated in the royal archives. These include the *Ancient Deeds*, series A–H, L, P (TNA E 40–2, E 326–9, C 146–8, E 210–12, LR 14–15, DL 25–7, E 354–5).[44] Most of these accumulated as part of the business of government; Series B and BB, however, consisted of some but not all monastic archives confiscated at the Reformation. The originals of some deeds enrolled were also partially preserved in TNA E 354–5 (Pipe Office) and C 146–8 (Chancery), but far more deeds survived by enrolment in several places. Probably the earliest are those enrolled on the Pipe Rolls from Henry II's reign onwards which have been printed down to 1224;[45] almost as early were the charters, mostly of royal grants to religious houses, copied onto the *Carte Antiquae* rolls (TNA C 52) which are partly printed;[46] for safe keeping, private deeds were increasingly copied onto the dorse of the Close Rolls (C 54) and by 1500 were the sole content of these rolls;[47] the Charter Rolls (C 53),[48] Patent Rolls (C 66) and Confirmation Rolls (C 56)[49] frequently contain copies of deeds certified as produced in court (*inspeximus* procedure).[50] The Charter Rolls are completely printed, as are the Close Rolls until 1509 and the Patent Rolls down to the 1590s. The Plea Rolls of Common Pleas begin in 1272 (TNA CP 40), earlier rolls being included in the *Curia Regis Rolls* (TNA KB 26) which have been printed from 1194 to 1250.[51]

Cartularies

For ease of reference and as security against loss or damage, many lords, secular, ecclesiastical and corporate, compiled copies of their deeds in deed-registers known as cartularies. There is a standard list of these cartularies, both ecclesiastical and secular, known to exist in Britain with their location and details; many have been printed and publication has continued since the first edition of the guide was published in 1958.[52] If you cannot find a cartulary it is still possible that the original deeds may have survived in TNA (see pp. 64–65), in the archives of the successor to the purchasers of the sixteenth century, in one of the great libraries (British Library, London; Bodleian Library, Oxford; University Library, Cambridge), or in a local library or record office.

Parish and chapelry

A useful pointer to identifying parts of larger manors, either subinfeudated or given to a religious body, is to ascertain the ecclesiastical status of their areas. Most old large manors had churches which, by the Norman Conquest or shortly afterwards, had the status of parish churches, i.e. their parish priests could perform all the major rites of christening, marriage and burial. If part of the parish was split-off, as a result of the constituent manor being subinfeudated or granted to a religious body, the portion of the manor thus separated generally became a chapelry of the parish church. Originally, the chapel priest might be appointed by, or had to be approved by, the parish priest, and the rites of baptism and burial would usually be reserved to the parish church. In the course of time, however, most old chapelries became parish churches whose priests were able to perform all the rites of the church, with the original parish church perhaps receiving a nominal annual fee as acknowledgement of its status as the mother church. In some areas, however, chapels did not become parish churches until the nineteenth century, especially in the north of England, though exceptional cases can be found elsewhere. For example, in south Gloucestershire, Westerleigh and Wick and Abson were technically chapelries of the parish of Pucklechurch until 1886, though their chapels had full rights of christening, marriage and burial since at least the sixteenth century and all became civil parishes.

The best sources to discover the exact status of a church in the Middle Ages are in documents ('*acta*') of the local diocesan bishops: these will be found in the bishops' registers from the date of their commencement; earlier episcopal documents are being printed in the ongoing *English Episcopal Acta* series which should be available in county and university libraries. Other sources which may yield data on the status of a particular church include ecclesiastical surveys such as the tax authorised by Pope Nicholas IV in 1291, the earlier but incomplete Valuation of Norwich in 1254, visitations of parishes by bishops or archdeacons from the thirteenth to the nineteenth centuries,[53] the *Valor Ecclesiasticus* of 1535 compiled by Thomas Cromwell,[54] the chantry certificates of 1546–8.[55] Another worthwhile source is clerical subsidies (down to 1660 clergy were taxed separately from laymen), some of which have been printed, but most remain unprinted in TNA E 179 and have been re-catalogued.[56]

Later medieval population decline

After about 1315, population decline was much more likely as a result of famine and successive epidemics of 'plague' which led to populations failing to reproduce themselves and, in extreme instances, ending in total depopulation and the emergence of 'deserted villages'.[57] If there are sufficient population estimates, it is worthwhile trying to establish when and why trends changed. There is an extensive literature on regional depopulation in late medieval England, and the background is set out in a pioneering study by Maurice Beresford and in two excellent recent books by Christopher

Dyer.[58] Did the local soil favour pastoral farming rather than arable husbandry? Indeed, was the soil so poor that it was only occupied under conditions of high demand for crops? Was the local lord of the manor still trying to maintain the tenants' more burdensome labour services and the servile position of the pre-plague period, or was he adapting to new conditions by leasing his demesnes and abandoning peasant labour services and personal serfdom in return for easier rents and a free peasantry? Was there a nearby town still attracting incomers with urban freedom, light money rents and opportunities for employment in crafts and trades? There is much more diversification in rural conditions in the fourteenth and fifteenth centuries, when it is therefore less easy or safe to generalise from a nearby local manor than before 1300. Some areas were already becoming 'industrialised', which needs to be explained.

Medieval household size

The best evidence on medieval household-size comes from the Spalding serf lists of the thirteenth century, which show an average household size of 4.68 people,[59] following a demonstration of the inadequate basis for Russell's household 'multiplier' of 3.5.[60] This conclusion was later supported by research on the bishop of Worcester's estates, on Durham Priory estates in south-east Durham, and on family entries recorded in the three surviving *libri vitae* and the *Rotuli de Dominabus*.[61] Even in the depths of depressed fifteenth-century England, the household size still remained around 4½–5 and the typical family was still clearly nuclear.[62] Although Jones' averages may be slightly high, there is no reasonable doubt about their order of magnitude.[63]

Until recently it was not believed possible to extend investigation of the average size of family and household back before the thirteenth century since it was believed that the necessary materials did not exist. This, however, I have myself shown to be an unnecessarily pessimistic conclusion. There are earlier sources available which can facilitate demographic conclusions: what has been missing is the openness of mind and the technical knowledge needed to evaluate old sources for new conclusions. Economic and social historians have rarely acquainted themselves with the unfamiliar sources for medieval history, and medieval historians have rarely been willing to acquire the necessary arithmetical expertise and quantitative approaches of the economic and social historian.

The *Rotuli de dominabus*

As we have noted in Chapter 2, 'listings' are a major source of information for early modern demography, but the existence of 'listings' for the medieval period has been, for the most part, ignored. In particular, those interested in medieval demography have failed to see the utility for population history of the *Rotuli de dominabus* of 1185. This 'Register of Rich Widows and Orphaned Heirs and Heiresses' is a unique list of the widows and minor sons and daughters of dead tenants-in-chief (those holding land by knight service directly from the Crown) in a large part of England in 1185. This was required so that the king could give or more usually sell the 'wardship' of unmarried sons and daughters and the 'marriage' of the widows and unmarried daughters. In order that the market value of the widows and wards could be accurately assessed, it was necessary to list and value their estates, and to note the ages of the widows and children. The resulting survey now survives for 12 counties, but can clearly be used to calculate family sizes. Indeed, J. H. Round, the editor of the *Rotuli de Dominabus*, who is often damned as a narrow-minded and reactionary 'feudal' historian, was at pains to point-out their value for demographic as well as genealogical purposes.[64] Nevertheless, I can claim, nearly 80 years later, to be the first historian to follow-up Round's hints. A statistical analysis of the *Rotuli* has shown that it is possible to reconstruct 128 Anglo-Norman families in 1185, of which 40 (31.3%) were baronial, 72 (56.3%) knightly, and 16 (12.5%) freemen; family sizes ranged from 2 to 15 if we include the dead husbands to obtain a figure at the end of marriage; the overall average family size was 5.2 persons.[65] Given that the richer groups of medieval society were healthier and better fed, thus more likely to survive longer, the slightly larger average family-size seems perfectly acceptable.

Libri Vitae

Another medieval source hardly used for demographic purposes consists of *libri vitae:* 'Books of Life'. These were records of benefactors to monastic bodies who, in return for a gift of land or money, had been granted 'confraternity' with the monks who prayed for the welfare of their souls. Such benefactors might be single individuals, but quite frequently the men's wives are included, and sometimes their children. Three English *libri vitae* have long been known to survive the Reformation (when most were destroyed), at Durham Cathedral Priory and at Thorney and Hyde Abbeys, and the relevant entries are also analysed in my article previously cited. At Hyde Abbey, 14 entries of families between *c.* 1060 and *c.* 1250 show families with 2–6 people and an average family size of 3.9 people;[66] at Durham Priory 81 entries between *c.* 1090 and *c.* 1250 show families with 2–9 people and an average family size of 4.26 people;[67] at Thorney Abbey 35 entries between *c.* 1100 and *c.* 1180 concern families of 3–12 persons and an average family size of 4.74.[68] All these results are broadly similar and show a fairly constant family (and by implication household) size comparable to Laslett's figure of 4.75.

Trends in population

The other, 'indirect', approaches to historical demography in the medieval and early modern periods all try to establish the direction and extent of demographic trends in the long-term, as well as the extent of short-term fluctuations around these trends, and to assess the reasons for the observed changes. The 'indirect' methods include the use of non-demographic evidence, especially long-run series of prices, wages and rents, as indicators of population-trends. This last approach, however, presents special difficulties to the historian since non-demographic indicators such as these may well reflect, at least in part, changes in non-demographic factors. Moreover, the calculation even of 'crude' birth- and death-rates requires both data on births and deaths which are difficult to find before 1538 but also an outside population-total which can only be derived from a contemporary estimate with the aid of a 'multiplier' (see Chapter 2 above) or from a local census or 'listing', of which only a few exist for the sixteenth or earlier centuries. Because there was no even rudimentary registration of 'vital events' (births, marriages and deaths) before 1538, all these methods rely on the use of a variety of proxies or substitutes for these vital events or combinations of them.

Unhappily, there are few substitutes for births, marriages, deaths or total population in the period before 1538. The local administrative machinery of the hundred or wapentake (units of several parishes roughly equivalent in area to later District Councils) which had once required all males over the age of 12 to 'come into the tithing' declined in the later Middle Ages. The lists of such young men enrolled in hundred court-rolls or of totals of payments by all men over the age of 12, the 'hundred pennies' which have been used, where they survive, by medieval historians as indicators of trends in total population, came to an end. In most areas the 'hundred penny' was long forgotten or had been commuted into a fixed 'common fine' (in the Somerset hundred of Taunton, this commutation had occurred by the 1320s), though in some parts of Essex and Leicestershire hundred-penny payments still reflected demographic changes in the fifteenth and early sixteenth centuries.

For deaths we may be able to utilise totals of wills proved in various probate jurisdictions from the fourteenth century onwards to suggest trends in mortality, a method first pioneered for England by Sylvia Thrupp in studying the merchants of later medieval England, then utilised by F. J. Fisher to study the influenza epidemic of the 1550s, and later applied by Gottfried to the study of East Anglian epidemics in the fifteenth century. There is no doubt that the raw material is plentiful: wills (and in some probate jurisdictions also administrations of intestates' goods) exist in large quantities from various parts of England since the later middle ages, and the existence of lists of wills and administrations, mostly in print and mostly arranged by the Old Style year of probate, permits the tabulation of annual numbers of wills (and intestate administrations where these exist) for each probate jurisdiction, though these are weighted towards eastern England.[69] For population trends we can, perhaps in the future, call on a reworking and extension of the Russell-Hollingsworth data from inquisitions post mortem, though no professional historian since Hollingsworth has seriously considered this approach.

Other areas of quantification

Besides population, there are other aspects of medieval life where an ability to handle figures comes in useful. Agriculture, the primary occupation of most medieval people, is the obvious starting point. The size of demesnes (home farms) and peasant farms can be easily extracted from surveys of various kinds, provided that the overall pattern is not distorted by sub-letting: this, however, is much more prevalent in the early modern period than earlier. Generally speaking, the lord's demesne will rarely comprise more than one-third of a manor's cultivated area. Land-use is more difficult to calculate: for demesnes, manorial account rolls will give an accurate picture of the demesne arable acreage sown and harvested, and of meadow mown, but assessing pasture is more problematic. In addition to 'several' pasture in fields entirely held by the lord of the manor, the lord also shared with his tenants in common pasture, both the common waste of soils never put under the plough and the one common field lying fallow in rotation. If the peasant holdings as well as the lord's demesne are cultivated under the communal 'open field' system, the relative percentages of arable, meadow and pasture will also be true for peasants as for lords. If, however, the lord's demesne has been enclosed and is held 'in severalty', it may well not be typical of local peasant agriculture, which may have to be approached either through studying peasant litigation (if the manorial court rolls survive), through probate inventories or tithe accounts if either of these survive for your area in the later medieval period, through deeds which generally specify the land-use for each area being conveyed, and through feet of fines (see pp. 64–5 above). If the account- and court-rolls exist, you can also collect figures for prices of goods bought and sold and the amount of daily wages for various jobs; prices will also appear in probate inventories.

Industry and trade

Industry and trade may be much more difficult to study in many areas. But it is clear that, in addition to rural craftsmen such as millers, millwrights, carpenters and blacksmiths to be found in most villages of any size, there were always some long-distance trade, especially in essentials like cloth, iron and salt, and various types of building craftsmen depending on the local tradition in vernacular architecture. From about the mid-thirteenth century, many industries which had been earlier undertaken in towns were migrating into the countryside, notably woollen textiles, in search of clean water and cheaper labour, and the extractive industries (mining and quarrying) where ores were accessible. Unless the lords are involved, in which case manorial account rolls will be useful, the court-rolls are the most likely source of information if they survive; but some subsidy rolls before 1334 and the 'inquisition of the ninths' in 1342 may also throw light on both local agriculture and industry.[70] Local wills and probate inventories, if they exist for your area in the later Middle Ages, should also tell much about all aspects of local life. Deeds are also a good source for occupations.

Fieldwork

Nor should local historians forget to put their boots on: relict features survive in the landscape such as disused dams, roads, footpaths, ponds and altered watercourses, while abandoned mineshafts and spoil-heaps may be the only tangible traces of rural industry apart from housing adapted to accommodate looms and other machinery. But housing will be considered in the next chapter: apart from the archaeological investigation of 'deserted villages' which, by definition, may not be typical of surviving villages, there is little documentary evidence available on this subject below the castle/'greater house' level until and unless local series of probate inventories begin in the fourteenth and fifteenth centuries. Another 'relict feature' of medieval and early modern open-fields is 'ridge and furrow', the corrugated surface of former open fields, often taking the shape of a reversed S: this pattern was the result of ploughmen for centuries starting the ploughing in exactly the same position in each field because they were constrained by the existence of the system of individually held scattered strips in the open or common fields.

Literacy

Finally, it may be possible to gather material on literacy from several sources: wills and probate inventories from the later fourteenth century onwards and deeds (charters) from the eleventh century onwards. But for this purpose only original charters will suffice: deeds in medieval cartularies will all be in one script, that of the copyist, and even modern editions may not show if the original 'signatures' are autographs.

Medieval towns

Probably no more than one-tenth of England's total population lived in towns in 1086, and perhaps 15% in the early fourteenth century, falling back towards 10% in 1524. Nevertheless, the important roles played by towns probably expanded throughout the Middle Ages, and in some respects there is more evidence for urban activities by the end of the medieval period. But the term 'town' has to be used with care: some of the larger towns, London, the regional capitals of York and Bristol, the county towns, grew in size and population, acquired varying rights of corporate local government as boroughs and played significant roles in the national economy; others were restricted by divided lordship – notably Coventry – and were late in acquiring full legal rights of self-government; most unincorporated market towns, governed by courts which had developed out of the parent manor, were little more than large villages with a weekly market and a yearly fair. Despite the apparent similarity of large villages with a market to the smaller towns in terms of size, however, there was an essential difference in function: a much greater proportion of the urban population earned a living not from agriculture but from industry, trade and administration (see Chapter 2). Many towns achieved varying degrees of recognition as self-governing bodies, some even gained MPs as Parliament evolved and the larger towns from the fourteenth century onwards began to acquire the higher status of 'counties in themselves'. Most of the large self-governing 'royal' boroughs acquired new revenues often levied on people and goods passing through the town gates as well as rents from urban properties acquired by the borough administration, and levied rates on the occupiers of borough tenements. If these records survive – sadly, Bristol's medieval accounts and council proceedings disappeared long ago – we may hope we can learn more about the size and the economic activities of the townsmen from various sources. Other bodies, merchant and craft guilds, local churches and charities may also have accumulated records which will aid the reconstruction of the community, its members and their main activities.[71]

Before Domesday?

It may seem fanciful to enquire into local history before the Norman Conquest, when the only contemporary historical sources for most parts of the countryside are the rare Anglo-Saxon charters and scattered mentions in various chronicles. Moreover, the charters that do survive are not a random selection of those that once existed: they are those that survived the Norman Conquest because they were preserved in ecclesiastical archives, of bishops and Anglo-Saxon monasteries: the archives of the Anglo-Saxon aristocracy have vanished as utterly as the aristocrats themselves.[72] Apart, obviously, from archaeological evidence, which requires specialist knowledge both to discover and to interpret, there are two areas where the amateur local historian can nevertheless make valuable contributions. The first is the local landscape as revealed in maps at varying periods and by field-walking in the present. Finberg and Hoskins have both shown how much we can learn from what Maitland called 'the Ordnance [Survey] map, that great palimpsest', such as the difference between a landscape of nucleated villages and an area of dispersed hamlets, or the reason why some old highways were diverted from what would seem to be the obvious course for a definite reason.

This evidence can sometimes the strengthened by 'pre-feudal' survivals. Thus in late fourteenth-century Gloucestershire there are two references to 'the lordship of Winterbourne and Frampton' as including Stoke Gifford, yet at no time since 1066 had these three manors been in common ownership. The underlying unit must therefore be 'pre-feudal'; on the map again, before the elimination of scattered 'outliers' in the later nineteenth century, the boundaries of these three parishes interlock to produce a coherent unit in which local meadows, the scarcest land in Domesday England, and woodland were carefully apportioned between the three manors and parishes. Later records also reveal the use of the name 'Winterbourne Giffard', yet at no time after 1066 was Winterbourne held by the Giffards of Stoke Gifford to which this name refers. Again, this is evidence of an earlier unit in which Stoke Giffard was regarded as part of Winterbourne: interestingly, one of the meanings of the Old English *stoc* is 'a secondary settlement'. Such survivals are rare and correspondingly valuable when they come to light.

Field- and place-names

Probably the most frequently occurring evidence for England before the Norman Conquest, present everywhere except perhaps in 'deserted villages', is that of the names of places and fields, which are recorded in deeds, leases, surveys, court- and account rolls as well as estate maps, Enclosure maps and, above all, the Tithe Maps where they exist. From such sources you will get hundreds if not thousands of field-names, and a precise location on a map, for each parish of any size. Admittedly, you will need expert knowledge to interpret these names, generally from the earlier forms: the modern name 'As(h)ton', for example, can represent several possible origins; only an expert's view of the earlier forms will reveal what is the more likely origin in any particular case (see Chapter 1, p. 7). Many counties have been covered by the *English Place-Names Survey* volumes, though most of the volumes in that series produced before 1939 now need revision; if your place is not covered adequately, it should be possible to get a regional linguistic expert to interpret your names if they have been adequately recorded and dated. The great benefit of the Tithe Maps and estate maps is that they allow field-names to be precisely located on the modern map even if both field and field-name have disappeared since the 1840s. Thus a parish map of field-names, properly recorded and interpreted, is a marvellous key to understanding the local history of Anglo-Saxon England, and often also Romano-British and earlier features.

Conclusion

It will be clear that much remains to be done in all parts of medieval England represented in Domesday Book before a broadly based picture of demographic changes in the four and a half centuries after King William's survey can be constructed. Much of the detailed history of industry and trade and the spread of new occupations in your area still remains to be investigated if adequate sources are available. In this task the work of local workers has a large part to contribute alongside that of professional historians and demographers, particularly in elucidating the precise later manorial and sub-manorial units which represent the manors of Domesday Book. Without such co-operation, achieving the necessary work will be impossible.

Notes

1 E. A. Wrigley (ed.) *Introduction to English Historical Demography* (London, Weidenfeld & Nicolson, 1966), xi.

2 J. S. Moore '"*Quot homines?*" The population of Domesday England', *Anglo-Norman Studies* 19 (1997), 307–34; R. Bartlett *England under the Norman and Angevin kings, 1075–1225* (Oxford, OUP, 2000), 290–7; M. Prestwich *Plantagenet England, 1225–1360* (Oxford, OUP, 2005), 9, 531–2; G. Harriss *Shaping the Nation. England, 1360–1461* (Oxford, OUP, 2005), 218–25. The most recent set of estimates given in G. Clark, 'The long march of history: farm wages, population and economic growth, 1209–1869', *Econ. Hist. Rev.* 60 (2007), 97–135, is accepted by Pamela Nightingale 'Gold, credit and mortality: distinguishing deflationary pressures on the late medieval economy', *Econ. Hist. Rev.* 63 (2010), 1081–1104).

3 W. G. Hoskins 'The population of an English village, 1086–1801', in his *Provincial England* (London, Macmillan, 1963),182–3, 186.

4 D. C. Douglas and G. W. Greenaway (eds), *English Historical Documents, II: 1042–1189* (London, Methuen, 2nd edn, 1981),168.

5 *Ibid.*, 946.

6 J. S. Moore, 'Domesday slavery', *Anglo-Norman Studies* 9 (1989), 191–220.

7 T. H. Aston 'The origins of the manor' *Trans. Roy. Hist. Soc.* 5th ser. 8 (1958), 59–83.

8 See Bibliography, section 3 (i) 5.

9 See *TNA Research Guide*, Legal Ser., 12–14, 20, 36 for the *Curia Regis* and Assize Records; for the hundred rolls, S. Raban *A Second Domesday? The Hundred Rolls of 1279–80* (Oxford, OUP, 2004); for the *quo warranto* proceedings, D. W. Sutherland *Quo Warranto Proceedings in the reign of Edward I, 1278–94* (Oxford, OUP, 1963).

10 P. D. A. Harvey, (ed.) 'Manorial Records of Cuxham (Oxfordshire), *c.* 1200–1359', *Oxfordshire Rec. Soc.* 50, 1975 is a model edition.

11 See the later discussion of 'Medieval household size' (pp. 68–9 above).

12 Moore, 'Domesday slavery', 192–211.

13 See references cited in n. 27 below.

14 J. S. Moore 'Anglo-Norman Garrisons', *Anglo-Norman Studies* 22 (2000), 205–59.

15 See Bibliography, section 5 (ii) 8.

16 See Bibliography, section 5 (ii) 3.

17 See *TNA Research Guide*, Legal Ser., 1, 10, and references in n. 10 above.

18 Bartlett, *England ... 1075–1225*, 377; J. C. K. Cornwall *Wealth and Society in Early Sixteenth-Century England* (London, Routledge, 1988), 123.

19 M. Howell, *Regalian Right in Medieval England* (London, Athlone P, 1962), 5–59.

20 The best known is the survey of the Peterborough abbey estates in 1125

(T. Stapleton (ed.) 'Chronicon Petroburgense', *Camden Society*, OS 47 (1849), 157–83).

21 Howell, *Regalian Right*, chap. 4; for a rare example, see *ibid.*, 69, n. 8.

22 See Bibliography, section 5 (ii) 2.

23 See Bibliography, section 5 (ii) 3.

24 A. Conyers (ed.) 'Wiltshire Extents for Debts, Edward I – Elizabeth I', *Wiltshire Rec. Soc.* 28, 1973; M. Carlin (ed.) *London and Southwark inventories, 1316–1650* (London, Centre for Metropolitan History, 1997).

25 *Calendar of Miscellaneous Inquisitions* (London, HMSO, 7 vols, 1916–69).

26 Raban, *A Second Domesday?*, 183–9 (appendix 1) lists all the surviving returns and where they have been printed. These should not be confused with the returns of 1254–5 also printed in W. Illingworth and J. Caley (eds), *Rotuli Hundredorum* (London, Rec. Comm., 2 vols, 1812–8).

27 F. M. Stenton, *The First Century of English Feudalism, 1066–1166* (Oxford, OUP, 2nd edn, 1961), chap. 2; C. Given-Wilson, *The English Nobility in the Later Middle Ages* (London, Routledge, 1987), chap. 4; K. Mertes, *The English Noble Household, 1250–1600* (Oxford, Blackwell, 1988), esp. appendix C.

28 For monastic populations, see D. Knowles, *The Monastic Order in England* (Cambridge, CUP, 1950), appendix 17; D. Knowles and R. N. Hadcock, *Medieval Religious Houses: England and Wales* (London, Longman, 1971), in detailed notes to each monastic house.

29 R. Lennard, *Rural England, 1086–1135* (Oxford, OUP, 1959), chap. 10.

30 Raban, *A Second Domesday?*, 175–6.

31 This meaningless mantra is reiterated several times in C. R. J. Currie and C. P. Lewis (eds) *A Guide to English County Histories* (Stroud, Sutton, 1994).

32 I. Sanders, *English Baronies: their origin and descent, 1086–1327* (Oxford, OUP, 1960).

33 V. Gibbs and G. E. Cokayne (eds), *The Complete Peerage of England, Scotland, Ireland, Great Britain and the United Kingdom* (London, St Catherine's P, rev. edn, 14 vols, 1910–59).

34 H. Hall (ed.) 'The Red Book of the Exchequer' (*Rolls Ser.* 99, 3 pts, 1896); the *cartae baronum* are printed in pt. 1, 189–444. For the Pipe Rolls, see n. 43.

35 *The Book of Fees* (London, HMSO, 3 vols, 1921–31); *Feudal Aids* (London, HMSO, 6 vols, 1899–1921).

36 Illingworth and Caley (eds), *Rotuli Hundredorum*.

37 W. Illingworth and J. Caley (eds) *Placita de Quo Warranto* (London, Rec. Comm., 1818); Sutherland, *Quo Warranto Proceedings*. For useful guidance on manorial history see R. B. Pugh, *How to Write a Parish History* (London, Allen & Unwin, 6th edn, 1964), 43–68; W. G. Hoskins, *Local History in England* (London, Longman, 3rd edn, 1984), chap. 4.

38 Note, however, that on large estates, especially baronies, a subinfeudated section might not be contiguous to, or even near, the parent manor, and often comprised geographically dispersed estates.

39 J. Caley and J. Hunter (eds) *Valor Ecclesiasticus temp. Henrici VIII* (London, Rec. Comm., 7 vols, 1810–34); 'List of lands of dissolved religious houses', *Supplementary Lists and Indexes* III, 7 pts, 1964; M. Jurkowski and N. Ramsay (eds) 'English monastic estates, 1066–1540: a list of manors, churches and chapels', *List and Index Soc.* Supplementary Ser. 40–42, 2007; *TNA Research Guides*, Domestic Ser. 12, 14.

40 See Bibliography, section 5 (i) 1.

41 C. Platt, *The Monastic Grange in Medieval England: a reassessment* (London, Macmillan, 1969); R. A. Donkin, *The Cistercians: studies in the geography of medieval England and Wales* (Toronto (Canada), Pontifical Institute of Medieval Studies, 1978); D. Robinson (ed.), *The Cistercian Abbeys of Britain: far from the concourse of men* (London, Batsford, 1998); G. Coppack, *The White Monks: the Cistercians in Britain, 1128–1540* (Stroud, Tempus, 1998); J. Bond, *Monastic Landscapes* (Stroud, Tempus, 2004).

42 See Bibliography, section 5 (ii) 1–5.

43 *TNA Research Guide*, Legal Ser. 2.

44 *TNA Research Guide*, Legal Ser. 7.

45 See Bibliography, section 5 (i) 5.

46 L. Landon (ed.) 'The *cartae antiquae*, rolls 1–20', *Pipe Roll Soc.* ns 17, 33, 1938, 1960.

47 T. D. Hardy (ed.), *Rotuli Litterarum Clausarum* (London, Rec. Comm., 2 vols, 1833–4; *Calendar of Close Rolls, Henry III – Henry VII* (London, HMSO, 60 vols, 1892–1963).

48 T. D. Hardy (ed.), *Rotuli Chartarum ... 1199–1216* (London, Rec. Comm., 1837; *Calendar of Charter Rolls* (London, HMSO, 6 vols, 1903–27).

49 T. D. Hardy (ed.), *Rotuli Litterarum Patentium ... 1201–1216* (London, Rec. Comm., 1835); *Calendar of Patent Rolls* (London, HMSO, 55 vols, 1891–1976). The Confirmation Rolls are unlisted after 1514.

50 *TNA Research Guide*, Legal Ser., 7.

51 F. Palgrave (ed.), *Rotuli Curiae Regis* (London, Rec. Comm., 2 vols, 1835; *Pipe Roll Society* vols 14, 24, 1891, 1900; *Curia Regis Rolls,* 1–20 (London, HMSO, 1923–2000, in progress). A useful guide to private deeds is N. W. Alcock, *Old Title Deeds* (Chichester, Phillimore, 1986).

52 G. R. C. Davis, *Medieval Cartularies of Great Britain and Ireland*, eds C. Breay, J. Harrison and D. M. Smith (London, British Library, 2nd edn, 2010). For future additions, see *Monastic Research Bulletin* (York, Borthwick Institute, 2010–in progress).

53 See Bibliography, section 5 (ii) 11.

54 Caley and Hunter (eds), *Valor Ecclesiasticus.*

55 A. Kreider, *English Chantries: the road to dissolution* (Cambridge (USA), Harvard UP, 1979), lists all the printed chantry certificates, to which C. J. Kitching (ed.) 'London and Middlesex Chantry Certificate, 1548', *London Rec. Soc.* 16, 1980, should be added.

56 *TNA Research Guide*, Domestic Ser. 10.

57 M. W. Beresford, *The Lost Villages of England* (London, Lutterworth, 1954, repr. Gloucester, Sutton, 1983): M. W. Beresford and J. G. Hurst, *Deserted Medieval Villages: Studies* (Woking, 1971, repr. Gloucester, Sutton, 1989).

58 C. Dyer, *Everyday Life in Medieval* England (London, Hambledon, 1994); C. Dyer, *Making a Living in the Middle Ages. The People of Britain, 850–1520* (New Haven (USA), Yale UP, 2002); C. Dyer, *An Age of Transition? Economy and Society in England in the Later Middle Ages* (Oxford, OUP, 2005).

59 H. E. Hallam 'Some thirteenth-century tensuses', *Econ. Hist. Rev.* 2nd ser. 10 (1958), 340–61.

60 J. T. Krause 'The medieval household: large or small', *Econ. Hist. Rev.* 2nd ser. 9 (1957), 420–32).

61 C. Dyer, *Lords and Peasants in a Changing Society: the estates of the bishopric of Worcester, 680–1540* (Cambridge, CUP, 1980), 230–2; T. Lomas 'South-east Durham: the late fourteenth and fifteenth centuries', in P. D. A. Harvey (ed.), *The Peasant Land Market in Medieval England* (Oxford, OUP, 1984), 257–8.

62 E. D. Jones 'Going round in circles: some new evidence for population in the later Middle Ages', *Journal of Medieval History* 15 (1989), 329–45.

63 M. Bailey, 'Blowing up Bubbles: some new demographic evidence for the fifteenth century', *Journal of Medieval History* 15 (1989), 347–58.

64 J. H. Round (ed.), 'Rotuli de Dominabus et Pueris er Puellis de XII Comitatibus', *Pipe Roll Society* 35 (1913), xxv, xxxviii–ix.

65 J. S. Moore 'The Anglo-Norman family: size and structure', *Anglo-Norman Studies* 14 (1992), 157–69.

66 *Ibid.*, table 3 (175).

67 *Ibid.*, table 3 (175–7).

68 *Ibid*, table 3 (178–9).

69 S. L. Thrupp 'The problem of replacement-rates in late medieval England', *Econ. Hist. Rev.* 2nd ser 18 (1965), 101–19; F. J. Fisher 'Influenza and inflation in Tudor England', *ibid.*, 120–9; R. S. Gottfried, *Epidemic Disease in Fifteenth-Century England* (Leicester, Leicester UP, 1978).

70 G. Vanderzee (ed.), *Nonarum inquisitions in Curia Scaccarii* (London, Rec. Comm., 1807).

71 S. Reynolds, *An Introduction to the History of English Medieval Towns* (Oxford, OUP, 1977) is an excellent survey; for more details for comparative purposes, see D. M. Palliser (ed.), *The Cambridge Urban History of Britain, I: 600–1540* (Cambridge, CUP, 2000).

72 See Bibliography, section 3 (i) 2.

CHAPTER 4

The Parish Register Era, 1538–1837

The civil parish

As we have already seen, Wrigley and Schofield remarked that 'the dark ages of English demographic history ended in 1538' when parish registers were authorised by Thomas Cromwell. Nevertheless, we do not step at once from darkness into light. The first registers were generally written on rather fragile paper and many had been partly or totally lost before the government of Queen Elizabeth in 1597–8 ordered them to be copied onto parchment, a much more durable material. Unfortunately they added a proviso 'but especially since the beginning of her majesties reign', with the result that only about 100 or so paper registers now start in 1538, and only about 1500 parchment copies start in 1550 or earlier, of which half have substantial earlier gaps in either christenings or burials or both series. After 1558–9 the quality of most registers improves, with far more registers surviving, though later careless keeping has often created gaps or total losses. The Civil War period (1642–53) was a notable period of poor registration, partly because the Anglican church was regarded as royalist and therefore disloyal, and partly because many Anglican clergy were expelled from their parishes after 1645, whilst many Puritan clergy were ejected in 1662. On both occasions, some registers were removed and subsequently lost.

Nevertheless, parish registers survive for most parishes from about 1560 onwards and, if complete, provide good local series of christenings (births), marriages and burials (deaths).[1] Throughout the period 1538–1837 many registers were lost or damaged because of clerical absenteeism, carelessness, theft, fire, floods, mildew and rats and mice; others are now partly or wholly illegible because of the later use of gall and similar restorative fluids to enhance faded writing. Although official copies of parish registers known as Bishop's (occasionally Archdeacon's) Transcripts were supposed to be made annually and sent to diocesan registrars, few exist before 1600 and there are none for the period 1642–60; some dioceses are well represented by Transcripts, while other have very few; they usually end in the first half of the nineteenth century. Where they exist, however, such Transcripts should be compared with the parish registers: I have found occasional entries in the Transcripts which are not in the original registers, probably because both the fair copy register and the Transcript were copied from an original rough register. Given that there were about 9250 parishes in existence in the early seventeenth century, you will be very unfortunate if no registers survive for any local parishes.[2] J. C. Cox, a notable authority on the history of parish registers, calculated the number of registers starting in 1538 or 1539 from the 1833 official return as 877, of which he reckoned at least 95% were copies on parchment made in 1597 or later; he did not give any estimate of the total number of registers, which was at least 9250 in the seventeenth and eighteenth centuries.

But the period from 1538 is historically important for other reasons beside the introduction of parish registers. The parish, previously an ecclesiastical unit with purely ecclesiastical functions, now became also a secular unit with civil powers: in part this reflected the state's assumption of control over the Church of England. In addition, the *Highways Act* of 1555 and successive acts dealing with poor relief from 1572 onwards created new secular parish officials, the surveyors of highways or waywardens and the overseers of the poor, and gave supervisory civil powers to the churchwardens and to the parish vestry. The parish thus became the main unit of local administration below the county, a position which it retained until the late nineteenth century.[3]

Parish registers and historical demography: aggregative analysis

From the sixteenth century onwards the parish registers can be exploited for population history in several ways, as we have seen in Chapter 2. The first method is 'aggregative analysis', the annual and monthly tabulation, perhaps even weekly in populous urban parishes, of christenings, marriages and burials from the registers, together with a derived series of 'Natural Change', that is, christenings minus burials.[4] Your task will be greatly eased, of course, if you put your figures into a spreadsheet which will immediately produce totals, averages, etc, and various graphical illustrations. The 'Natural Change' series should be a good guide to the overall long-term trend in population, but may not be, because it necessarily assumes that the parish is a closed, isolated community. In reality, no parish was entirely isolated from its neighbours, for migration was not a feature which suddenly appeared as Britain began industrialising in the seventeenth and eighteenth centuries: historians can demonstrate its occurrence throughout the medieval and early modern periods.[5]

The second method is 'family reconstitution' which has both strengths and weaknesses. If the registers are of sufficiently high quality and consistently identify children by their parents' names, the calculation of age-related birth- and death-rates is possible. But these results are likely to be greatly affected by two factors. The first is that relatively few registers consistently name the parents of children christened or buried; the second factor is migration, so that most reconstitutions only cover perhaps one-fifth at most of the local population, normally an atypical selection.[6]

Migration

There are basically three forms of migration, 'desperation migration', migration in search of work, any work, or in its international form, to escape from persecution, or the result of 'involuntary migration' (criminal transportation to North America and the West Indies and later to Australia). By contrast, 'betterment' migration is the usually voluntary move to various forms of work, and in particular, movement to obtain marketable skills by means of apprenticeship to an industrial craft or commercial trade. In higher social levels this can be by means of taking articles for barristers, attorneys, solicitors and accountants, often going to train either in the Inns of Court and Chancery or the two universities, where, after the Reformation, nearly all Anglican clergy had graduated before ordination. Younger sons of farmers often went to the grammar school in a nearby market town or to one of the 'Dissenting Academies' which, after 1660, provided a more practical and utilitarian curriculum than most grammar schools. From the 1660s until the 1870s there was also compulsory migration created by the 'removal' of paupers under the *Settlement Acts* from 1662 onwards (see below).

Migration may therefore also affect the usefulness of christenings as a guide to overall population change: if those moving into a parish are mainly young men and women of childbearing age, the christenings will be artificially boosted above previous levels; if, on the other hand, the local young people are moving out in search of work, christenings will be lowered and burials boosted as the average age of the parish's inhabitants rises. Because of the effects of migration, the calculation of birth and death rates can only usefully be attempted for two or three years each side of a year with a known population-total.

Changing vital rates

Sudden changes in any of the three series of vital events will be significant: a sudden rise in burials usually means an epidemic disease has appeared which may be indicated in the registers by its supposed name, 'pox', 'plague', 'fever', etc, and by the clustering of burials within a few weeks or months in a particular season. The period when this clustering occurs is a partial guide in determining the nature of the main prevalent disease: for example, plague is usually a summer disease and influenza is normally a disease of winter. A gradual but sustained rise in burials may be the result of a population getting older, either because younger people are moving out in search of work or because older people are moving in (retirement to the south coast!), often being repatriated because they are unemployed. But if christenings have been rising for 20–30 years before, the increase in the number of burials is to be expected without any necessary change in the rate of burials per 1000 population.

Likewise, a sustained rise in christenings may result either from women of childbearing age moving into the area with their husbands, as noted above, or that the age at marriage is going down, thus increasing their period of legitimate fertility. A sudden rise in marriages may be the result of more immigrants marrying as soon as they have found work, or that previous high burials have created vacant holdings or gaps in services to be filled. But before 1754 it could also indicate that the local incumbent was operating a 'marriage shop', encouraging outsiders to marry in his church so that he could collect more fees. The acid test in such cases is to see if any of these newly married couples either are outsiders or have children christened in the same parish in the next five years; if most do not, then your parson was indeed running a 'marriage shop'.

Even if we can calculate the crude birth- and death-rates from the parish registers, we will not usually know why these rates have changed over time. Nevertheless, tabulating the three main series and the derived series of 'Natural Change' is the first step in studying changes in local population; it will be assisted if you put on to a graph both the raw data and a 13 year 'moving average' of all the series which will smooth out sudden fluctuations. If you are using a spreadsheet program on a PC to record your data, the program will do this easily, quickly and accurately for you as well as summing the monthly and yearly vital events.

Incomplete registration

Although Thomas Cromwell's Injunctions instituting parish registers only specified that the incumbent should fill-in his entries every

Sunday, it is likely that most incumbents soon began writing-up vital events as they occurred, particularly in more populous urban parishes where many such events might occur daily. However, the survival of these documents was often very uncertain. As we have seen, the original registers were written on paper, then a rather fragile material, and when the Elizabethan government in 1597 ordered that the registers should be recopied on parchment, the unfortunate proviso 'but especially since the beginning of her Majesty's reign', resulted in over three-quarters of the copy-registers now in existence starting in the years 1558–60. Even where the registers start before 1558, fewer than one in 1 in 7 is complete from 1538–9. Many of these have large gaps between 1557 and 1559 caused by the breakdown of registration as a result of an epidemic of influenza and typhus; the Civil War (1642–6) and the republican regime (1649–60) meant that relatively few registers were continuous during the 1640s and 1650s. As mentioned, there have been many partial or total losses of registers throughout the period due to fire, flood, and careless keeping of registers which have had to withstand the perpetual enemies of all archives: fire, floods, rats, mice, and uncaring men and women in search of free wrapping or cleaning materials. Many have been adorned with childish scribbles or the parish clerk practising his handwriting. As recently as the 1980s in one Gloucestershire parish, the incumbent's childrens' toys were kept in the parish chest alongside the registers; when I queried this, the priest's wife indignantly rejected my criticism of 'her' chest! Finally, far more parish registers both start early and are relatively detailed south of the Trent and Humber; in the north, partly because of distance from London and partly because of Catholic survival, registers started later and were less complete.

Under-registration

To what extent were there other possible causes of under-registration of either christenings or burials? The process of registration of christenings, marriages and burials was not in any way a contentious issue in religious terms: it was being implemented in the sixteenth century in Catholic as well as Protestant states.[7] Christenings became more problematic in the seventeenth century with the rise of the Baptists, who rejected infant baptism, and the Quakers, who did not accept any baptism but did record births. The process of registration did not involve recording what were, in any sense, secret or sensitive events (with the possible exception of christenings and burials of bastard children, and the weddings either of brides obviously pregnant or of grooms and brides who were for some other reason anxious for privacy). But the first of these exceptions was undoubtedly numerically insignificant. Laslett calculated that the bastardy ratio per 1000 unmarried women for most of the sixteenth and seventeenth centuries was under 3.0, and only rose significantly after 1760 to around 6 by 1851, then declining to 4 by 1900 before a dramatic rise to over 20 in 1971.[8] Bridal pregnancy, by contrast, was apparently so common that it could hardly have raised many eyebrows in Tudor England, with nearly 1 in 3 of all brides being pregnant when they married, and in some parishes 4 out of 10 brides.[9] When I was working at Keele (Staffs), I noticed that one nearby agricultural parish had a large number of obviously pregnant brides. I asked the vicar why this should be so, and received the answer, 'They are mostly farmers; they need to know that their wives, like their heifers, will drop a good 'un!' This vicar was one of the last parish priests to farm his own glebe land, he knew how his flock thought, with the result that farmers and farm-labourers from miles around came to his church while closer churches were half-empty. In fact, nearly all marriages before *c.* 1850 did take place in church because of the legal and social disabilities attached to the bastard status of children of unmarried unions as much as the penalties, again both legal and social, attached to 'fornication', whether or not this led to children being born.

Clandestine marriages were not a substantial problem in the sixteenth and earlier seventeenth centuries, probably because of the continuing effectiveness of ecclesiastical visitation and the enforcement of discipline by the church courts, but became more obvious in the eighteenth and nineteenth centuries as the church's prohibitions became less effective together with the rise of 'marriage shops', especially those attached to the London prisons.[10] Burial registration also declined after 1690 and especially after 1760, partly again because of the church's declining control, but also because many churchyards, particularly in towns, were full and were being replaced by burial grounds outside church control.[11]

Another possible cause of under-registration of christenings would be delayed baptisms, so that infants might die (and be buried) before they could be christened. If this happened, it would have a doubly punitive effect on vital statistics: not only would there be no recorded christening but an infant would be buried who apparently had not been born in the parish, thus unduly lowering what was normally a natural increase resulting from an excess of christenings (births) over burials (deaths). In later centuries the period of such delayed baptism would become increasingly longer, up to a month or more between birth and baptism in the later eighteenth and nineteenth centuries, but in the sixteenth century it is thought that christenings normally took place no later than a week after birth and usually on the day of birth or the next two days, although the earliest register so far examined for such data started in 1574.[12] This belief can now be confirmed by the first register for Tunstall (Kent) in which the average interval between birth and christening in the two periods of Catholic domination (1539–47, 1553–8) was under one day, and was just over two days in Edward VI's reign (1548–53); it did not rise above three days in the early part of Elizabeth's reign (1559–69), and even when Anglicanism was becoming well-established (1577–1610), christening was roughly a week after birth.[13] Further evidence on the interval between births and baptisms is to be found in the register of Tickenham (Som.). From 1538 to 1554 when the married vicar, William Mathew, was deprived, he consistently used the formula 'borne and baptised' or 'borne and christened' on [presumably] the same day for all children. The only two exceptions are his own two sons, both also named William, the first born on New Year's Day 1551/2 and christened the next day and the second born on 30

March 1553 and baptised on April 2nd. Even for an incumbent of relatively advanced views, the interval was only 1–3 days and for his congregation the norm was christening on the day of birth. After mid-1554 no further information is available until the period 1588–1601, when another married vicar, William Slater, recorded both dates of birth and dates of baptism for 10 children. If these 10 entries for 1588–1601 are representative of all christenings at Tickenham, then the interval between births and baptisms ranged from zero to three days, and averaged one and a half days. Even at the end of the Elizabethan period, Tickenham was considerably more conservative in this matter than Tunstall.[14]

There remain for consideration the official exceptions to burials in consecrated ground, originating before the Reformation but continuing afterwards: excommunicates and suicides. Marchant estimated the number of excommunicates at any one time at about 5% of the total population of Tudor England; the proportion of excommunicates at death would be much smaller, probably under 2%.[15] The proportion of suicides in the population was even smaller. Various attempts have been made to evaluate the suicide rate in early modern England, although some major towns such as London, Norwich and Bristol, made no returns of coroners' inquests to King's Bench.[16] These estimates range from four per 100,000 population to 10 per 100,000, which suggest that the suicide rate in Tudor England was of the same order as the modern English rate of about 8 per 100,000 population. Given a crude death rate which was generally between 24 and 30 per 1000 population in sixteenth-century England,[17] the omission of suicides from Anglican burials would have little effect on the overall death-rate calculated from such burials. Moreover, we cannot be certain that the more charitable clergy did exclude suicides from the burial registers. The incumbent of Tenterden (Kent) thus recorded in 1585, 'John Whitfelde havinge drowned himselfe was laid in a grave but noe service saide the 28th of Maye'.[18]

Interpolation

The existence of all these factors presents considerable difficulties when trying to quantify 'vital events' (births, marriages and deaths). Losses may range from an entire chest to a single volume or a few pages in a volume. If only a few months' entries are missing but the record in surrounding years is complete, you can interpolate the missing entries by calculating the average share of each month's events in the surrounding fully registered years, bearing in mind that your estimate must be in whole numbers. If the gap is more than a year, you need to look at all the surrounding parishes in the same area with complete registers in order to ascertain the general regional trend year-by-year. This trend can then be applied to each of the missing years in the incomplete series. But I would be dubious about interpolating for more than 4–5 years in any one period, or if there is obviously a crisis, signalled by a sudden rise in burials, in any of those years. There are times when you must bite the bullet and say 'regretfully the registers of parish 'X' are too fragmentary or too poorly kept to yield usable data' and either rely on what figures you have for total population or say that 'the good-quality figures from nearby parishes 'Y' and 'Z' are the best guide we have to the likely demographic trends in parish 'X'.' If you are more fortunate, you will have a complete record for most years which can be tabulated to show monthly and yearly totals of christenings, marriages and burials, and derived annual totals of natural change (christenings less burials). These figures, when graphed and also converted to 13-year moving averages (a few keystrokes with a spreadsheet program on a computer!), will immediately give you a visual picture of long-term developments in population since the sixteenth century, which you may be able to supplement with some figures for medieval population if your quest for medieval manorial records has been successful, and to compare with census figures for your parish from 1801 to 2011.

Family reconstitution

Migration also affects the second main method of exploiting parish registers, which is 'family reconstitution'. As the name implies, this involves sorting individual register entries into married couples, starting with the christenings of the husband and wife, then their marriage, followed by the christenings of each child in turn, and finally each burial.[19] In practice, however, even with good quality registers stating the parents' names of each child baptised and buried, only a minority, at most 20%, of local families will be fully reconstituted, and these are unlikely to be typical of all local families as we shall see. Finally, for the method to be used profitably, the registers have to identify the children by their parents consistently over long periods: a couple born around 1540 and being married in the late 1560s may still be alive after 1600; their children, born between about 1568 and 1580, may still be alive in James I's reign (1603–25). Only a minority of registers will meet these exacting requirements. But the method does have one great advantage over aggregative analysis, because it gets round the problem of requiring an outside population figure in order to calculate vital rates (which, moreover, are age-specific, not the crude 'all ages' rates) in an elegant and ingenious way: the total population figure is the sum of all recorded persons who are alive at the date chosen for analysis. Whilst most attempts at family reconstitution in the past have been achieved using large index cards or sheets of paper, using a computerised database is easier and more certain in its results: again, calculations can be made easily and correctly. The chief problem is deciding which contemporary surname-spelling should be adopted at the standard surname; variants should be listed and cross-referenced to the standard form, especially if you are using any computer program – computers are rigid in their spelling requirements. Morever, it is thought that these reconstituted families may not be typical, and therefore representative, of the whole community: they are likely to be landholding families who remain resident for several generations or craftsmen with a stake in the land.[20]

Parish registers and local history

Parish registers are of course an invaluable guide to many aspects of local history. Besides their essential value for historical demography as recording christenings, marriages and burials which was their original purpose, parish registers usually, though not invariably, are useful for other, more historical purposes. Their variety arises from several factors: it partly reflects the state's lack of interest in parish registers, apart from the *Marriage Duty Act* of 1695 (widely disregarded) which ordered particular details to be recorded for each family, Lord Hardwicke's *Marriage Act* of 1753 regulating marriage, and George Rose's *Registration Act* of 1812 requiring the use of standard printed christening and burial registers, which included a column in the christenings register for the occupation of the father of children christened and a column for age at death in the burials register. Before 1813 many incumbents had already often added status or occupational labels and ages to many of the names recorded in the registers. The nobility and gentry were prominent, not surprisingly given the importance of status in contemporary society and the parson frequently being a relation or associate of the lord of the manor who was commonly the owner of the advowson, the right to nominate to the vacant living. But many parsons were adding details to most of those named in their registers partly presumably to aid identification, since population growth often meant that more than one person bearing the same name was alive at the same time who needed to be separately identified.

In addition, Lord Hardwicke's *Marriage Act* of 1753 also prescribed printed *pro forma* marriage registers which included a space for the marital status of the groom and bride, but in a large number of cases (over 50% in Gloucestershire for example) the clergy instead inserted an occupational or social status description ('gentleman', 'yeoman', 'husbandman', etc).[21] In some cases the motives for annotation of parish registers seems to have been simple curiosity and the desire to know their congregation; one vicar of Thornbury (Gloucs) in the later eighteenth century even included both sets of grandparents of the child being christened. Some registers ended up as virtual parish memoranda books giving details of the weather, local noteworthy happenings and natural disasters.

Apart from the three acts of Parliament in 1695, 1753 and 1812 just mentioned, there was virtually no regulation of parish registers by higher authority in either Church or State. Proposals by Lord Burghley for copying local registers to a national centre were dropped after his death in 1596;[22] although bishops and their archdeacons tried to enforce the annual transmission of register entries, the Bishop's (or occasionally Archdeacon's) Transcripts, to diocesan centres, there is no evidence that these Transcripts were scrutinised by the bishop's staff except for payment of fees or that suggestions for their improvement went back to parish clergy. In the event their principal utility was to provide copies to be used if the original registers were damaged or destroyed; they rarely exist before the seventeenth century and cease during the Civil War and the Interregnum, being restored in 1660. Some were still being supplied to registrars in the second half of the nineteenth century. Equally there was nothing to prevent parish clergy inserting additional information into their registers, which they frequently did. Apart from inserting 'senior' and 'junior' to distinguish fathers and sons with the same name, the most common addition was an occupation or a status label; because of the parsons' class consciousness, nobility and gentry were the most likely to be identified, references to them often being written in larger, darker or more ornate handwriting. Besides age and parenthood, a few registers even included grandparents, as noted above. Finally, in parishes with several hamlets within its area, the place of residence of the parents of a child being baptised and of the parents of a child being buried or of an adult would usually be stated. Registers, in addition to their obvious utility for demography, therefore need to be scanned to extract any additional information.

National and local records

As in the medieval period, national records remain important sources for local demography. The diocesan surveys of 1563 (which

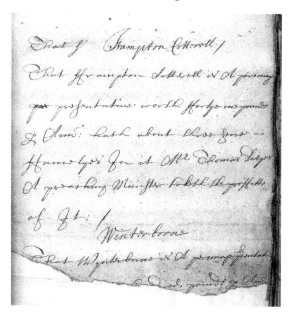

That for Frampton Cotterell.

That Frampton Cotterell is A parsonage

presentative worth Fortye one pounds

per Ann[um]: hath above three score

Famelyes In it. Mr Thomas Davyes

A preaching Minister

Taketh the proffetts

of It.

Figure 2 Commonwealth Church Survey of Frampton Cotterell, 1650 (Lambeth Palace Library Comm. XIIa, p. 191). Copyright (C) The Trustees of Lambeth Palace Library.

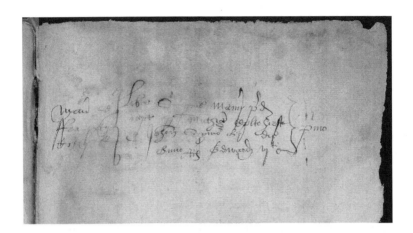

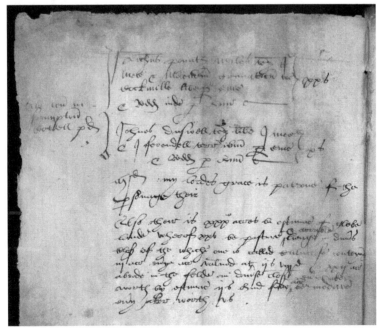

Figure 3 Survey of the Manor of Frampton Cotterell, 1547 (TNA SC12/2/46, pp. 139r, v). Original MS. Crown Copyright (C)

Translation:

(p.39r)

Manor of
Frampton
Cotterell

(p.39v)

| Free tenants in Frampton Cotterell Aforesaid | Sir Nicholas Poyntz, knight, holds a messuage and corn-mill there called Cockmille there by services and yearly rent of |
| | 20s. |

John Duswell holds freely a messuage and fardel of land by services and yearly rent of 10s.

Be it remembered that my Lord's grace is patron of the parsonage there.

Also there are 30 acres by estimation of glebe land whereof 25 be pasture and arable lying in various closes of which one is called Culverclose containing 3 acres, each acre valued at 2s. 8d, and 22 acres abroad in the fields in diverse closes everywhere each worth by estimation 2s. And five acres be meadow, each acre worth 5s.

recorded the number of households per parish) and of 1603,[23] Bishop Compton's Census of 1676[24] (both of which recorded the number of communicants), and the Commonwealth Church Survey of 1650[25] (see Fig. 2) are invaluable sources often overlooked by local historians and demographers. Later diocesan surveys,[26] and glebe-terriers from the sixteenth to the nineteenth centuries[27] will also provide the ecclesiastical status of each unit. Do not be surprised if some sources contradict others about the status of a particular place, partly the result of human frailty but also reflecting the general upgrading of populous places to be parishes. This in turn had a partly secular explanation: for poor law purposes a parish was defined as a place 'maintaining its own poor', which supplied another good motive for claiming parochial status. Manorial surveys remain a useful source for local demography if the manor and parish are identical units (see Fig. 3).

Diocesan population records

Because every parish was part of an archdeaconry, a diocese and a province (archdiocese), local records such as parish registers can be supplemented by records of superior jurisdictions. Archbishops, bishops and archdeacons had been undertaking 'visitations' (formal inspections) of parishes since at least the thirteenth century, though the first visitations to include any details of parish populations occur in 1551 (Gloucester diocese) and 1557 (Canterbury diocese).[28] The two following national diocesan censuses of 1563 and 1603, though conducted by bishops and their staffs, were in response to requests from the Privy Council, as was Bishop Compton's Census of 1676. Nevertheless, Anglican bishops had finally embraced numeracy, and several later visitations included details of parochial populations, probably stimulated by continued requests from government for numbers of 'Papists', and after the *Toleration Act* of 1689, by fears of growing nonconformity. Several such visitations have been printed, whilst many others remain unprinted: they are also valuable sources for other aspects of parish life.[29] There is, however, no up-to-date and comprehensive national list of episcopal archives; some dioceses have good printed catalogues (Bristol, Chichester, Gloucester, Lichield, Lincoln, Salisbury), but for most you will have to investigate what catalogues exist in the appropriate Record Office.[30] The task is not made easier by the variety of possible names for this type of record: 'survey' is common, though the predominant usage of the word refers to land, 'diocese book' often occurs as well as 'visitation book' (or 'return'), and the Latin *speculum* is also found. The only safe course is to examine for yourself all possible visitation records after *c.* 1550 in your diocese as it was constituted in the period 1547–1800 in order to find any population details; they are more frequent after 1660 and continue into the second half of the nineteenth century, though after 1801 the population details usually come from the last decennial census before the visitation. Often the records of questions for and returns to visitation are bound together as volumes, but in some dioceses the original returns remain as unbound sheets. Generally, bishops' visitations are much more likely to have details of population, usually numbers of 'families' or 'households', than archdeacons' visitations which tend to focus on the parish church, its clergy and services.[31]

County histories

Local historians and demographers ignore previous county histories at their peril. Of course their quality varies: some authors are clearly riding hobby horses of their own making; there is often a clear desire to enhance the importance of their county, their town or their village; their deductions about the derivation of place-names are usually wrong, and they will often be trying to trace a particular place back to a supposed Roman origin. As 'history' they may be tendentious, but in the midst of the dross you will often find accurate information from a source that has now disappeared, especially relating to manorial history. As one example, Nichol's history of Leicestershire includes a copy of some original hundred rolls of 1279 that have disappeared since his time.[32] Several county historians included data on contemporary populations in their county,[33] and other figures are often available in unprinted manuscript collections of source-materials.

Literacy

The classic measurement of literacy was the ability to sign one's name instead of putting a mark on various documents, especially the post-1754 marriage registers which enable mass-coverage of a community, but earlier from a variety of documents which required attestation by signature or mark: wills, probate inventories, court depositions, bonds and poor law records. Do not forget that though the brides and grooms can only attest from 1754 onwards, literacy in the preceding generation is often documented in the attestation of their witnesses. But the simple division of attestations into signature (= literacy) or mark (= illiteracy) is now regarded as rather crude. A better subdivision is partly qualitative, between a fluent signature (= habitually literate), a poorly formed signature (literate but not frequently), a mark consisting of the initials of the person's name (= reading literacy only) and a general mark X (= totally illiterate). Since most marriages take place when the bride and groom are in their 20s or early 30s, the ability to sign, especially to sign fluently, is not likely to be affected by weakness associated with old age.[34]

Besides the marriage registers after 1754, there are numerous other sources that provide information on literacy because there was a legal obligation to 'attest' either by signature or by a mark. Many of the 'Protestation Returns' made in 1642 by those opposing the ritualistic changes introduced by Archbishop Laud provide what in some cases at least is an almost complete directory of householders in the parish attesting by signature or mark; but since those protesting were mostly Puritan, royalists often refused to sign, and in two counties, Gloucestershire and Herefordshire, royalists apparently prevented the Protestation from being circulated locally.[35] It is well worth experimenting with the totals from parish Protestation returns and a household 'multiplier' and comparing the results with, first, those from the reliable Hearth Taxes of the 1660s and 1670s,[36] and, secondly, with the estimates of households from the Commonwealth Church Survey of 1650 where these exist.[37]

Wills, then as now, required both the maker of the will and the witnesses to attest; again, registered copies can be misleading and originals (or photographic or digital copies) are preferable to registered copies for this purpose.[38] Probate inventories are a rich source of information on this as on other matters: they had to be attested by at least two 'appraisers' who were rarely professional valuers; bonds of any kind (e.g. marriage, probate administration, tuition and debt) had to be attested by the person(s) creating the bond and by two witnesses (Bondsmen); poor law documents, especially apprenticeship indentures and a variety of settlement documents, also required attestation. All these documents listed in this paragraph are also good sources for social rank (Peer/Baronet/Knight/Esquire/ Gentleman/Profession/Yeoman/Craftsman/Husbandman/Labourer) as well as occupational information.

Even if all the local records (registers and poor law records) have been lost, probate records (wills, probate inventories, administration and tuition bonds) were held at diocesan centres and generally have survived well: the only major losses were the probate records for Cornwall, Devon and Somerset which were destroyed in the Exeter 'blitz' of 1942, and some of the Chester diocesan probate documents for Lancashire and West Yorkshire in the eighteenth century were lost during their removal from Richmond to Lancaster.

The national ('Prerogative') probate series at Canterbury and York have also generally survived well, though the main series of PCC probate administrations are preserved only from 1559 and inventories mostly from 1660. Statements by witnesses were preserved especially in ecclesiastical deposition books now to be found in diocesan record offices from the fifteenth century onwards for most of the next two centuries: in many cases witnesses are identified not only by present status or occupation and residence but also by past status or occupation and residence, thus helping also to illuminate migration. Wills are valuable in other ways besides providing evidence on literacy and occupations: whilst kinship relationships between members of a will-maker's extended family will be apparent from the parish registers, links based on friendship are more likely to be revealed in wills than any other source apart from diaries and letters which are rare below the upper and middle classes. Literacy, finally, is an obvious field for using graphs to illustrate the gradual progress towards the achievement of full literacy in most places by 1900. Usually the progress towards literacy will be more apparent earlier in towns than in the surrounding countryside: not only is the provision of education greater in most towns but urban occupations are more likely to need a literate labour force.

Occupations

Many of the sources likely to yield information on the occupational composition of the local population have already been mentioned: parish registers, wills and probate inventories, deeds, poor law documents, especially registers of pauper apprentices and documents relating to 'settlement'. In addition, for the upper and middling groups of society, oath rolls record the name and occupation of those taking an oath (especially to defend the monarchy and the Church of England, and after 1662 everyone holding an official position had to be recorded as taking Holy Communion in their parish church, which was recorded by the incumbent and the churchwardens in Oath Rolls and Sacrament Certificates which are now mostly in TNA.[39] For non-pauper apprentices, details of occupation and residence of both the master and the father of the apprentice, as well as the apprentice's trade are preserved in a series of volumes in TNA from 1710 to 1774.[40] It is probably best to keep such information on a database which will assist in attempts to link occupations with other factors: parentage, point of origin, etc. But, given that computers are very literal machines, you do need to record variant surname spellings and cross-reference them to the preferred form. Wide variations in surname forms are to be expected in a mainly pre-literate society in which much information is transmitted orally, and very often in a local dialect, to a literate recorder who may well be an outsider.

If records exist (farm accounts in agriculture, factory records in industry, business records in trade and industry, you may be able to say more about these local activities, or perhaps benefit from work done in similar nearby parishes. Broadly speaking, industry produces a better general standard of living, including better housing, than in purely agricultural parishes which in the eighteenth and nineteenth centuries were often depressed and poverty-stricken. New industry, especially if based on factories and mines, could lead initially to poor living conditions as a result of overcrowding and poor quality speculative building, but even in the urban slums wages were usually higher than in the countryside.

Agriculture and 'enclosure'

Agriculture was to remain one of the major occupations throughout the early modern period, since it was a major employer as well as a significant supplier of foodstuffs and of industrial raw materials. It used to be thought that this situation was largely the result of the enclosure of open fields and common wastes under acts of Parliament after 1760, but it is now clear that half of England had already been enclosed before 1500, and that much additional land was later enclosed by private agreement before the era of Parliamentary enclosure after 1760.[41] As in the medieval period, deeds and leases will provide information on land-use and field-names as well as on buyers and sellers; land-use and farm-sizes will also be shown on any surviving maps and surveys, both those made by local landowners and the maps accompanying Enclosure awards. More detail will come from any surviving farm accounts although these are rare.[42] It is also possible to interpret the varying formulae used in feet of fines to state land-use if the preceding deeds 'to lead the uses of a fine' or the subsequent deeds 'to declare the uses of a fine' are also available. This period also sees the rise and decline of the probate inventory with its manifold uses as a source in agriculture, industry and housing. If rate books exist either as separate documents or within the accounts of churchwardens, overseers and highway surveyors these will provide information on the owners and/or occupiers of land within the parish over perhaps 2 or 3 centuries. For the period 1780–1832, and in some cases earlier, Land Tax assessments can sometimes also be helpful.[43] Even where open fields or common fields survive throughout the early modern period, do not assume that they have existed unchanged from the late Anglo-Saxon period: at Keele (Staffs), for example, I was able to show that though three open fields survived until the early nineteenth century, their outlines and constituent furlongs underwent re-arrangement after the dissolution of the Knights Hospitallers in 1540 and the coming of the secular landlords, the Sneyds, who began building a new 'Hall' on what had been 'East field', the remainder of which now became 'Hall Field'.

Industry

Apart from probate inventories which will be very useful for any craft or industry where the work is carried out at home, whether you can say much will mainly depend on the survival of factory or industry records. The preceding section on 'Occupations' will help reveal what industries did exist in your area, but it is fair to say that factory records are even rarer than farming records. The Business Archives Council is listing all known industrial and commercial records, the Royal Commission on Historical Manuscripts has produced two volumes on the *Records of British Business and Industry, 1760–1914*, and Manchester University Press has produced three volumes of *Studies in British Business Archives*.[44] Industrial methods and events may also appear in local newspapers (do not forget the advertisements as well as the main news columns) and in encyclopaedias or guide-books especially after *c.* 1750.

Housing and the standard of living

The later medieval period is the first in which the position of houses within a plot generally becomes fixed, as peasant houses become much more permanent with the use first of timber framework, then of stone and brick. Yet again, probate inventories are a major source, as over half proceed to list furniture and other possessions in named rooms, from which the layout and the number of storeys can usually be deduced. The ordinary house or cottage is the principal subject of the periodical *Vernacular Architecture*, and the evidence of any surviving local buildings which are recognisably of this period should be examined and recorded.[45] But it is quite possible that older local houses below the manor-house level have been either demolished and replaced or so much altered and 'improved' that little of the original building survives. On the other hand, the stripping of plaster or rendering from walls may reveal structural features previously unknown. One cottage in Frampton Cotterell which was stripped of both exterior cement rendering and interior plaster before modernisation was shown to be a later medieval 'long house', divided in two by a cross-passage, in which the human living rooms occupied two-thirds of the length: the remaining one-third was for animals, as shown by an open drainage-channel running its length. Any cottages with no more than two rooms per storey and one or two storeys are probably originally labourers' houses and any surviving examples should be photographed and recorded if at all possible.

Since housing at this level did not change markedly before the twentieth century, dating may be difficult: beware of assuming that date stones necessarily refer to the date of building; in some cases they simply record the date that a newly married couple began living there. If your parish was partly or wholly owned by a large estate, its records may include details of the houses on the estate, when they were built and repaired, who the tenants were and what rents were paid. If you are able to reconstitute any of the families living in the houses, you will be able to calculate how many people lived in the house at any one time: at some parts of the life-cycle, most cottages and even some farmhouses will be grossly overcrowded. Other aspects of the standard of living may be difficult to document: inventories and accounts may enable you to produce some series of prices for foodstuffs and other commodities, but data in budgets giving an idea of how much was bought are much more difficult to find before the late eighteenth century, but should be exploited when available. Wage-rates (per hour, day, week or year) may be available, but the length of employment may be difficult or impossible to establish. In default of employment records, you will have to use wage-rates to produce a 'real wage index', by comparing local wage-rates with local prices.[46] The results may well be problematic and not directly comparable with a modern 'cost of living' index for two main reasons: the wage-rates do not allow a calculation of money income because usually we do not know how many days in the year the person actually worked; the prices similarly do not allow for the overall expenditure in a year when, as we have seen, unemployment will affect the ability to buy. Family 'Budgets' are rare.

Parish and people

As I said earlier, it is in this period that the parish becomes a civil unit of local government, and the powers of the vestry were extended into local government. There were new officials with new duties, the surveyors of highways or waywardens dealing with local roads and the overseers of the poor, but the churchwardens acquired extra duties and responsibilities, particularly for the 'non-settled' poor; churchwardens', overseers' and surveyors' accounts were to be audited by the vestry. In addition, new responsibilities were added, including the apprenticeship of pauper children and the extermination of vermin. After the passing of the *Acts of Settlement*, churchwardens and overseers were jointly responsible for issuing Removal Orders, to ensure that any unemployed poor not 'settled' in the parish were 'removed' to their 'place of settlement', and Settlement Certificates to natives working elsewhere guaranteeing that if they became 'chargeable' (in need of poor relief) the home parish would either receive them or reimburse the cost of their relief. Some parishes will have more detailed records for building poor houses and caring for the elderly poor, for clothing poor children and so on. If your parish does have a good collection of civil parish records, they will throw light on many aspects of ordinary community life; if you are unlucky, it is worth looking at the civil parish records in neighbouring parishes, which will give you a good idea of how the system functioned and may well mention many inhabitants of your parish who have been 'removed' to their home parish. Because appeals from the decisions of the vestry or parish officials went to the Quarter Sessions of the county or borough, their records will certainly have some mentions of inhabitants whose removal to or from your parish was in dispute, or arguments about the levying of rates: these will often include copies of the rates levied in a particular year, of which copies have not survived among the local parish records. Listing and identifying the parish officers, especially churchwardens, overseers and surveyors, will be desirable if it is possible, which will throw much light on local government. Whether you can say much about the official activities of the vestry and its officers depends on the survival of vestry minutes and churchwardens', surveyors' and overseers' accounts. Moreover, many parishes had, and some still have, local charities for helping the poor in various ways: besides assisting apprenticeship, these included provision of clothing and food. Local knowledge and the files of the Charity Commission are the best guides. Finally, the original responsibilities of churchwardens for the church building, its services and reporting to bishops' or archdeacons' visitations on parish affairs have continued to this day after their added secular duties were removed in the nineteenth century.[47]

Towns

Towns continued to be established in the early modern period and often to acquire borough status until the later seventeenth century; at the same time, some older towns had failed, or were failing, to keep up with their earlier success and were declining into the 'rotten boroughs' of the Georgian period. If towns survived and flourished, their constituent parishes would acquire the same civil powers as their rural counterparts in relation to poor relief and the highways. Those towns which became chartered boroughs with rights of self-government recorded their activities in Council minutes and

Registers, account rolls, deeds of urban property and numerous files. Because of disputes between urban parishes over their responsibilities and often complicated interlocking parish boundaries crossing and re-crossing major roads, the larger towns led the way in creating Unions of parishes such as Bristol's Incorporation of the Poor founded in 1696, and in the eighteenth century the urban élite sponsored acts of Parliament to establish 'Improvement Commissioners' with special powers. They often supported the foundation of Turnpike Trusts and Canal Companies to improve communications with their hinterland and with other similar towns. A corporate town or borough was therefore likely to be much better documented than a market town; in addition to the records of the borough and the new bodies just mentioned, many towns had craft guilds covering the predominant local industries and trades, and also charities, all keeping their own records, and in addition many urban churches had feoffees or trustees with charitable functions. By contrast, an unincorporated town had usually evolved out of one of the neighbouring manors and its powers, such as they were, were derived from the parent manorial court and its lord. Power was likely to reside more in the civil parish authorities or even in a 'shadow government' disguised as a club or society.

Travellers' reports

A final source of information, and one often overlooked by local historians, consists of reports by travellers in England both native and foreign. Some, such as William of Worcester in the fifteenth century and Lady Celia Fiennes in the seventeenth century, were simply curious about England, their native country; John Leland's *Itinerary* was the by-product of a royal commission to track down manuscripts from now dissolved monastic libraries; Daniel Defoe was primarily interested in the economy of Queen Anne's England. Foreign travellers are a mixed bag, some not venturing far from London, but some were interested in the economy and society of a rising imperial power, the Duc de Rochefoucald for example, and from about 1750 onwards many foreigners came to discover the agricultural, industrial and commercial secrets which had created the English Industrial Revolution: they were in effect industrial spies. Other foreigners were attracted by the political structure underlaying the economic triumph, Great Britain being the only great power in the early modern period with a strong representative assembly, Parliament. Such travellers are a mixed bag, some being very useful, others less so, but they did reveal points that were strange to them, even if commonplace to the English: that the average English labourer in the eighteenth century drank tea with sugar or beer, smoked tobacco, ate white bread, and lived in a cottage with glass windows and some security of tenure amazed them, though to the English these features were commonplace; that noble titles only descended to the eldest son, not, as on the continent, to all male children, was astounding.[48]

Besides 'travel' literature, much of interest will be found in diaries, autobiographies and correspondence. As we shall see in the next chapter, official records blossomed in the nineteenth century, but the 'information explosion' began in the previous century. Apart from the foreign and native tourists already mentioned, the long-running *Gentleman's Magazine* frequently contains useful regional or local information, which is accessible through the multi-volume indexes of G. L. Gomme.[49] Arthur Young's *Annals of Agriculture* (1784–1808) and other publications are full of reports on local agriculture, contrasting the existing norms with examples of best practice.[50] The *County Reports* of the Board of Agriculture are a valuable source and not just for agriculture: there were two series of these *Reports*, one in the 1790s, the other in the early 1800s, written by knowledgeable enthusiasts for agricultural improvement, whose findings can be compared with any surviving Home Office Returns in the same period.[51] Another well-known and influential propagandist for agricultural improvement was William Marshall.[52] Increasing press freedom was reflected in critical publications such as William Cobbett's *Political Register* (1802–36), which included the *Rural Rides* later separately republished.[53] Cobbett was of course a political Radical, violently opposed to 'The Thing' (the

Unreformed Parliament and aristocratic control of political affairs), but he had an unrivalled knowledge of the lives and conditions of the cottagers and the poor.

Conclusion

Unless you are very unfortunate in the non-survival of any parish records apart from the registers, or of any town records, it should be possible to study a considerable amount of local history in the early modern period, and in many cases to enhance the history with appropriate tables, graphs and maps, perhaps also pictures, prints and drawings, and photographs. (Bear in mind that if you are aiming at publication, reproducing any illustration in colour and pictures even as black-and-white photographs is expensive and may put the price of your production beyond what most people might be prepared to pay: black-and-white line-drawings and maps are far cheaper and can be more effective as illustrations.) As yet, national records will add relatively little to the local picture: Parliament passed the acts authorising various powers to local authorities, initially the parish which now became a unit of civil government, but later also a variety of *ad hoc* bodies such as Turnpike Trusts, canal and railway companies and Improvement Commissioners which were called into being as economic expansion led to the creation of new towns (or new suburbs outside the bounds of the parent boroughs) which had to wait until the nineteenth century to achieve borough status. The central government after 1660 did not interest itself much in local affairs until the nineteenth century, a situation that was to change radically in the modern period when, as we shall see, the *Blue Books* of the national government become an important source of local information.

Notes

1 The best lists of parish registers are the *National Index of Parish Registers* series published by the Society of Genealogists and the lists in C. Humphery-Smith, *The Phillimore Atlas and Index of Parish Registers* (Andover, Phillimore, 3rd edn,

2010). Each Record Office will have an up-to-date list of registers in its custody and their covering dates.

2   R. N. Swanson, *Church and Society in Late Medieval England* (Oxford, Blackwell, 1989), 4, 45, stated that there were *c.* 9500 parishes in 1291 and *c.* 8800 in 1535, but he overlooked Cardinal Wolsey's list of 1520 with 9407 parishes (W. Camden, *Britain, or a Chorographicall Description of the most Flourishing Kingdomes England, Scotland and Ireland* ... (London, Bishop & Norton, 1610), sig.O₁v). This may have been based on the 1291 list, which was still the most up-to-date official list for ecclesiastical taxation until the 1535 *Valor Ecclesiasticus*. The 1603 total of 9244 is based on A. Dyer and D. M. Palliser (eds), *The Diocesan Population Returns for 1563 and 1603* (Oxford, OUP, 2005), lxxxiv–v.

3   The classic introduction, though now in need of revision, is W. E. Tate, *The Parish Chest: a study of the records of parochial administration* (Cambridge, CUP, 3rd edn, 1969, repr. Chichester, Phillimore, 1983). For parish registers, see J. C. Cox, *The Parish Registers of England* (London, Methuen, 1910).

4   For this method see E. A. Wrigley (ed.), *An Introduction to English Historical Demography* (London, Weidenfeld & Nicholson, 1966), chap. 3, and E. A. Wrigley and R. S. Schofield, *The Population History of England, 1541–1871* (London, Arnold, 1981, repr. Cambridge, CUP, 1989).

5   See Bibliography, sections 6 (v) 3 and 7 (iv) 3. For alien immigrants see also *TNA Research Guides*, Domestic Ser. 50.

6   For this method, see Wrigley (ed.), *Introduction to English Historical Demography*, chap. 6 and E. A. Wrigley *et al.* (eds), *English Population History from Family Reconstruction, 1580–1837* (Cambridge, CUP, 1997).

7   T. H. Hollingsworth, *Historical Demography* (London, Hodder & Stoughton, 1969), 159–66, 168–78.

8   P. Laslett, *Family Life and Illicit Love in Earlier Generations* (Cambridge, CUP, 1977), 112–7, 125, 134, 137–45; P. Laslett *et al.* (eds), *Bastardy and its Comparative History* (London, Arnold, 1980), 14, 18, 96–7, 124; E. A. Wrigley *et al.*, *English Population History from Family Reconstruction* (Cambridge, CUP, 1997), 219.

9   P. E. H. Hair, 'Bridal pregnancy in rural England in earlier centuries' (*Population Studies* 20 (1966), 233–43); P. E. H. Hair, 'Bridal pregnancy in earlier rural England re-examined' (*Population Studies* 24 (1970), 59–70); Laslett, *Family Life and Illicit Love*, 130; Laslett *et al.* (eds), *Bastardy and its Comparative History*, 23–4, 109, 164; M. Ingram, *Church Courts, Sex and Marriage in England, 1570–1540* (Cambridge, CUP, 1987), 161–3, 219–37.

10 R. A. Houlbrooke, *Church Courts and the People During the English Reformation, 1520–1570* (Oxford, OUP, 1979), chaps 2–3; Ingram, *Church Courts, Sex and Barriage in England, 1570–1540*, esp. pts 2–3; A. Tarver, *Church Court Records* (Chichester, Phillimore, 1995); R. B. Outhwaite, *Clandestine Marriage in England, 1500–1850* (London, Hambledon, 1995); D. Cressy, *Birth, Marriage*

and Death. Ritual, Religion and the Life-Cycle in Tudor and Stuart England
(Oxford, OUP, 1997).

11 Wrigley and Schofield, *The Population History of England*, 4, 15–16, 89, 96–102;
Cressy, *Birth, Marriage and Death*, 100–6.

12 B. M. Berry and R. S. Schofield, 'Age at baptism in pre-industrial England'
(*Population Studies* 25 (1971), 453–63); Wrigley and Schofield, *The Population
History of England, 1541–1871*, 96–102. E. A. Wrigley, 'Births and baptisms:
the use of Anglican registers as a source of information about the numbers of
births in England before the beginning of civil registration' (*Population Studies*
31 (1977), 281–312), deals with allowances to be made for delayed baptism,
mostly after 1660.

13 Centre for Kentish Studies, Maidstone, P 375/1/1.

14 Somerset Heritage Centre, Taunton, D/P/Tick/2/1/1.

15 R. A. Marchant, *The Church Under the Law: justice, administration and discipline
in the diocese of York, 1560–1640* (Cambridge, CUP, 1969), 227. Houlbrooke,
Church Courts and the People during the English Reformation, 1520–1570, 50,
stated that 'the proportion of excommunicates signified remained small'; Ingram,
Church Courts, Sex and Marriage in England, 1570–1640, 341, 343, argued for
raising Marchant's estimate to 15%, but also shows that excommunication
was often allowed to lapse, and that attendance levels at church courts after
summons remained high, 69–93% (*ibid.*, 350–1).

16 P. E. H. Hair, 'A note on the incidence of Tudor suicide' (*LPS* 5 (1970), 36–43);
Hair, 'Deaths from violence in Britain: a tentative secular survey' (*Population
Studies* 25 (1971), 5–24, esp. 15–16); J. A. Sharpe, 'The history of violence in
England: some observations' (*Past and Present* 108 (1985), 209–11); M. Zell,
'Suicide in pre-industrial England' (*Social History* 11 (1986), 303–17); S. J.
Stevenson, 'The rise of suicide verdicts in south-east England, 1530–1590:
the legal process' (*Continuity and Change* 2 (1987), 38–76); Stevenson, 'Social
and economic contributions to the pattern of "suicide" in south-east England,
1530–1590' (*Continuity and Change* 2 (1987), 232–30); M. Macdonald and
T. R. Murphy, *Sleepless Souls. Suicide in Early Modern England* (Oxford, OUP,
1990), 238–58, 360–6.

17 Wrigley and Schofield, *The Population History of England*, 528.

18 Centre for Kentish Studies, Maidstone, P 364/1/1, 350.

19 See n.6 above.

20 Wrigley (ed.), *An Introduction to English Historical Demography*, 110–1; Wrigley
et al. (eds), *English Population History from Family Reconstitution*, chaps 3–4.

21 J. S. Moore, 'Rural housing in the north Bristol region, 1600–1850', in M.
Baulant *et al.* (eds), *Inventaires après deces et ventes de meubles. Apparts a une
histoire de la vie economique et quotidienne (XIVe–XIXe siecles* (Louvain (Belgium),
Academia, 1988), 197–209).

22 H. M. Registrar-General, *The Story of the General Register Office and its Origins
from 1538 to 1937* (London, HMSO, 1937), 6, citing 'Report of the House of

Commons Select Committee on Registration' (*Sessional Papers of the House of Commons, 1833*, no. 669, 3–4).

23 Dyer and Palliser (eds), *The Diocesan Population Returns for 1563 and 1603*.

24 A. Whiteman (ed.), *The Compton Census of 1676: a critical edition* (Oxford, OUP, 1986).

25 J. Houston (ed.), *Catalogue of Ecclesiastical Records of the Commonwealth, 1643–1660, in Lambeth Palace Library* (Farnborough, Gregg, 1968), 81–181.

26 J. Gairdner, 'Bishop Hooper's Visitation of Gloucester Diocese, 1551' (*English Hist. Rev.* 19 (1904), 98–121) and L. E. Whatmore (ed.), 'Archdeacon Harpsfield's Visitation, 1557' (*Catholic Rec. Soc.* 45–6, 1950–1) are the two earliest diocesan surveys giving details of local population. For later diocesan surveys, see Bibliography, section 6 (iv) 7.

27 To be found in local diocesan record offices and sometimes also in local parish records,

28 See n. 26 above.

29 See nn. 23–6 above.

30 I. M. Kirby, *Records of the Diocese of Bristol* (Bristol, Diocese of Bristol, 1970); F. W. Steer, I. M. Kirby, *A Catalogue of the Records of the Bishops, Archdeacons and former exempt jurisdictions of the diocese of Chichester* (Chichester, West Sussex County Council, 1966); I. M. Kirby, *A Catalogue of the Records of the Bishop and Archdeacons of the Diocese of Gloucester* (Gloucester, City Corporation, 1968); K. Major, *A Handlist of the records of the Bishop of Lincoln and the archdeacons of Lincoln and Stow* (Oxford, OUP, 1953); P. Stewart, *Guide to the records of the Bishop, the Archdeacons of Salisbury and Wiltshire* (Salisbury, Wiltshire County Council, 1973).

31 D. M. Owen, *Records of the Established Church in England Excluding Parochial Records* (London, British Rec. Association, 1970, repr. 1996) is a good introductory guide.

32 J. Nichols, *The History and Antiquities of the County of Leicester* ... (London, Nichols, Son and Bentley, 4 vols in 8 parts, 1795–1811).

33 Some of this data has been analysed in R. Wall, 'Mean household size from printed sources', in P. Laslett and R. Wall (eds), *Household and Family in Past Time* (Cambridge, CUP, 1972), chap. 5, but this is far from a complete list: for example, for nearly all Gloucestershire towns and villages, population figures are available in Atkyns' *Ancient and Present State of Glostershire* (London, Gosling, 1712, repr. Wakefield, EP, 1974) for *c.* 1711.

34 Wrigley (ed.), *Introduction to English Historical Demography*, 121, 152; the statement that 'Work on literacy ... is not possible until ... after the passage of Hardwicke's Marriage Act (1753)' is simply wrong. For further information see Bibliography, section 7 (v) 8.

35 J. S. W. Gibson and A. Dell, *The Protestation Returns, 1641–2, and other contemporary listings* (Birmingham, Federation of Family History Societies, 1995) is an excellent guide. See also A. Whiteman, V. Russell, 'The Protestation

Returns of 1641–42' (*LPS.*, vol. 55 (1995), 14–27; vol. 56 (1996), 17–29.

36 For the Hearth Tax, see *TNA Research Guides*, Domestic Ser. 10, 32, and J. S. W. Gibson, *The Hearth Tax, Other later Stuart Tax Lists and the Association Oath Rolls* (Birmingham, Federation of Family History Societies, 1987). For published Hearth Tax assessments, see Bibliography, section 6 (iv) 6.

37 See n. 25 above.

38 See *TNA, Research Guide*, Legal Ser. 46; A. J. Camp, *Wills and their Whereabouts* (Canterbury, Phillimore, 2nd edn, 1963); T. Arkell *et al.* (eds), *When Death Do Us Part: understanding and interpreting the Probate Records of early modern England* (Oxford, Leopard's Head P, 2000).

39 See *TNA Research Guide*, Domestic Ser. 4 and Gibson, *The Hearth Tax ... and the Association Oath Rolls*.

40 See J. Lane, *Apprenticeship in England, 1600–1914* (London, UCL P, 1996), and *TNA Research Guide*, Domestic Ser. 80.

41 J. R. Wordie, 'The Chronology of English Enclosure, 1500–1914' (*Econ. Hist. Rev.* 2nd ser. 36 (1983), 483–505).

42 In addition to the local Record Offices, the Museum of Rural Life in the University of Reading has a nationwide collection of farm accounts.

43 J. C. Cox, *Churchwardens Accounts* (London, Methuen, 1913); A. Foster, 'Churchwardens' Accounts of early modern England and Wales', in K. L. French *et al.* (eds), *The Parish in English Life, 1400–1600*, Manchester, Manchester UP, 1997), chap. 5. J. Gibson and D. Mills, *Land-Tax Assessments, c. 1690–c. 1960* (Birmingham, Federation of Family History Socs, 1983) and Gibson, *The Hearth Tax, Other Later Stuart Tax Lists and the Association Oath Rolls* are all useful guides. Rate books are covered by L. M. Munby (ed.), *Short Guides to Records* (London, Hist. Association, 1972), no. 1, and other civil parish records in K. M. Thompson (ed.), *Short Guides to Records (Second Series)* (London, Hist. Association, 1997), nos 25–30.

44 These so far cover brewing: A. Turton (ed.) (1990); shipbuilding: L.A. Ritchie (ed.) (1992); and pharmaceuticals: L. Richmond, J. Stevenson and A. Turton (eds) (2003). E. Kerridge, *Textile Manufacture in Early Modern England* (Manchester, Manchester UP, 1985), is an excellent survey. For coal see J. Hatcher, *The History of the British Coal Industry, 1. Before 1700* (Oxford, OUP, 1993) and M. W. Flinn, *The History of the British Coal Industry, 2. 1700–1830* (Oxford, OUP, 1984). Studies of stone relate mainly to its architectural use but say little about quarrying.

45 M. W. Barley, *The English Farmhouse and Cottage* (London, Routledge, 1961), W. G. Hoskins, *Provincial England* (London, Macmillan, 1963), chap. 7, and A. Clifton-Taylor, *The Pattern of English Building* (London, Faber, 4th edn, 1987) are classic introductions; for the proliferation of regional studies, see the journal *Vernacular Architecture*. One example is Moore, 'Rural Housing in the North Bristol region, 1600–1850'. See Bibliography, section 6 (v) 6.

46 E. H. Phelps-Brown and S. V. Hopkins, *A Perspective of Prices and Wages*

(London, Methuen, 1981) and J. Burnett, *A History of the Cost of Living* (London, Grigg, 2nd edn, 1993) are the best guides.

47 See n. 43 above.

48 For foreign travellers in England, see R. C. Richardson and W. H. Chaloner, *British Economic and Social History: a bibliographical guide* (Manchester, Mancchester UP, 2nd edn, 1996), 54, 113; for all travellers see G. E. Fussell, *The Exploration of England. A Select Bibliography of Travel and Topography, 1570–1815* (London, Mitre P, 1935), which now needs revision. Much topographical information will be found in diaries and autobiographies: W. Matthews, *British Diaries: an annotated bibliography of British diaries written between 1442 and 1942* (Cambridge, CUP, 1950); W. Matthews, *British Autobiographies: an annotated bibliography of British Autobiographies Published or Written before 1951* (Berkeley (USA), California UP, 1955); A. Ponsonby, *English Diaries from the 16th to the 20th Century* (London, Methuen, 1923); A. Ponsonby, *More English Diaries* (London, Methuen, 1927).

49 The *Gentleman's Magazine* ran from 1731 to 1922 and should be available in major libraries, as should the indexes in G. L. Gomme (ed.), *The Gentleman's Magazine, Being a Classified Collection of the Chief Contents of the* Gentleman's Magazine *from 1731 to 1868. Indexes: Topographical History* (London, Elliott Stock, 11 vols, 1891–1904).

50 G. E. Mingay, *Arthur Young and his Times* (London, Macmillan, 1975), appendix, lists all his writings.

51 *Board of Agriculture, Reports* (London, Board of Agriculture, many volumes in different bindings, 1794–1817).

52 P. Horn, *William Marshall (1745–1818) and the Georgian Countryside* (Abingdon, Beacon Publications, 1982).

53 G. Spater, *William Cobbett: the Poor Man's Friend* (Cambridge, CUP, 2 vols, 1982). W. Cobbett, *Rural Rides* (standard edition in 3 vols, 1930; later editions by G. Woodcock (Harmondsworth, Penguin, 1967) and by Asa Briggs (London, Dent, 1973).

CHAPTER 5

Modern Times, 1841–2011

....

The increase in central government power

Although what happened in the history of English and Welsh population from the mid-nineteenth century, at local, regional or national level, is well-established, historians are still arguing about causes and effects. Before 1841, and even more before 1801, we move into a period where, as we have seen in Chapter 4, much investigation is still required to establish, at various geographical levels from the whole country to its constituent parishes, what happened in the history of population, why it happened, and what were the results for the people in each area. In and after the eighteenth century the state became increasingly interested in ascertaining the numbers and 'condition' of the people as England united with Scotland to become by 1714 an imperial power as 'Great Britain' with world-wide political and commercial interests. In the sixteenth century Sir William Cecil had been almost alone in trying to estimate trends in a quantitative fashion, whereas by the eighteenth century intellectuals and politicians were regularly using 'political arithmetic' to consider problems from a mathematical viewpoint.

The coming of the parish registers in 1538 coincided with a change in the nature of the parish clergy: from being, often, barely literate in 1500, they had become an overwhelmingly graduate profession by 1700 who not only recorded the christenings, marriages and burials but often commented on them either in the registers or in print.[1] The clergy were, with their cousins the gentry, at the centre of local society at county and parish levels, well placed to comment effectively on its doings. As the power of the state apparatus grew, government and the ruling classes became increasingly concerned with the condition of the majority of the population because of possible rioting and disorder. This led to increasing government reports to Parliament, to the decennial census after 1801, and the introduction in 1834 of a nationwide 'new poor law' based on new regional units, the 'unions' of several parishes.[2] In 1837 a national system of registration of births, marriages and deaths began, which is regarded as complete from the 1860s. From 1841 onwards census-information was collected from individual heads of household on all members of their households. Following the introduction of the *New Poor Law*, the 'unions' became the major administrative units below county level in the country; these frequently took on additional powers as Highway Boards, Sanitary Authorities and School Boards. After 1889 the counties, until then mainly judicial units (as Quarter Sessions), again became important administrative units, and from 1894 the boundaries of either Urban or Rural District Councils coincided with those of most unions; the parish, for so long the local centre of civil administration, now lost most of its civil power, becoming merely a unit for collection of rates for a higher body.[3]

All these new bodies served as collecting centres for information required by central government which increasingly was utilised for its purposes and presented as Official Publications generally known as *Blue Books* from their covers. Once Parliament had established its sovereignty, the extra powers often required were obtained by 'Local and Personal' or 'Private' acts of Parliament after the proposed acts had been scrutinised by Parliamentary committees whose records of evidence, including in many cases large-scale maps and reference-tables, remain a fertile and underused source in the Parliamentary Archives, formerly known as the House of Lords Record Office. A very useful guide to much of this material exists and many public libraries as well as university libraries will have runs either of these *Blue Books* or of the reprinted series produced in the 1970s which were re-arranged by subject-matter.[4]

Two warnings are necessary at this point: in the first place all subject-indexes, especially of major subjects as in the 1970s reprints, are not fully inclusive, so that it is always worthwhile reading through any papers which refer to your area regardless of their major topic: witnesses have been known to wander off the point, but what they are saying is often still good evidence of contemporary events and beliefs! Secondly, place-indexes are not always complete at parish level or below (e.g. hamlet, chapelry): you should, to be safe, also recheck by the local hundred or wapentake, by the Poor Law union, by any known local geographical regions, e.g. the Vale of Gloucester, Sherwood Forest, and by county, both the old historic counties and the changes resulting from transfers of outlying and detached sections between counties which became increasingly common in the nineteenth and twentieth centuries before the radical changes introduced in and after 1973. A useful guide to most of these changes before 1973 will be found in the county chapters of the *Domesday Geography* regional volumes (bear in mind that Domesday Book did not include the northern counties of Cumberland, Durham, Northumberland and Westmorland, and its coverage of Lancashire was scrappy).[5]

The expansion of government publication

From 1837 official registers of births, marriages and deaths were established in England and Wales which are regarded as complete from the 1860s, and the recording of causes of death became more reliable with growing medical knowledge. Although entries relating to named individuals can be traced in the official indexes to each series of registers and copied, this is a facility only useful to genealogists; the free access to all the local registers necessary for family reconstitution at parish level or below is still denied to historical demographers, a deplorable situation. The results of the new registration system were also summarised in printed *Reports of the Registrar-General* which can also be consulted in university and major local libraries. The recording of migration into and out of Britain also markedly improved in the nineteenth and twentieth centuries, though recent experience has showed that immigration in times of crisis can be massively under-recorded.[6] The availability of the enumerators' schedules to the census from 1841 to 2011, now all available on-line, makes possible the reconstruction of local households and the 'kinship-network' linking them to other households in the same and different generations, also the size of agricultural, industrial and commercial enterprises, individuals' status and occupations, and from 1911 the number of rooms occupied by one household.[7]

Even at village or small town level, it will generally be found that most places had more, and more varied, shops available in Victorian times than at any earlier or later period, partly because many goods were made 'on site' by local craftsmen or supplied by local farmers and partly because most local people could not afford the time or the money to shop further away from home. The only useful facilities for supplying goods from a distance were either by getting a country carrier to buy on behalf of a customer or buying from a travelling salesman: both required mutual trust between the buyer and seller. A weekly market within about 10–15 miles (16–24 km), if still functioning in the modern period, was another resource. Similarly, unless an area was blighted by the Temperance movement, there were far more taverns and inns open locally in the nineteenth century than after the First World War, most of which were local concerns, although especially in the towns chains of inns ('tied houses') were being created by brewers competing with each other for business. Eventually, cut-throat competition between brewery chains and tighter licensing regulation during and after World War I reduced the number of local pubs open, helped by a tendency towards more drinking at home and the decline of institutions such as local friendly societies and trades union branches that had previously used local pubs as convenient meeting places.

Particularly in the towns, local shops apart from general stores, bakers and butchers found it difficult to compete with larger urban shops offering a wider range of cheaper goods or, in some areas, expanding Co-operative shops, though even these found it more and more difficult to compete with the chain stores which appeared after 1918 especially as access by villagers to the local towns became easier with motorised busses after 1918 and the expansion of private car ownership after 1945.[8] In the larger towns prestigious department stores evolved, and were joined by chains of stores such as *Woolworth's* and *British Home Stores* competing on price and the range of goods offered.[9] Many villages were growing with the expansion of middle-class building especially between the wars, the beginnings of new towns such as Welwyn Garden and other London suburbs in the inter-war period ('Metroland') and the 'new town' movement after 1945 leading to such developments as Basildon, Crawley, Harlow, Milton Keynes, Stevenage and Telford. Even in rural villages, there was much new house-building between the 1950s and the 1980s, as many villages became dormitories for skilled workers from older industrial areas. Most of the 'new' inhabitants of Frampton Cotterell from the 1950s, for example, were skilled workers in the aero-engineering industry in nearby Filton, which became an industrialised suburban village after 1900 when Sir George White's 'Bristol' aircraft factory was joined by the aero-engine factory of *Rolls-Royce*.

Parish/hamlet/neighbourhood

The growth of local population after 1801 may make it possible and perhaps even desirable to select a smaller unit of study than the traditional parish or chapelry without necessarily sacrificing any relevant details: if the area is a new ecclesiastical parish or district, its boundaries will be given in the issue of the *Gazette* containing the Statutory Instrument which established the new area on a map with defined boundaries. Once the boundaries have been ascertained, any necessary adjustments in the census enumerators' schedules can be made to produce a consistent series of population statistics for the new area, which may well suggest ideas for its formation.

Given the amount of fragmentation in all the local churches, – the Church of England being increasingly divided between the 'high' (Anglo-Catholic or Tractarian) and the 'low' (Evangelical) factions while the Methodists' increasing divisions after John Wesley's death were not reversed until the reunion of the 1920s – religious observance was very often a major reason for new settlements in what increasingly were suburban areas.[10] One of the early industrial immigrants to Frampton Cotterell told me that when he and his wife arrived in 1937 all that the locals wanted to know about them was 'were they Church or Chapel?' (It would be exceptional now for such a question even to be asked: organised religion's hold on the majority of people has simply evaporated.) In areas where Irish immigration was strong,[11] Roman Catholicism witnessed expansion; in many areas there were local variants of Christianity which enjoyed much support at least for a time.

Long-distance migration was also often significant locally: Jews were re-admitted to England by Oliver Cromwell and Louis XIV's persecution of Huguenot Protestants drove many of them to settle in England: in both cases their contribution was out of all proportion to their numbers. In some financial and industrial centres Jews were a significant and important minority, reinforced by Jews fleeing from Tsarist pogroms in the later nineteenth century and enlarged in the 1930s by German Jews fleeing Nazi persecution. Since 1948 immigrants from the West Indies and the Indian sub-continent have become highly significant in industrial and commercial urban communities.[12]

Besides religion, another motive for new settlement was often the paternalist desire to provide housing of reasonable quality for the workers of a particular employer – *Cadburys* at Bournville, *Frys* at Keynsham, *Lever Bros* at Port Sunlight and Titus Salt at Saltaire are well-known examples – though trade unions often regarded such schemes with suspicion as disguised bribery.[13] But the increasing rise of a middle class desirous of renting and, if possible, owning its own homes also meant there was increasing speculative building to meet this demand for new housing, either for rent or for sale, which was increasingly evident throughout the nineteenth and twentieth centuries. The 1851 Census *Report* had highlighted the fact that by then more people now lived in urban than in rural areas, and the urban percentage of population has continued to grow ever since. Equally, so has house-ownership: even in towns, flats are common only in areas of municipal housing, of large numbers of upwardly mobile young professionals and of retirement apartments. Census

Reports for each parish include statistics on the numbers of houses 'inhabited' 'uninhabited' and 'building' which enable the rate of local building to be precisely measured each decade.[14]

The increased level of migration, and the increasing distance travelled by new immigrants, partly of course affected by new means of transport – canal boats, country carriers and later bus services, above all the railways – also produced new strains on family life. No longer were the vast majority of one's relatives and in-laws likely to be living no more than about 10 miles (16 km) from the family home, if not in the same village or urban neighbourhood then in the next one or two. In the meantime, long-distance migration frequently weakened contacts between the generations which were difficult to maintain given the rather low levels of literacy of the working class before universal primary education became compulsory and free in the 1880s and before the new cheap postal service began in 1840.[15] Increasingly, people looked for support to their neighbours who were often either new in-laws or friends working locally in the same industry or trade. Such new links were strengthened by new associations like the expanding and now legal trade unions, who often absorbed or replaced the older local friendly societies, and the new national friendly societies such as the Ancient Order of Foresters;[16] the middle classes equally tended to gravitate towards bodies like the Freemasons, the Rotary Associations and the local Conservative or Liberal Clubs. The expansion of house-building around expanding towns and later in middle class enclaves in small towns and villages was often an unexpected boost to landowners whose wealth had been depleted by declining agricultural rents, rising death-duties and punitive taxation.[17]

Law and order

Population-growth and continued urbanisation in the modern period inevitably raised the problems of maintaining law and order. Previously the parish constable, in medieval times a manorial appointment, was an elected official chosen annually by the parish vestry (originally by the manor court) and having very few effective powers. For positive support he needed to rely on the local Justices of the Peace who had since Tudor times acquired considerable judicial and administrative powers, albeit in a rather haphazard manner, in response to new emergencies.[18] If public disorder occurred, the county musters might be called out, usually not very effectively in the period 1500–1650, and army detachments were sent to deal with outbreaks of violence, notably during the 'rule of the Major-Generals' after Cromwell's death. From 1660 a standing army came into being, whose role and numbers greatly increased as Britain acquired an overseas Empire; units of the regular army and the Militia, later the yeomanry regiments, could be called-on to suppress serious disorder and rioting as at Peterloo.[19]

Apart from the occasional employment of army or militia detachments sent 'to aid the civil power' during times of disorder sufficiently serious to be officially classified as 'riotous', there was no force with national powers and responsibilities, and no force with an efficient investigative team. The nearest thing in both cases was the 'Bow Street Runners' founded in 1751 by Sir John Fielding, magistrate at Bow Street. The troubles associated with the Napoleonic wars and the post-war depression led to the foundation of the Metropolitan Police Force in 1829 and of the county police forces from 1839, often against considerable opposition from ratepayers' groups who organised county petitions, whilst the Borough 'watches' developed into borough police forces.[20]

The records of most English police forces are mainly in local record offices or still at Police Headquarters; the records of the Metropolitan Police are divided between TNA and Scotland Yard;[21] the records of the British Transport Police and its predecessors of the separate railway police forces for each company are in TNA among the records of British Rail and its predecessors.[22] Before the *Rural Constabulary Act* of 1839, crises or serious problems of law and order would be reported in the State Papers Domestic, later the Home Office Papers, and in Privy Council Records, possibly also in the Treasury Solicitor's Records. After 1839, the Home

Office Correspondence would deal with most problems, though the Treasury Board Papers might be worth perusing.[23] As Britain became a predominantly urban and industrialised country, the police were more concentrated in the towns, but many country people continued to have a different attitude to crime.

One of the major factors in rural crime was poaching, seen by the poor as exercising a right to the fruits of nature, not least on what had often been common land before enclosure, but regarded by the landowners as a major attack on their property-rights. High rates of population-growth combined with urbanisation and, especially after the Napoleonic wars, falling living-standards as food costs in particular escalated, resulted in food riots in the period 1780–1840 of an intensity not seen in England since the 1590s; these were often exacerbated by riots over the Parliamentary enclosure of commons between 1760 and 1845.[24] This, coupled with the ending of transportation as a criminal punishment, led to the development in England and Wales of a modern prison system steering a middle course between rigorous punishment of criminals and their reformation.[25] Industrialisation and law and order not only influenced the new prisons but provided another problem for the police, as lawyers increasingly came to regard industrial disputes as a criminal offence, thus apparently involving the police on the side of industrial employers, a trend culminating in Mrs Thatcher as Prime Minister using the police to break the Miners' strike in 1984.[26]

Economic activities

Many, though not all, of the sources for economic activities mentioned in previous chapters still remain useful in the modern period: farm and factory accounts where they survive are important but the survival of such accounts depends mainly on the survival of either the farming or landowning families involved or the business enterprise, and on these families' willingness to allow access to their records.[27] My own experience suggests that landowners are usually willing to allow access to their records if presented with a reasoned case whereas farmers are generally uninterested in local history and disinclined to help local historians. Other important sources for agriculture and land-use are the 'Invasion Returns' of the 1790s and 1801–4 which list the individual farms, giving areas, land-use and livestock for each farm; these are rare, but where they survive are very useful.[28] Apart from records held locally, most will be found in TNA HO 42 and 67.

The next major source comprises the Tithe Awards and Maps made between 1836 and the mid-1840s for all parishes which still had land liable to pay tithes; the principal areas excluded are those parishes where tithes had been commuted by an earlier *Enclosure Act* or by a long-established redemption money-payment known as a *modus*. There are parishes where most land was still titheable but a portion, often but not always a detached 'outlier', had been subject to a *modus* at some time in the past. (Earlier glebe terriers may show you when this commutation occurred but it may be of medieval origin 'whereof the memory of man runneth not to the contrary'). Generally the Award consists of a list of numbered fields giving area, land-use, name and amount of tithes payable, usually arranged alphabetically by owner and within each owner alphabetically by occupier (e.g. the farmer or cottager). At the end the individual returns are summarised by owner and by occupier; it is quite possible for an owner to occupy part or all of his or her land and also land owned by others; if this is apparent you must adjust the summaries accordingly. Apart from any copying errors, the figures are as good as you are likely to find; the field numbers are also given in the Tithe Map and thus enable you to reconstruct the boundaries of the estates and their constituent farms in early Victorian England. Tithe-free land is generally listed and usually indicates former possession by a monastic house in the Middle Ages. Where the tithe-owner is also the sole landlord, he may choose to attribute all his tithe-liability to one or two fields rather than the whole parish: Stoke Gifford (Gloucs), for long the property of the Dukes of Beaufort, is a case in point; if one is not aware of this possibility, the landowner's role will be unduly diminished.

Three copies of the Tithe Award and Map for the relevant parishes were made: the first set for the Tithe Commissioners is now in TNA IR 29 (Awards) and IR 30 (Maps); the second set was for the local Anglican bishop and is now in the appropriate diocesan record office; the third set was for the local parish authorities and is with the parish records, normally now in the local record office. The third set is the one most likely to have suffered damage or to have been lost; diocesan copies are usually in a better state of preservation, and the set in TNA is said to be complete. It is also worth looking at the Tithe Files (TNA IR 18) which exist for all parishes in England and Wales, not just those for which Awards and Maps exist; the Files may explain why no award was made, usually because of abolition under previous enclosure acts, or any particular local problems. Although the Tithe Maps and Awards are mainly valuable for agricultural history, these will include industrial establishments such as mines, factories and early railways.[29]

Further details of land-use in the Victorian countryside from the 1850s to the 1880s can be obtained from the *Parish Books* compiled by the Ordnance Survey to accompany the first edition 25 inches to the mile maps: these books contained a numbered list of individual fields for each parish with their land-use and areas; these can be mapped and compared with the Tithe Maps for the same parish 20–30 years earlier.

From 1866 onwards, new agricultural returns were required every year of both numbers of livestock and areas under crops which are still being compiled today; the original returns were destroyed though parish summaries were compiled which can be consulted for 1866–1988 (TNA MAF 68). Later parish returns survive electronically (UKNDAD CRDA/4) and will be available 30 years after they were compiled. Following Lloyd George's first Budget of 1909–10, a detailed survey of all land in England and Wales was ordered, which was made for every individual property; its voluminous records have not all survived and those that do survive are not all in TNA. Record Plans for each property will eventually be transferred from local Valuation Offices to TNA; Working Plans which survive are held by local record offices, as are Valuation Books ('Domesday Books') where they survive; those for London and Westminster, however, are in TNA, which also has the final Field Books (IR 58). Where they survive, the final valuations, Form 37 Land, are also in local record offices. It is usually necessary to locate the local properties from lists for each Valuation Office area in TNA IR 121, 124–35. Provided that adequate records survive, it should be possible to recreate the pattern of local landownership before the First World War and Lloyd George's 'death duties' began the transformation of landed estates after 1918. But some local Valuation Offices are known to be dragging their feet in transferring out-of-date records to local record offices.

The 1930s, mired in agricultural depression, saw a further survey of the countryside in the semi-official *Land Utilisation Survey* conducted in the 1930s by Sir Dudley Stamp and his colleagues using local teachers and schoolchildren as volunteers; a national survey was published and most of the original parish maps are preserved in the Library of the London School of Economics as 'Archives LUS'. Fears of severe food-shortages during the Second World War led to a National Farm Survey in 1941–3 which produced several useful results: individual farm records are in TNA MAF 32 together with individual parish maps, but maps showing farm boundaries are in TNA MAF 73; the parish maps are listed in the TNA Index, but no individual farm records are indexed by place. Although the coverage and usefulness of the Ordnance Survey maps greatly increased after World War II with the introduction of the 2½ inches to the mile maps and swifter re-surveying of the older scales (1 inch, 6 inches, 25 inches to the mile), there were no further attempts at recording land-use. All the above records of land-use, though mostly introduced to assist the 'agricultural interest', are often also useful as indications of rural industrialisation and therefore the eventual expansion of the national urban area.

Local industry and trade

Towns, especially in the nineteenth and twentieth centuries, will generally have a much wider range of trades and industries than in earlier times, since the Industrial Revolution saw increasing subdivision of labour as the complexity of industrial processes and commercial specialisation increased. Unlike the 'agricultural interest' which had always been represented in both Houses of Parliament, the 'commercial interest' was much slower to become a pressure group, though bankers such as the Hoares, army contractors such as the Godolphins and financiers like Sir Stephen Fox were moving up the social ladder from the later seventeenth century onwards, and by the nineteenth century big brewers, the 'beerocracy', had risen into the peerage. Already in the seventeenth century the 'East India interest' was pushing its concerns on government, joined later by the 'West India' interest in Bristol and Liverpool, the two greatest slave-trading centres in England. By the nineteenth century, with the Industrial Revolution based on coal, iron and textiles, industry was a massive creator of wealth, initially for its entrepreneurs, but with wealth and benefits gradually filtering down to its suppliers, to the middle class and finally to its work-force. From the historian's viewpoint this was not well co-ordinated and in so far as national government was involved in recording or regulation was divided between several bodies. Initially at least, some of the older departments of national government were involved: the State Papers, Domestic Series, from 1714 to 1782,[30] were continued by the Home Office Papers. These included papers dealing with financial and commercial policy but also on law and order since governments tended to believe, and were encouraged by unscrupulous industrialists and merchants to believe, that the industrial working classes were in a state of riotous disorder.[31] The Privy Council was also involved, and its letters and registers (TNA PC 1–2) also included relevant material, including the records of the Central Board of Health, 1831–4.[32]

Responsibility for regulating an industry frequently shifted: the inspection of coal mines after 1850 was in the hands of the Home Office until 1920, when the responsibility passed to the Mines Department of the Board of Trade until 1942, then to the Ministry of Power and its succeeding ministries and departments. The interests of coal owners was represented in the Coal Mines Reorganization Committee, 1930–6, and the Coal Commission, 1938–47; for the 40 years of nationalisation the National Coal Board was responsible for overall management of the coal industry, but the records of individual coalmines, if they survive, are in local record offices. Other record series with mention of coalmining include State Papers, Domestic (TNA SP 10–29), Treasury Board Papers (TNA T1), and in various papers of the Ministries of Power and Labour.[33] Other minerals in private ownership escaped government notice until the *Mines Act* of 1842: from then on, regulation became more intense and widespread.[34]

More general records for business history include the records of the former railway companies nationalised in 1946 (TNA RAIL 1-1204) and company records among Chancery Masters Exhibits (TNA C 103–114; J90), though more will be found in local record offices.[35] Canal records also are often found among the records of the railway companies who took them over; from the 1850s the Board of Trade and later the Ministry of Transport regulated canals before they were also nationalised in 1947 and transferred to the Docks and Inland Waterways Executive.[36]

Labour history ought to be a fruitful counterpart to business history, but the relevant *TNA Research Guide*, Domestic Series, 125, is rather poor, omitting the references to 'three related guides'. In all these areas, whilst records held centrally may be useful, their utility is greatly improved if relevant local records, e.g. of local employers' associations and local trade union branches, are available. Finally, the records of the new local government bodies, the County Councils introduced in 1889 and the District and Parish Councils started in 1894, may be useful if they survive: county council records are usually well preserved, but considerable losses of some District Councils' records are known to have occurred after the local government reorganisation of 1973 and Parish Council records have often not survived too well, partly because they have rarely been consulted by local historians.

Contemporary commentary on local events is always worth tracking down. Before the nineteenth century widespread illiteracy among the 'lower orders' meant that most comment would come from members of the upper and middle classes who at best could only express the views of the majority of people at second hand:

nevertheless there was often considerable sympathy and understanding of popular conditions and feelings in, for example, the writings of Daniel Defoe, Arthur Young, the local correspondents to the Board of Agriculture and, above all, William Cobbett, as well as in many of the county newspapers appearing from the 1730s. Following the reduction of the stamp duty on newspapers from 4d to 1d in 1836 and its final abolition in 1855, both local and national newspapers proliferated, and working-class literacy also expanded with the rival activities of the National (Anglican) and British (Nonconformist) Societies in founding local primary schools culminating in free and compulsory public elementary schools in and after the 1880s.[37] Such comment will often be partisan but nevertheless illuminating, and local newspapers often preserve opinions as well as facts otherwise hard to find. Much more useful and generally reliable, is the evidence from local directories, which start for towns in the late seventeenth century and by the mid-nineteenth century cover the whole country, including rural villages, generally in one volume for each county. They are useful for identifying the local elites (gentlemen, farmers, professionals, major shopkeepers) from the beginning and by the end of the nineteenth century cover virtually all householders. The urban directories cover every street, often indicating junctions with other roads; as with newspapers, their advertisements are often a neglected source of information.[38] From the late 1930s to the early 1950s, a source underused by most local historians are the reports regularly submitted to the Mass Observation Survey organised by Tom Harrison: not every correspondent had the percipience or perseverance of Nella Last, but the Survey was the nearest thing to a record of genuine public opinion in its period.[39] Its records survive in the Library of the University of Sussex and are well worth checking for any local correspondents in your area of interest.

As we saw in the last chapter (see. p. 109), the 'agricultural revolution' of the eighteenth century and the troubled period of the Revolutionary and Napoleonic period generated a considerable amount of both factual statements and critical comment which provide much information on local developments in the countryside.

Cobbett's role as champion of the agricultural labourers passed later in the nineteenth century to Richard Jefferies whose *Hodge and Masters* was a classical critical outline of the basis of Victorian rural society.[40] Other notable commentators followed more in Arthur Young's footsteps, focussing on 'improving' landlords and farmers; these include Edward Caird, whose *English Agriculture in 1850–51* was a masterpiece,[41] while H. Rider Haggard's *Rural England …1901 and 1902* tended to favour the landlords and farmers at the expense of the laborours.[42] An under-exploited source which local historians could usefully explore is the local influence of agricultural societies, both national (e.g. the Royal Agricultural Society of England) and local (e.g. the Royal Bath and West Society).[43]

In addition to written and printed sources, there is also, of course, 'oral history', in my view better called 'spoken opinion'. Old age is no guarantee of either truthfulness or wisdom, nor can it guard against biased questioning designed to elicit a particular opinion, as it sometimes clearly is. On the other hand, spoken opinion inevitably has a short lifespan, and once a contributor is dead or has lost all contact with reality, he or she cannot be re-interrogated or confronted with opposite opinions. Unless the recollections can be checked at least in part, they should not be regarded as even probably true. Bias can only too easily creep in unrecognised. Fifty years ago, I was researching the village of Laughton (Sussex) and was told that the local parson was 'totally awful … a dreadful Hun': it subsequently transpired that the parson was a German Lutheran refugee from Hitler and that his main traducers were the parents of an airman maltreated after being shot down in Germany; the opinion was therefore understandably biased. Obviously relatively few old people are suffering from dementia: some may be perfectly sane and sensible even in their 90s, and may preserve valuable insights which may not be recorded anywhere else. Indeed, paradoxically, old people's memory of childhood and earlier adulthood may be good to excellent whilst they have forgotten what happened yesterday or recently. My own approach, for what it's worth, is to slip in some questions to which you already know the answers to test for veracity:

often too, 'wrong' answers may result from a well-meaning desire to please you by telling you what they think you want to know.[44] The best that one can realistically expect from oral history is a pointer towards a possible fact or opinion whose validity needs to be checked as far as possible by other evidence.

Notes

1   A. Smyth, *Autobiography in Early Modern England* (Cambridge, CUP, 2010) notes extensive autobiographical commentary by parish priests in parish registers. For the clergy themselves, see Bibliography, section 6 (v) 4.

2   For the *New Poor Law*, see A. Brundage, *The making of the New Poor Law … 1832–8* (Ann Arbor (USA), Michigan UP, 2nd edn, 1999) and D. Fraser (ed.), *The New Poor Law in the Nineteenth Century* (London, Macmillan, 1976).

3   V. D. Lipman, *Local Government Areas, 1834–1945* (Oxford, Blackwell, 1949).

4   W. R. Powell, *Local History from Blue Books: a select list of the sessional papers of the House of Commons* (London, Historical Association, 1962). For the records in the Parliamentary Archives (formerly the House of Lords Record Office) see M. F. Bond, *Guide to the Records of Parliament* (London, HMSO, 1971) and M. F. Bond, *Select List of Classes of Records in the House of Lords Record Office* (London, House of Lords Record Office, 1973).

5   See Bibliography, section 4 (ii). For the four main areas excluded, see J. Nicholson and R. Burn, *The History and Antiquities of the Counties of Westmorland and Cumberland* (London, Strachan and Cadell, 2 vols, 1777, repr. Wakefield, EP, 1976–77); J. Raine (ed.), *History of North Durham* (London, Bowyer, 2 vols, 1852); *Northumberland County History* (Newcastle upon Tyne, Reid, 15 vols, 1893–1940); L.W. Hepple, *History of Northumberland and Newcastle* (London, Phillimore, 1976). For the background to the boundary changes, see V. D. Lipman, *Local Government Areas, 1834–1945*.

6   For alien immigrants see *TNA Research Guide*, Domestic Ser. 50, and Bibliography, sections 6 (v) 3 and 7 (iv) 3.

7   See Bibliography, section 7 (iv) 1.

8   See Bibliography, sections 6 (v) 5 and 7 (v) 5, 10.

9   See Bibliography, section 7 (v) 5.

10 See Bibliography, section 7 (v) 6.

11 R. Swift and S. Gilley (eds), *The Irish in Britain, 1815–1939* (London, Pinter, 1989); R. Swift, *The Irish in Britain, 1815–1914* (London, Hist. Association, 1990).

12 See references in n. 6 above.

13 J. Tann, *The Development of the Factory* (London, Cornmarket P, 1970); P. Joyce, *Work, Society and Politics. The Culture of the Factory in late Victorian England* (Aldershot, Gregg Revivals, repr. 1991).

14 See Bibliography sections 6 (v) 6 and 7 (v) 7. I have excluded the extensive literature on country ('great') houses and urban terraces for the upper classes since 1750.

15 See Bibliography, section 7 (v) 8.

16 P. H. J. H. Gosden, *The Friendly Societies in England, 1815–75* (Aldershot, Gregg Revivals, repr. 1993); Gosden, *Self-Help: Voluntary Associations in the Nineteenth Century* (London, Batsford, 1973); S. Cordery, *British Friendly Societies, 1750–1914* (Basingstoke, Palgrave Macmillan, 2003).

17 H. A. Clemenson, *English Country Houses and Landed Estates* (London, Croom Helm, 1982); M. Beard, *English Landed Society in the Twentieth Century* (London, Routledge, 1989); H. J. Habakkuk, *Marriage, Debt and the Estates System: English Landownership, 1650–1950* (Oxford, OUP, 1994).

18 W. E. Tate, *The Parish Chest: a study of the records of parochial administration* (Cambridge, CUP, 3rd edn, 1969, repr. Chichester, Phillimore, 1983), pt. 2; see Bibliography sections 6 (v) 1 and 7 (v) 9.

19 L. Boynton, *The Elizabethan Militia, 1558–1638* (London, Routledge, 1967); J. R. Western, *The English Militia in the Eighteenth Century. The story of a Political Issue, 1660–1802* (London, Routledge, 1965).

20 See Bibliography section 7 (v) 9.

21 *TNA Research Guide*, Domestic Ser. 52; D. G. Browne, *The Rise of Scotland Yard: A History of the Metropolitan Police* (London, Harrap, 1956).

22 *TNA Research Guide*, Domestic Ser. 97; see also P. Appleby, *The History of the British Transport Police, 1825–1995* (Malvern, Images, 1996).

23 See *TNA Research Guides*, Domestic Ser. 18–19 (State Papers, Domestic, 1660–1782), 28–9 (Privy Council Registers and Papers), 39 (Treasury Board Letters and Papers), and *TNA Research Guide*, Legal Ser. 31 (Treasury Solicitor's Records).

24 R. Wells, *Insurrection. The British Experience, 1795–1803* (Gloucester, Sutton, 1984); S. Palmer, *Police and Protest in England and Ireland, 1780–1850* (Cambridge, CUP, 1988); D. C. Richter, *Riotous Victorians* (Athens (USA), Ohio UP, 1981).

25 C. Harding *et al.*, *Imprisonment in England and Wales. A Concise History* (London, Croom Helm, 1985); J. E. Thomas, *The English Prison Officer since 1850. A Study in Conflict* (London, Routledge, 1972); W. J. Forsythe, *The Reform of Prisoners, 1830–1900* (London, Croom Helm, 1987); W. J. Forsythe, *Penal Discipline. Reformatory Projects and the English Prison Commission, 1830–1900* (Exeter, Exeter UP, 1991).

26 R. Geary, *Policing Industrial Disputes, 1895–1985* (Cambridge, CUP, 1985); J. Morgan, *Conflict and Order. The Police and Labour Disputes in England and Wales, 1900–1939* (Oxford, OUP, 1987).

27 Readers are again reminded that, in addition to the major libraries and the local record offices, a large specialist collection of farm accounts will be found in the Museum of Rural Life, University of Reading.

28 For an example in print, see J. S. Moore (ed.), *The Goods and Chattels of Our Forefathers* (Chichester, Phillimore, 1976), 271–2.

29 Tithe Maps and Maps are also useful for earlier phases of local history, because nearly every numbered field is named: the field-names are a valuable source for local history, particularly before the Norman Conquest: see above, Chap. 3.

30 See *TNA Research Guides*, Domestic Ser. 19–20. The State Papers, Domestic, should be checked in the printed *Calendar* volumes by place, including alternative spellings and names of its region. For Henry VIII's reign, see J. S. Brewer *et al.* (eds), *Letters and Papers, Foreign and Domestic, of the Reign of Henry VIII* (London, HMSO, 24 vols in 36 pts, 1864–1932); for Edward VI–Anne, see *Calendar of State Papers, Domestic* (London, HMSO, 94 vols, 1856–2006). The State Papers, Domestic, for the reigns of Edward VI and Mary have been recently re-edited: C. S. Knighton (ed.), *Calendar of State Papers, Domestic, 1547–1558* (London, HMSO, 2 vols, 1992–8).

31 See *TNA Research Guide*, Domestic Ser. 47. Printed for 1760–75 in J. Redington and R. A. Roberts (eds), *Home Office Papers, George III* (London, HMSO, 4 vols, 1878–99).

32 See *TNA Research Guides*, Domestic Ser. 28–9. The Privy Council under the Tudor and Stuart kings exercised wide jurisdiction over internal affairs; its acts are printed in J. R. Dasent *et al.* (eds), *Acts of the Privy Council of England* [1542–1631] (London, HMSO, 46 vols, and 200 micro-opaques 1890–1964).

33 Details of all these record series are in *TNA Research Guide*, Domestic Ser. 35. Most coalmining records, however, will be in local record offices or still with the descendants or representatives of the pre-nationalisation owners.

34 See *TNA Research Guide*, Domestic Ser. 64. Most records will be found in local record offices or still in private hands.

35 See *TNA Research Guide*, Domestic Ser. 122. This contains a particularly good list of Further Reading.

36 See *TNA Research Guides*, Domestic Ser. 69, 83. Both these contain useful lists of further reading in a field where collectors' books greatly outnumber serious historical works.

37 See *TNA Research Guide*, Domestic Ser. 123, and Bibliography, section 7 (v) 10. Most major public libraries will have lists of their holdings of local newspapers; in default, the British Library's Newspaper collection at Colindale is the obvious resource.

38 For directories, see Bibliography, section 7 (v) 13.

39 P. Malcolmson and R. Malcolmson (eds), *Nella Last's War. The Second World War Diaries of Housewife, 49* (London, Profile, 2006); P. Malcolmson and R. Malcolmson (eds), *Nella Last's Peace. The postwar diaries of Housewife, 49* (London, Profile, 2008).

40 R. Jefferies, *Hodge and his Masters* (London, Smith Elder, 1850 repr. Stroud, Sutton, 1992).

41 E. Caird, *English agriculture in 1850–51* (London, Longman, 1852).

42 H. R. Haggard, *Rural England ... 1901 and 1902* (London, Longman, 1902, repr. 1906).

43 N. Goddard, *Harvst of Change: the Royal Agricultural Society of England* (London, Quiller P, 1988); K. Hudson, *The Bath and West* (Bath, Moonraker P., 1976).

44 See Bibliography Section 7(v) 14.

CHAPTER 6

Researching, Writing, Publishing

....

Beginning

As I said in the *Introduction*, if you are new to local history, it is a good idea to read this chapter first rather than plunging into research straightaway. Much depends on your circumstances. Are you a novice to any kind of history, or are you someone with some historical knowledge who wants to contribute to the history of a particular place? Perhaps most important of all, are you working alone or as part of a team from the Local History Society? If there is no local history society in your town, village or neighbourhood, why not try to get one up and running? Writing and research is much easier and more fulfilling, indeed more fun, if you are not alone but part of an enthusiastic team. However, I am certainly not suggesting that every member of a Local History Society should be a diligent researcher: some people for reasons which seem good to them may not wish, or be able, to give much time to the necessary research, and their views should be respected. Those who attend meetings, who serve coffee and biscuits at meetings, who support the society with an annual subscription, who help deliver mailshots of your society's newsletter, are in their own way doing much to keep the society in the forefront of local people, and to encourage new members to join. Any worthwhile Local History Society needs both sorts of members if it is to flourish and prosper in the future. I was once a member of a society where the organiser was so fanatically enthusiastic that he was putting-off existing members by appearing to belittle their activities, with the result that membership was falling. This view is far too limited: the non-researchers can and do commit much time and energy to helping the society just by being members; if *you* think you can do more, fine; you will be appreciated by many other members who cannot.

Where to start?

As you will see from the *Contents*, this book, like most history books, moves forward in time, so that starting at the beginning in the remote past on the borderline between archaeology and history may seem obvious and logical. In fact, it inevitably means that you plunge into the remote past with very few mental or physical guideposts to lighten your journey. I am quite certain myself that what the great medieval historian Maitland called 'that retrogressive method "from the known to the unknown" of which Mr Seebohm is the apostle' is preferable in researching: in other words, start with the recent past where much of its local landscape, personnel and society is familiar and not much different from your own world.[1] Once you have mastered that period (with, on the whole, excluding doctors, legible handwriting and many sources in print), then you can move on to earlier periods and increasingly unfamiliar handwriting often in contemporary English or Latin or perhaps even Old French.

Even then, help is at hand: there are several good books which will help you to understand old handwriting and medieval languages. It will take some time, but perseverance pays off: my supervisor when I was a postgraduate told me that learning old handwriting was like learning to ride a bike – you fell off several times and then found you were riding without realising it. It's true! The forms of official documents change quite rarely – official scribes tend to be conservative in terminology – the words mean the same, only the language has changed. Thus, many of the documents you will encounter follow the same format even if the language changes: if you compare a manorial court roll written in Latin in, say, 1730, with a roll written in English after 1733 (when the use of Latin in legal documents was no longer required), you will see how close the latter resembles the former though it is in English. Medieval and early modern scribes' Latin vocabulary was not necessarily better than ours: I remember coming across in one account roll of the manor of Keele (Staffs) '*unum ollam cenapiam (anglice a mustarde pott)*' ('in English a mustard pot') where the original scribe was obviously unsure that his Latin would be understood. Quite frequently you will find the modern schoolboy/ girl method of translation: when in doubt give the English word a Latin ending (*-us, -a, -um*). Medieval estate administrators or scribes were not trying to emulate Cicero's half-page sentences ending with a string of verbs: their vocabulary was restricted mainly to administrative and agricultural matters used in fairly rigid layouts. Medieval Latin is much simpler than classical Latin and English word order often occurs (subject, verb, object) rather than the classical order (subject, object, verb). There is a well-known and very useful *Revised Medieval Latin Handlist* and good guides to both medieval (and early modern) Latin and to medieval and early modern scripts. Chronology, the stating of dates, is also different from modern usage. You may have dates with months and calendar years, but beware: down to 1752 in Great Britain, years usually begin at Lady Day (25 March), and to avoid confusion a date in the period 1 January–24 March 1301 should be written as 1300/01 to avoid obscurity.[2] Nevertheless, just to confuse you, New Year's Day was always celebrated on 1 January! Medieval dates are frequently expressed in relation to a church festival, which can be deciphered in the *Handbook of Dates*, and years are often in relation to the year of the monarch's reign (regnal years), details of which are again in the above *Handbook*.

Usually though not invariably, both landscape and society get simpler as one goes back in time, but understanding both may well become more difficult in the past. Sometimes, however, the reverse is true: understanding the detailed layout of a common or open field-system with its multitude of small strips in furlongs and rotating common rights over one field in turn is much more difficult to understand than surveying a dozen or so farms inside their own boundaries and totally under the control of the owner or farmer (what contemporaries called 'in severalty'). On balance I am sure it is better to move back in time in stages, but there is one great difficulty to beware. It may be obvious to you, with the benefit of hindsight, that factor A led to effect B, but you must not assume that this outcome was inevitable or obvious to contemporaries at the time. For them, effect B was unknown, still in the future.

Researching

The first essential is to decide what you hope to achieve in the future. Are you simply trying to find about more about your area, either on your own or as part of a group? Are you or they hoping eventually to produce a book or series of pamphlets on the history of your area or perhaps an article or articles on certain aspects of your area for a local history journal either national (e.g. *The Local Historian* or *Local Population Studies*), regional (e.g. *Northern History; Midland History*, and *Southern History*) or local (your county historical society or a local newspaper or magazine)? Obviously with more research under your belt you may decide to abandon the book as too ambitious or impossible to publish, and prefer a series of articles on more defined topics. Alternatively, you may start with articles which are so well received that a book seems a viable proposition.

Defining your publishing objective will immediately raise questions about length: commercial publishers will very rarely accept a non-fiction book of more than 100,000 words, if that, and would prefer a length of 50–80,000 words including notes, and most historical journals, whether national, regional or local, will have a limit for articles of 8–10,000 words including footnotes. It is often wise to start with a topic that attracts you, and then go on to another topic afterwards. There is no golden rule about this: it is entirely up to you what approach you adopt.

Having decided your immediate objective, you obviously need to acquire sufficient background knowledge about the topic being studied: inevitably other people have tried to study that topic in their own area or for the whole country, so it is worthwhile finding out what approaches they used and what records they consulted. The Bibliography at the back of this book will be a start, followed by Richardson's *British Economic and Social History. A bibliographical Guide*.[3] Your county or town may have a local bibliography either in print or on file in a local reference library. Do not be surprised if you find that your area does not have the same records as another area; it may have other, perhaps better sources. So long as you feel you can make a useful contribution in your area, do not give up.

Equipment

Once you have decided what you want to do, you must consider what equipment is necessary. You can still produce good text with a typewriter, preferably an electric typewriter (less effort in typing!), and include where necessary any tables or calculations worked-out on an electronic calculator, *but* if you type-in a wrong figure this will mean re-doing the calculation and probably re-typing the table too. Assembling the evidence for a topic can be done with pencils and paper in a Record Office or Library (their custodians forbid pens and ballpoints or gellpens with good reason: spillages from these are extremely difficult to remove from parchment or paper). Still, permanent record-notes ought to be typed or word-processed; recopying pencil notes at home inevitably leads to possible error best avoided, and unnecessary expenditure of time. If you have a laptop or notebook computer (which nearly all libraries and record offices now permit you to bring-in and use),[4] you can immediately enter the data you have found, check your entry, verify that its reference is correct, and carry on. A laptop, like a PC at home, also enables much more efficient use of data to be achieved: tables can be created and calculated using a spreadsheet program, and illustrated with graphs, pie-charts, etc, by using a few keystrokes.

Equally, indexes and record-keeping of various kinds can still be carried out using index cards or printed forms, as devised by Wrigley and Schofield in the 1960s for both 'aggregative analysis' and 'family reconstitution', but nowadays, given the availability of both spreadsheet and database programs which can process data quickly and accurately to produce any graphs, figures or tables required instantly, it makes more sense to enter data straight into your laptop, keeping the original sources (if transcripts or photocopies). Using a laptop or notebook computer to record data in record offices and libraries is therefore efficient: it saves time in recopying data, and eliminates the possibility of copying errors when transferring data from notes at home. It is not a cardinal sin, if you have a bright idea away from your computer, to jot it down in a paper notebook or on the back of the proverbial envelope, but do transfer the thought onto your computer as soon as possible. Never, ever, think 'I know this so well, I need not write it down' – you will forget it, alas!

The other great advantage of word-processing is that you do not have to produce finished prose output immediately: get your main ideas down on a word-processed file, ensuring that you have not left out anything important. If you later realise you have omitted something of value, you can simply insert it at the appropriate place and the existing text will automatically re-align itself. When you come to write-up your chapter or article, these will be based on the structure of your notes; if you feel a different order would be better, you can easily shuffle your main points into a better order. When you are writing up your chapter or article paragraph, consider what you are trying to portray and explain; having written some beautiful prose, you may want to shuffle the order of sentences or whole paragraphs: this will be easy with a word-processing program. You may wish to add footnotes or endnotes (see pp. 147, 151), which again can easily be done on a word-processor: these do not have to be finished notes, just sufficient to remind you what you want to include.

Finally three tips:

1. Before you start, make sure all your computer programs are compatible with each other, so that you can add tables or graphs to your text easily. The simplest way to do this is to use a suite of 'Windows' programs such as Microsoft Office.
2. Whatever programs you are using, make frequent back-ups (every 5 minutes is a good interval) so that if there is a power-cut your PC will not lose an enormous amount of work; if you are using a laptop, its battery, if fully charged, will enable you to save and shut down

safely with no loss of data. And every week do a back-up to another PC, an external hard drive, a memory stick, or an internet storage facility, so that all is not lost if your PC is stolen, the hard-drive fails, or the PC simply won't start-up.

3. Also make sure your laptop's battery is fully charged when you start work even if there is access to a mains supply in the library or record office or at home. It will prevent the loss of whatever you have been doing since the last back-up if there is a mains power-cut and enable you to save all your work and shut down safely.

Computers and computer programs

If you already have a satisfactory laptop, you can skip the rest of this section except the last paragraph. If you are new to computers, do not rush to buy the first laptop you see advertised. Ask advice from friends who have computers, even your children who have grown up with computers since primary school. Resist, however, attempts by your children to push you towards a powerful, fast and therefore expensive PC which just happens to be ideal for their games: not only are they more expensive than what you require but you will find the machine is permanently occupied by James and friends fighting World War III. In any case, PCs, including their screens, are not easily transported. What you need is what is termed an office (small o) machine, which should not cost more than about £450 (as of June 2012); this will happily cope with any compatible suite of programs running word-processing, spreadsheet and database programs under Windows and accessing the internet. Do not waste money on a 'netbook', 'tablet' or 'ultrabook': these are all smaller than a laptop and therefore cheaper, but the first two do not have the capacity and computing power nor the screen-size of a laptop: a screen smaller than 15.6–17 inches diagonal screen-size may make images difficult to read especially if you are running two or more files or applications simultaneously. Your main requirements, apart from a fairly large screen-size, are: enough RAM to cope with several programs running at once (3–4 gigabytes (Gb), a largish hard-drive (300–500 Gb)) and lightness (not more than about 2–3 kg (4½–7 lb)): you will spend a fair amount of time carrying it around. Do not be tempted by the latest and fastest processor: most if not all processors are perfectly adequate now, though dual-core processors are now becoming standard and 4–6 core processors are starting to appear: most single-core processors (e.g. the Pentium) are sufficiently powerful and are considerably cheaper. The battery 'life' (the time to become discharged under working conditions) should be at least 6 hours. Ask for advice from any knowledgeable IT (Information Technology) person you know (your son or daughter's College or school will have at least one) and read magazines like *Computer Shopper*, *PC Pro* or *PC Advisor* which regularly review new PCs, including laptops, and software.

It is always worthwhile checking prices on the internet, which are normally lower than high street shops, but consider the cost of delivery and maintenance: some 'bargains' are not what they seem. Is the product new or outdated? Most magazine advertisements are covered by the magazine's guarantee if any advertiser goes out of business. You should expect a manufacturer's guarantee to last at least 1 year: some makers and retailers offer more. The new machine should come with Windows 7 or 8 installed: insist on getting the system disks (a CD or DVD nowadays) and preferably with a usable suite of Windows software including a word-processor, spreadsheet and database programs. If there is no such suite on offer, beware: buying MS Office separately will cost you at least £100 extra, probably more. If it is not included, a carrying case is essential for transporting the laptop and its battery-charger. You will also need a printer which can live at home: for black-and-white printing, either a laser or inkjet printer will do, but if you anticipate any colour-printing, go for an inkjet: colour laser-jets are more expensive than inkjets. Finally, some 'memory sticks (at least 1 Gb each) are essential for backing-up your machine: two or three should not cost you more than £50, but if your laptop is broken or stolen you will not have lost your previous work before the last back-up. In all you will not need to spend more than about £500. Do not buy both a PC and a laptop: you will get very little change out of £1000.

Finally you may think it worthwhile investing in an electronic ('digital') camera for copying documents, which most record offices and libraries now allow. I know it is an extra expense but look at the costs of 'in-house' photocopying which can easily rise into three figures. The camera should include a tripod to avoid shaky pictures. The camera should be at least 10 mega pixels, have a LCD screen to review your shots quickly, have internal memory, and come with a suitable carry case. Nowadays you can go into your local supermarket and buy a suitable camera for as little as £50, but check it meets the minimum specification above. As it will be used in the move, the risk of damage or loss is greater, but a replacement will not cost you the earth.

Getting started

Once you have acquired your equipment and familiarised yourself with the programs, it is well worth your while reading some useful books first. *Using Computers in History* is the title of two good books on the subject, one by Lewis and Lloyd-Jones published in 1996, the other by Cameron and Richardson published in 2005. Both are good, though Cameron and Richardson is slightly cheaper and to my mind better. Rather more advanced guides are Pat Hudson's *History by Numbers. An Introduction to Quantitative Approaches* (2000) and C. H. Feinstein and M. Thomas' *Making History Count. A Primer in Quantitative Methods for Historians* (2002). Both are good, but the amateur will probably find Hudson easier to read.

You can now decide on the initial topic to be studied. You first need to put down what exactly you hope to find out in note-form. In the case of population, for example, this might be:

(a) What sources are available?
(b) What dates do they cover?
(c) Where are they to be found?
(d) What should they contain?
(e) Have they been printed anywhere?
(f) What methods should be used.
(g) What results do you hope to obtain?

Your answer will look something like this:

(a1)   medieval 'extents' and surveys.
(a2)   Parish registers.
(a3)   *Census Reports.*

(b1)   1238; 1279; 1322; 1349; 1370; 1442; 1547.
(b2)   1559–1973 (gap: 1642–60).
(b3)   1801–2011.

(c1)   TNA, references; County Record Office, reference.
(c2)   County Record Office, references.
(c3)   County Library (Government Publications).

(d1)   Free and villain/customary tenants at all dates.
(d2)   CMB, 1559–1973 (gap, 1642–60); parents of children baptised given, 1559–1641, 1685–1705, 1783–1812; listing, 1775.
(d3)   National and local summaries.

(e1)   MSS at all dates.
(e2)   CMB, 1559–1812 (*Blankshire Parish Register Society* vol. 5).
(e3)   1801–20011: printed at all dates.

(f1)   extents and surveys: calculate total number of households at each date and estimated population (spreadsheet).
(f2)   CMB: transcribe (word processor);
(f3)   Tabulate local (parochial), regional and national totals from 1801; include non-local items to assess typicality of local results.

(g1)   Graph estimated manorial populations (all dates);
(g2)   CMB: tabulate monthly and annual totals; calculate natural change; graph trends in population (all spreadsheet); listing: copy with link to appropriate CMB entries (database).
(g3)   National Censuses: 1841–2011: decennial totals by parish; household details, 1801–2011; family details, 1841–2011 (spreadsheet).

You now have a clear idea of what needs to be done and the sort of answers you hope to find, to which you can always refer if you get dazed with facts and figures and lose sight of the intended objective (which is easily done!). You do not have to follow my outline: invent your own so long as it is clear and complete. This will also mean that if for some reason you cannot finish what you have started, someone else can take over without duplicating what you have already finished. In the ideal world, of course, you never get intoxicated with facts and figures, but in the real world you can get so immersed in the subject that you get over-tired (and will then be prone to make mistakes). Stop – make a brief note of where you have stopped so that you can carry on another day, and start doing something quite different: have a drink and relax with your wife, husband, girl-/boyfriend or whoever.

Eventually you will end up with a transcription of the register or other records which may also be useful for a different topic. This is not absolutely necessary, but it is the best way of getting to know your primary source and any of its peculiarities and also different handwriting scripts, a tabulation of christenings, marriages, burials and natural change with illustrative graphs, and the contents of the listing entered on a database and linked to the appropriate register entries. This analysis can be extended into the next two centuries using the census totals, possibly also the Registrar-General's births, marriages and deaths annual totals for urban and rural districts, and possibly backwards using any manorial statistics for the Middle Ages (see Appendix). For other sources dealing with other topics, the same approach is useful: the outline I have suggested as a model will help you to keep to the point.

When you have written-up your article or chapter on population, you will have a much clearer idea of where to go next. Are there any oddities in the population trend that need to be examined and explained? Was the sudden rise in population between 1680 and 1700 due to the arrival of Huguenot refugees from France? Does this explain why silk-weavers as well as the traditional woollen weavers appear in records after about 1695? In this instance, if the records are sufficient, you may perhaps want to start on industrial history next. But it really does not matter what you do next: whatever turns you on. There is no golden rule for the correct way to write-up a topic.

So long as your records are clear and entered under appropriate file names, it can be retrieved and if necessary finished by someone else. Incidentally, one of the virtues of the later versions of Microsoft Office is that you can use multiword file-names to indicate their contents instead of the earlier one word of eight characters. But do have a break, before starting to tackle another topic. It is probably a good idea to do a draft write-up while it's fresh in your mind: include any queries or unsolved problems which need more work: italics or, better, bold type or 'bullets' pinpoint the problems easily.

At some stage you may want to share your results with the rest of your society: preparing a text for a talk forces you to be intelligible, will benefit other members, may inspire some to join in research and, best of all, may inspire you to further efforts in communicating your findings. Speak clearly, simply and fairly slowly; do not gabble! Nobody expects you to be a professional orator or lecturer, but you can and should communicate clearly to your audience. Hopefully, this may also inspire you to communicate your ideas to a wider audience in print, which is also good publicity for your society. After perhaps several years of researching and writing-up your results and covering all the topics that you feel can be covered properly, it may be time to consider publication in book or perhaps serial form.

Writing

Professional authors tend to make writing into a great mystery that only they understand. This is, to be frank, arrogant snobbery. Your writing has only one purpose, to tell everyone who needs to know what you have found, where you have found it, any obvious problems in using the data, and what you think are the conclusions to be drawn from them. If you have done all this, you have done all that a professional could do: he or she may well have a wider knowledge of sources but if your reasoning is sound and your use of local sources is good, you cannot be faulted. Do not fall into the trap of believing that second or third thoughts must be better from the first; make up your mind as best you can and put it down. Do not delay in the spurious hope that new sources may appear in the future: they may indeed do so, but no fair-minded person will expect you to know what professionals will not know themselves before the new discovery. If you delay unduly by seeking perfection, you may well never finish anything. That would be a sad waste of energy and hard work. Rather than getting too involved with one topic, it sometimes helps to do something else quite different for a while and return to the original task with renewed energy and enthusiasm: sometimes you will find that your subconscious has been mulling over the problem and throwing out new ideas and new approaches.

Once you feel you are ready to put pen to paper, or paper into your printer, make a brief plan of what you hope to do (no more than two sides of A4 paper), whether in one chapter or the book as a whole. This is not a waste of time: it will stop you straying off the point because you can see at a glance where the particular point fits into the whole. It hopefully will allow you on re-reading to add any points which you have omitted, change their order, etc. All this is very difficult using pens or a typewriter but very easy using word-processing.

Next, length: if your total word-length for a book is over 100,000 words including notes and preliminary matter (title page, copyright notice and ISBN number, contents, preface), that project, unless you have your own press, is almost certainly too long. Have you or anyone else written any articles that deal in detail with particular topics? Could you shorten one or more chapters by referring to the detailed treatment in these articles and simply summarise the main points and methods used? Apart from anything else, it will shorten that chapter of your book and may well make it more readable. Is your text clear and comprehensible? Ask your wife/husband and friends for a frank opinion: even if this means a complete rewrite of a chapter, this is child's play with a word-processor. A tip here: keep the original on file and copy it for rewriting in a different file: if you mess up the rewriting, you have still the original version safe. Can some numerical or arithmetical points be better made with a table, graphs and pie-charts? Your spreadsheet will instantly oblige; again, keep the original file intact and copy it to another file with a different file-name. Hopefully, this will help to shorten your text to a more acceptable word-length. If you are writing an article on one aspect of your local history, 8–10,000 words, including notes, is the maximum number of words any history editor will accept (see p. 138 above): I would suggest you aim for 5–7000 words including notes: this will allow you some leeway if the editor decides some points need rewriting, you should be able to keep within the journal's word-limit.

Submitting a text

Then you are ready to submit to the editor of the publisher (book) or periodical (article). *Do not send* your text unsolicited to him or her: it will almost certainly go straight into his/her wastebin. Instead, write a preliminary letter saying you have written a book/article on such-and-such, length so many words, and ask if s/he is interested; if s/he is, ask for her/his book/article conventions. These differ widely in the publishing world: you may think it is pettifogging, but if you follow the guidelines, you will keep the editor happy (always desirable!). The guidelines will also tell you how to submit: either hard copy (word-processed/typed) or as an email attachment, or both, and, if hard copy, the number of copies required. Check if s/he wants left justification (straight line left border, with every line starting at the same place with the right edge having a jagged pattern) or body-text (both edges being justified and varying spaces between words to allow this as in a printed text). Does s/he want your notes as footnotes (at the bottom of each page) or endnotes (at the end of the text)? How do they want you to present quotations from original sources? Normally, short quotes (less than about 50 words) are put in the text inside inverted commas, which may be double or single according to editorial taste, while longer quotes are usually indented five spaces from the left-hand margin without inverted commas. Again, the publisher's guidelines will tell you. Do send a clean hardcopy: make sure your printer has enough ink (inkjet) or toner (laser printer) and produces a clear easily read text: look at the fonts available in your word-processor for possible options. Do not worry if you fail occasionally to keep to the guidelines: if all authors were perfect, sub-editors would be out of their jobs. If your work is accepted, the sub-editors will call your attention to what needs to be amended.

Editing for publication

Assuming that the publisher/editor has agreed to consider your book/ article, s/he will send it to one or more referees who are experts in your general area or field for their opinions, which could take up to 3 or 4 months: referees are normally hard-working academics who have little free time during university terms. The referee(s) will read your work, note any faults (factual errors) or where there is room for improvement (change of wording or additional text needed, or repetitions to be removed), and give an opinion on publication. If the publisher/editor agrees with the referee (or majority of referees), s/he will then write a letter of acceptance including any faults spotted or points raised by the referee(s), and if it is a book, a contract. Journals very rarely pay for publication unless it is a commissioned piece by a well-known authority; commercial publishers will not usually pay more than about 5–10% on sales (excluding review copies and the free copies (normally 3–6 for books, up to 12 for journals) which you will get as author). When you have re-submitted your work with any changes the editor wanted, your script will go to the editorial staff to check that you have kept to their conventions and mark it up for printing. At some point you will normally get 'first-copy proofs': read through them with great care; if you spot any errors, mark them accordingly to the printer's conventions; if you think a sentence could be improved in roughly the same number of words, insert and delete the previous wording. Check that a change from your wording is not a change by the editor: if it is, s/he will tell you in a covering letter. Do your reading and any changes thoroughly: changes at the next stage (page proofs) will either be forbidden or the high cost of the changes will be charged to you, *unless* it is a printer's mistake, which can happen; no charge will made to you in that case. At both proof stages, return the marked-up proofs to the editor as soon as possible: normally, editors supply two sets of each proofs, one for you, one for return. Mark-up both sets of proofs identically so that you can check that any agreed changes have been made in page proof.

Illustrations

Next, illustrations of all kinds. Unless you are a well-known author, colour photographs and illustrations are expensive and therefore very likely to be turned down by your publisher. Even half-tone black and white photographs may be too expensive; black-and-white line-drawings, maps and diagrams are much to be preferred because they are much less expensive to reproduce. These should be as clear and uncluttered as possible: if you are illustrating a series of changes over time, three or four successive simple drawings are preferable to one so cluttered with detail as to be incomprehensible. Your book-publisher is more likely to be liberal if you can produce a striking illustration in colour as the main background to the dust-wrapper or paper cover of your book: a good dust-wrapper or cover can sell more books.

Copyright

If any of your source-materials and illustrations, manuscript or printed, are in copyright you must ask the owner of the copyright for permission to reproduce unless you can show that you are engaged only in 'fair dealing': your publisher will advise on this. If necessary, write a polite letter to the copyright owner(s) saying you are not a professional historian and asking for permission to quote from their book/article/manuscript in your text, and if possible enclose a typescript of that part of your work in which the copyright text (whether in the text itself or the notes or a separate illustration) is highlighted. Remember that the copyrighted work is the owner's 'intellectual property': if it is stolen by unauthorised printing, you will be liable for damages and legal costs if the matter goes to court. Generally, and understandably, for articles either the first or last of your notes (see your Conventions yet again!) should include thanks to those who have helped you, and this is also the place to thank any owners of copyright for their agreement to publish: for a book this should go in the References unless you have already done this in the Preface.

Indexing

Whilst journals will normally be indexed by the editorial staff, indexes for books are usually the responsibility of the author. The easy but expensive solution here is to employ a professional indexer who will usually be a member of the Society of Indexers; your publisher will have a list of people s/he has used and found satisfactory. But you yourself will have to pay something between £500 and £1000, even more if yours is a complicated text. I recommend that you get on with indexing as soon as your final text has been accepted: you then have time to do the job thoroughly without too much pressure on time, whereas once final page-proofs are returned to the publisher time becomes increasingly short: the presses cannot roll until the corrected Index proofs have been returned.

But a reasonably powerful word-processor like MS Word will produce adequate indexes for words (places and people) to which you will probably want to add some phrases or subjects. Obviously, final indexing can only be done when page-proofs are available, but having a list of headings available saves time; if you can mark up the set of proofs you have retained with your word-processed pages, it will make the task much easier and quicker at a time when publishing editors are likely to be wanting proofs returned 'yesterday'. All named people and places should certainly be included, together with major subjects. Try to avoid entries like 'Farming: *see* Agriculture'; use one or the other as a main heading. Although you can mark-up texts word-processed by Microsoft Word or similar level programs for indexing, you will still have to adjust final page-numbers when printed page-proofs are available. If you have a copy of the final typescript showing indexed items to which you can add final page numbers and the beginning and end of each printed page from the page-proofs (I suggest in red or green, because easily seen), converting your draft indexes into page-proofs is easy. All being well, your publication will eventually end up on your desk: congratulations – next time will be a lot easier!

References and preliminary pages

Your text, if you are writing a book, also needs a table of contents, probably a Preface, including any necessary acknowledgments (be generous and truthful here), and References. These can be of two kinds: footnotes (at the bottom of each printed page) and endnotes (at the back of the book, divided into Chapters). Authors (and readers!) much prefer the former, and nearly all publishers prefer the latter (endnotes are easier to set and therefore cheaper). It does not matter which you use in your text (in fact composing with footnotes is preferable because you can see at a glance what the purpose of the footnote is; MS Word and other word-processing software of the same level enable you to change all footnotes to endnotes (or *vice versa*) with a few key strokes. In either case your reference should generally be restricted to a published or manuscript reference (accuracy here is essential!). If you need to argue the value of a particular reference, this should usually be done in the text immediately before the reference number. If on re-reading your text, you want to insert or delete a new reference in your text, most word-processing programs will insert a new reference and automatically renumber the remainder of your notes. If you are using abbreviations of journal titles, a table of abbreviations should be included in the preliminaries. You will discover from your reading the normal presentation of References: generally but not invariably book-titles are in the following form: J. Smith, *Title* (Publisher, Place and year of publication), chapter or page number(s); if more than one author, include both authors;

if it is a multi-authored work, use J. Smith *et al.* Editor(s) should usually be (ed.) or (eds) after their names. Articles and editions of sources should usually be in the following: J. Smith, 'Title' (*Journal Name*, series if more than one, volume number (Year of publication), chapter or page-number(s)). Again, read those Conventions!

Publishing

In order to get yourself published, you need only the appropriate and appealing product (whether book or article) of appropriate length (see p. 138 above). In both cases you need to identify potential journals and publishers. Apart from national journals such as *Local Population Studies*, the *Local Historian*, *History* and *History Today*, and regional journals such as *Northern History*, *Midland History* and *Southern History*, all of which have high standards, your most likely target will be local (county) history and archaeological journals. Go into a good public library in your area or the county library and look at recent issues which will give you an idea of how they operate. You do not need to be a professional academic to publish in these journals; people will judge you on what you write, not on who you are (in fact, referees do not generally know the names of authors of books or articles sent to them).

For publishers, names and addresses are in the latest issue of the *Writer's and Author's Handbook* which should be in all reference libraries. I would advise you first to try those publishers who specialise in local history: Amberley of Stroud; Bredon of Derby; History Press at Stroud, Oxbow/Windgather of Oxford and Phillimore's, formerly of Chichester, now of Andover. Do not send an unsolicited typescript book or article to an editor or publisher straightaway; as I have already said, this is a waste of your time and the editor's and it will almost certainly end in the wastebin. Instead, write offering a book/article on whatever your topic is, with a brief outline (1–2 pages of A4 at most) and request their list of Conventions (which you will find differ in some degree from everyone else's). Every publisher and editor will have a list of Conventions which they will supply on request if it is not on the back cover of a recent issue of the journal. If the topic sounds interesting the publisher of a book will probably want a draft chapter, a list of chapter headings and an estimate of the total number of words; a journal editor will ask for a draft of your article, which should meet their Conventions and adhere to the specified word-limit (if you can come in under the limit, they will bless you). Remember that your initial letter and the subsequent book or article are the only things the publisher or editor has on which to judge you. Do send them freshly printed pages, free of spelling mistakes or grammatical howlers, adhering to their Conventions and word-limit, securely packed and sent by Special Delivery to reduce the chance of loss in the post, or by email attachments if these are requested.

Apart from an acknowledgement of receipt, do not expect a swift reply: if the editor or publisher likes your offering, s/he will usually send it to one or two referees who are known experts for an opinion. If they think it is worthwhile, they will send the publisher/ editor a letter of approval, and probably suggesting some changes, and if the publisher/editor agrees, s/he will write to you accepting the book/article and requesting you to deal with the points raised by the referees. If you do this, they will accept the article, and issue a contract for a book. This will spell out the word-limits and any special requirements needed, and for a book will specify the final date for completing the typescript. Do not expect generous payment for a book, especially a first book: the current rate is about 5–10% of sales, and probably less for an unknown author. For an unknown, non-professional writer, your chances of getting a book published are, to be frank, slim; your chances of acceptance will be greatly increased if you have had some articles accepted by reputable journals or periodicals. If a publisher or editor suggests changes, it is because they think your work could meet their standards; otherwise they would not bother, but simply reject you. One final point: you must have in the preliminary pages a list of abbreviations you have used in the text or in the References. You do not need to include abbreviations in common use such as e.g. or i.e., but abbreviated article titles and acronyms such as BR for British Rail should be included. Again, ask your wife/husband and readers if there are any abbreviations they did not understand when reading your text and References; if there are, add them to your list which should of course be in strict alphabetical order; also include any abbreviated journal titles such as *EHR* (*English Historical Review*).

After publication

There is nothing more pleasurable to any writer, professional or amateur, than seeing their first work in print. It is of course a tangible sign of success for any author, but particularly for an amateur who has shown s/he can produce a scholarly and popular piece of work judged by exacting standards. A book may well be reviewed in the historical journals as well as the local newspapers, especially the latter for publicity increasing sales. You may be asked to appear on local radio and regional television, and perhaps invited to autograph copies in a local bookshop. I well remember doing this in Bristol for what I thought would have relatively little appeal, my translation of the Gloucestershire section of Domesday Book: I was pleasantly surprised to be signing copies of my translation for the whole of one day! Needless to say, do not turn down any offers of interviews in newspapers, or on local TV and radio: it's all publicity which is good for your self-esteem and will help sell more books! One of my colleagues once told me he nearly cut his throat and it was 'all my fault': when I asked how and why he replied 'I was shaving in my bathroom and I suddenly heard your voice booming out: it took me a minute to realise I was listening to Radio Bristol.' An article will of course have no money attached, but it will give you enormous confidence to go on to another article or to consider a book. Above all, it will generate good publicity for local history and your local historical society which will all help with future work. To conclude, I hope that you have enjoyed this book and that you will find it useful in your own local history activities.

Notes

1 F. W. Maitland, *Domesday Book and Beyond* (Cambridge, CUP, 1897), v.

2 See Bibliography, section 2 (a)–(c).

3 R. C. Richardson and W. H. Chaloner, *British Economic and Social History: a Bibliographical Guide* (Manchester, Manchester UP, 3rd edn, 1996).

4 A few conservative libraries and record offices still require you to produce an Electrical Safety Certificate before allowing your laptop on their premises; for this go to any registered electrician who will test your machine and issue a certificate: it should not cost more than about £40. It is wise to check by telephone or email whether such a certificate is required before your first visit to a new record office or library. In times of likely bomb-attacks by sundry terrorists, staff may well require you to demonstrate that your laptop is indeed a laptop and not a bomb: tedious, I know, but remember that most documents in record offices and books in libraries are rare if not unique; preserving them is the first duty of archivists and librarians.

Appendix

A Case Study: the population of Frampton Cotterell (Gloucs), 1086–1801

Table 1: Population of Frampton Cotterell, 1086–1547

Date	Unit of area	Free	Customary	Cottagers	Total
1086	Original manor	10	11	5	26
1301	Frampton Cotterell	N/A [?1]	16	2	19
1309	Frampton Cotterell	1	15	14	30
1321–2	Frampton Cotterell	[13]	16	12	41
1333	Gastelyns	12	0	0	12
1384	Frampton Cotterell	[?1]	10	0	11
1451, 1454	Frampton Cotterell	N/A	N/A	N/A	24
1522	Frampton Cotterell Parish	N/A	N/A	N/A	31 adult men men, 1 rector
1524–5	Frampton Cotterell Parish	N/A	N/A	N/A	30–1 heads of household, 1 rector.
1547	Frampton Cotterell	2	21	0	22
1556	Gastlyngs	0	7	0	7

Estimated number of tenants (both manors)	Total estimated population (both manors)	Note
26	140–145	1
33	155	2
45	215	
61	290	
36	170	
16–17	80	
36	170	
31	150	
30–31	150	
} 28	135–140	3

Sources

1086:   J. S. Moore (ed.), *Domesday Book, Gloucestershire* (Chichester, Phillimore, 1982), fol. 169a, *58*, 4; 'villagers' = 'Free'; 'smallholders' = 'Customary'; 'slaves' = 'Cottagers'.

1301:   TNA Exchequer, Ancient Extents, E 142/8;

1309:   E. A. Fry (ed.), 'Abstracts of Inquisitiones Post Mortem for Gloucestershire', *Index Library*, 40 (1910), 106–7;

1321:   TNA Exchequer, Ancient Extents, E 142/24, m.8v;

1333:   Fry (ed.), 'Abstracts of Inquisitiones Post Mortem for Gloucestershire', 246;

1384:   E. Stokes (ed.), 'Abstracts of Inquisitiones Post Mortem for Gloucestershire', *Index Library* 47 (1914), 144; at least one freeholder appears to have been omitted;

1451–54: TNA Chancery Inquisitions Post Mortem, Henry VI, C 139/143/30; C 139/154/28;

1522:   R. W. Hoyle (ed.), 'The Military Survey for Gloucestershire in 1522', *Gloucestershire Reccord Series*, vol. 6 (1993), 16;

1524–5: M. A. Faraday (ed.), 'The Bristol and Gloucestershire Lay Subsidy of 1523–1527', *Gloucestershire Record Series*, vol. 23 (2009), 160, 324;

1547:   TNA Rentals and Surveys (Portfolios), SC 12/2/46, penultimate section.

1556:   *Calendar of Patent Rolls, 1555–57* (London, HMSO, 1938, 410.

Notes

1. The building by 1086 of 'a church which was not there' in 1066 recorded in *DB* suggests that the lord (Walter the Crossbowman) was resident by 1086.

2. No freeholder is named in the extent, but since the recorded free rent is the same as that recorded as payable by Nicholas de Weston in 1321, one freeholder has been counted in 1301; since Frampton Cotterell manor after 1240 was two-thirds of the original manor, it has been assumed that it constituted two-thirds of the parish population throughout the period 1301–1547. The data for 1547–56, however, suggests that Gastlyngs manor then only accounted for one-fifth of the total manorial population.

3. One freeholder, Sir Nicholas Poyntz, lord of the neighbouring manor of Iron Acton, has been omitted from the calculated population-total for Frampton Cotterell manor. Of the 7 tenants of Gastlyngs manor in 1556, 2 are either present or represented by a widow in Frampton Cotterell manor in 1556, thus 5 households should be added to 'the 21 resident households in Frampton Cotterell manor to produce a parochial total of 26. Given that the estimated population in 1551 of 160 derived from the number of communicants, it is likely that there may have been at least 20 people, say 4–5 households, who were landless or sub-tenants, some of whom may well have been servants to Paul Bush as lord of Gastlyngs manor and possibly also to the rector.

Table 2: Population of Frampton Cotterell, 1551–1801
(data for Frampton parish)

DATE	TYPE OF DATA	DATA	MULTIPLIER	TOTAL POPULATION
1551	Communicants	120	1.33	160
1563	Households	31	4.75	150
1603	Communicants	100	1.54	155
1608	'Able men' aged 16–60	59	3.5	210
1650	Households	60–65	4.75	295
1662	Households	57	4.75	270
1672	Households	62	4.75	295
1676	Communicants	219	1.54	340
1711	Inhabitants	300	None	300
1735	Inhabitants	393	None	393
1779	Inhabitants	393	None	393
1801	Inhabitants	1208	None	1208

Sources:

1551: J. Gairdner (ed.), 'Bishop Hooper's Visitation of Gloucester', (*Eng. Hist. Rev.* XIX (1904), 118). For the multiplier, assuming a first age of communion at 10, see E. A. Wrigley and R. S. Schofield, *The Population History of England, 1541–1871* (London, Arnold, 1981, repr. Cambridge, CUP, 1989), 565–6.

1563: A. Dyer and D. M. Palliser (eds), *The Diocesan Population Returns for 1563 and 1603* (Oxford, OUP, 2005), 166. For the multiplier, see P. Laslett (ed.), *Household and Family in Past Time* (Cambridge, CUP, 1972), chaps 4–5.

1603: A. Dyer and D. M. Palliser (eds), *Diocesan Population Returns*, 335. As Dyer and Palliser remark, the communicants' number seems low (*ibid.*, 335, n.39). For the multiplier, assuming an age at first communion of 16, see E. A. Wrigley and J. Schofield (eds), *Population History of England*, 569.

1608: J. Smith, *Men and Armour for Gloucestershire in 1608* (London, Sotheran, 1902, repr. Gloucester, Sutton, 1980), 200. For the multiplier, see

J. S. Moore (ed.), *The Goods and Chattels of Our Forefathers* (Chichester, Phillimore, 1976), 11.

1650:   See Fig. 2. Multiplier as in 1563.

1662:   TNA Exchequer Lay Subsidies, E 179/116/554, m.116r. Multiplier as in 1563.

1672:   TNA Hearth Tax Assessment Rolls, E 179/247/13, m.3v (Lady Day, 1672); E 179/247/14, mm.48v, 49r (Michaelmas, 1672); E 179/329 (Exemption Certificates, 1670, 1674). Multiplier as in 1563.

1676:   A. O. Whiteman (ed.), *The Compton Census of 1676: a critical edition* (Oxford, OUP, 1986), 535. Multiplier as in 1603.

1711:   R. Atkyns, *The Ancient and present state of Glostershire by Sir Robert Atkyns* (London, Gosling, 1712), 444.

1735:   J. Fendley (ed.), 'Bishop Benson's Survey of the Diocese of Gloucester, 1735–50', *Gloucestershire Record Series*, 13 (2000), 28. This figure is repeated in 1779 by S. Rudder, *A New History of Gloucestershire* (Cirencester, Rudder, 1779, repr. Stroud, Nonsuch, 2006), 456, without updating.

1801:   *Parliamentary Papers, 1802, vol.* VII (London, Luke Hansard, 1802), 121.

Bibliography

The purpose of this is to help you if you want to know more about particular topics; it is not a compulsory reading list. The details of place of publication, publisher, and date of publication are given because these details will often be required by inter-library loan librarians if a local library does not have the books in stock. Bear in mind that all bibliographies are out of date once they leave the writer's desk; at the end there is advice on updating.

The bibliography is arranged in numbered sections: 1. Introduction to Local History; 2 (a) Handwriting; 2 (b) Language; 2 (c) Dating; 2 (d) Computing and History; 3. Anglo-Saxon England; 4. Domesday England; 5. Medieval England, 1135–c. 1525; 6. Early modern England, c. 1525–c. 1750; 7. Modern England, c. 1750–2011. Sections 4–7 are further subdivided into sub-sections (i)– (v): (i) sources, (ii) the countryside, (iii) towns, (iv) population and (v) economic and social developments. Paragraphs within these sub-sections are numbered in Arabic numerals (1, 2, ...). Note that the bibliography is not a comprehensive listing of all printed sources or of studies based on these sources: fuller coverage is attempted only for the main printed sources for population and manorial history, which are arranged in alphabetical order of pre-1973 counties.

1 Introductions to Local History

R. B. Pugh, *How to Write a Parish History* (London, Allen & Unwin, 6th edn, 1955) is the classic work; see also

W. G. Hoskins, *Local History in England* (London, Longman, 3rd edn, 1984), an excellent guide, though now in need of revision;

W. B. Stephens, *Sources for English Local History* (Chichester, Phillimore, 2nd edn, repr. 1994) is the best guide to most sources;

W. R. Powell, *Local History from Blue Books: a select list of the sessional papers of the House of Commons* (London, Hist. Association, 1962).

163

C. Kitching, *Archives: the Very Essence of our Heritage* (Chichester, Phillimore, 1996) is an excellent basic guide to various types of English archives, public and private; see also

P. Carter and K. Thompson, *Sources for Local Historians* (Chichester, Phillimore, 2003);

D. Iredale and J. Barrett, *Discovering Local History* (Princes Risborough, Shire, 2nd edn, 2003) will encourage beginners;

D. Hey (ed.), *Oxford Companion to Local and Family History* (Oxford, OUP, 1996) is excellent;

A. Hinde, *England's Population. A History Since the Domesday Survey* (London, Hodder Arnold, 2003) is a brave attempt at a history of England's population.

P. Slack and R. Wood (eds), *The Peopling of Britain: the shaping of a human landscape* (Oxford, OUP, 2002).

C. R. J. Currie and C. P. Lewis (eds), *A Guide to English County Histories* (Stroud, Sutton, 1997) is an excellent guide to published county histories.

2 *(a) Handwriting*

J. Barrett and D. Iredale, *Discovering Old Handwriting* (Princes Risborough, Shire, 1995) is a good introduction, as is

H. Marshall, *Palaeography for Family and Local Historians* (Chichester, Phillimore, 2004, repr. Andover, 2010).

For more detailed work, see

A. Rycraft, *English Medieval Handwriting* (York, Borthwick Institute, 2nd edn, 1973);

H. E. P. Grieve, *Examples of Handwriting, 1150–1750* (Colchester, Essex Record Office, 2nd edn, 1974);

G. E. Dawson, *Elizabethan Handwriting, 1500–1650* (Chichester, Phillimore, 3rd edn, 1981);

L. M. Munby, *Tudor and Stuart Handwriting* (Chichester, Phillimore, 1988);

J. F. Preston and L. Yeandle, *English Handwriting, 1400–1650* (Ashville (USA). Pegasus, 2nd edn, 1999);

P. M. Hoskin, *Reading the Past: sixteenth- and seventeenth-century handwriting* (York, Borthwick Institute, 2001).

2 (b) Language

For medieval Latin, consult

D. Gosden, *Starting to Read Medieval Latin Manuscript* (Felinfach, Llanerch, 1993).

K. C. Sidwell, *Reading Medieval Latin* (Cambridge, CUP, 1995).

A. C. Mantello and A. G. Rigg, *Medieval Latin: an introduction* (Washington DC (USA), Catholic University of America Press, 1996).

D. Stuart, *Latin for Local and Family Historians* (Chichester, Phillimore, 2006, repr. Andover, 2010).

The standard dictionary is

R. E. Latham, *Revised Medieval Latin Word-List from British and Irish Sources* (Oxford, OUP, 2nd edn, 1965, repr. 1973). Note that this dictionary only includes classical Latin words if used with a non-classical meaning; for classical Latin words, see

C. T. Lewis and C. Short, *A Latin Dictionary* (Oxford, OUP, 1879), available in most reference libraries.

The local historian is very unlikely to encounter Anglo-Saxon (Old English), Middle English or Medieval French; if you do, my suggestion would be a polite letter to the nearest University departments of English and French asking for their help.

2 (c) Dating

You will frequently encounter dates in medieval documents using Saints' days and other church festivals and dating by regnal years (the Xth year of a king or queen's reign), and less frequently the classical Roman calendar; for all these see

C. R. Cheney and M. Jones, *A Handbook of Dates for Students of British History* (Cambridge, CUP, 2nd edn, 2000).

2 (d) Computing and History

2 (d) 1. Quantification and History

P. Hudson, *History by Numbers. An Introduction to Quantitative Approaches* (London, Hodder, 2000).

C. H. Feinstein and M. Thomas, *Making History Count. A Primer in Quantitative Methods for Historians* (Cambridge, CUP, 2002). (Hudson is more reader-friendly than Feinstein and Thomas).

2 *(d) 2. Computers and History*

M. J. Lewis, *Using Computers in History. A Practical Guide* (London, Routledge, 1996), or

S. Cameron and S. Richardson, *Using Computers in History* (Basingstoke, Palgrave, 2005) (the best choice).

3. Anglo-Saxon England

3 *(i) Sources*

3 *(i) 1. Chronicles*

You are very unlikely to encounter documents in Old English: there is a standard translation of the Anglo-Saxon Chronicle.

D. Whitelock, D. C. Douglas and S. I. Tucker (eds), *The Anglo-Saxon Chronicle* (London, Eyre and Spottiswoode, 2nd edn, 1965), which is also included in D. Whitelock (ed.), *English Historical Documents, c. 500–1042* (London, Eyre Methuen, 2nd edn, 1979), 145–261 and D. C. Douglas (ed.), *English Historical Documents, 1042–1189* (London, Eyre Methuen, 2nd edn, 1981), 103–215.

These volumes also include translations from other chronicles which may be of local significance. There is an excellent study of medieval English Chronicles in A. Gransden, *Historical Writing in England* (London, Routledge, 2 vols, 1974–82).

3 *(i) 2. Charters*

Your place, if held by a bishop or monastery before 1066, may have a charter or will, and perhaps a set of bounds: these are listed with details of printed editions in

P. Sawyer (ed.), *Anglo-Saxon Charters* (London, Roy. Hist. Soc., 1968). A new edition is being prepared. Most of these charters are listed and discussed in the works of Professor Finberg and his collaborators:

H. P. R. Finberg, *Early Charters of Devon and Cornwall* (Leicester, Leicester UP, 1954);

C. R. Hart, *The Early Charters of Essex (Saxon period)* (Leicester, Leicester UP, 1957);

H. P. R. Finberg, *The Early Charters of the West Midlands* (Leicester, Leicester UP, 1964);

H. P. R. Finberg, *The Early Charters of Wessex* (Leicester, Leicester UP, 1964);

C. R. Hart, *The Early Charters of Eastern England* (Leicester, Leicester UP, 1966);

H. P. R. Finberg, *The Early Charters of the East Midlands* (Leicester, Leicester UP, 2nd edn, 1971);

C. R. Hart, *The Early Charters of Northern England and the North Midlands* (Leicester, Leicester UP, 1975);

M. Gelling, *The Early Charters of the Thames Valley* (Leicester, Leicester UP, 1979).

Sources useful both for this and other periods include aerial photography and place- and field-names.

3 *(i) 3. Aerial photography*

For aerial photography see

M. W. Beresford and J. K. St Joseph, *Medieval England. An Aerial Survey* (Cambridge, CUP, 1958), and

M. Aston, *Interpreting the Landscape from the Air* (Stroud, Tempus, 2002).

3 *(i) 4. Visual records*

For other photographs, prints and drawings, consult

M. W. Barley, *A Guide to British Topographical Collections* (London, Council for British Archaeology, 1974).

3 *(i) 5. Place- and field-names*

For place- and field-names, first consult

V. Watts (ed.), *The Cambridge Dictionary of English Place-Names* (Cambridge, CUP, 2004) or

A. D. Mills, *A Dictionary of English Place-Names* (Oxford, OUP, 1991): both deal with names down to parish level.

For more local names, especially field-names, you need to consult the *English Place-Names Society* series for the historical (pre-1973) county, if published. Note that the coverage of field-names is generally much better in E.P-N.S. volumes published after World War II than before, and the derivation and meaning of words even by earlier experts have often changed quite radically in the last half-century. If there are no E.P-N.S. volumes for your county, or if they were produced before 1945, again a polite letter to the nearest University Department of English should bring help. Many of the changes in meaning, and their significance for history, are explained in two books by M. Gelling:

Place-Names in the Landscape. The Geographical Roots of England's Place-names (London, Dent, repr. 1991) and

Signposts to the Past: place-names in the history of England (Andover, Phillimore, 2010)

Surnames are another useful source of historical information:

B. Cottle, *Penguin Dictionary of Surnames* (Harmondsworth, Penguin, 2nd edn, 1978);

P. Hanks and F. Hodges, *A Dictionary of Surnames* (Oxford, OUP, 1988);

R. McKinley, *A Dictionary of British Surnammes* (London, Longman, 1990);

P. H. Reaney, *A Dictionary of English Surnames* (London, Routledge, 3rd edn, 1991).

The existence of groups of hundreds or hundreds linked to a central manor is often historically significant: see

H. M. Cam, '*Manerium cum hundred*: the hundred and the hundredal manor' and 'Early groups of hundreds' in her *Liberties and communities in medieval England* (Cambridge, CUP, 1944), chaps.V–VI.

3 *(i) 6. Fieldwork and archaeology*

Fieldwork is an essential complement to documentary study, though sadly most archaeologists still ignore the evidence of place- and field-names. See

F. T. Wainwright, *Archaeology and Place-Names and History. An Essay on Problems of Co-ordination* (London, Routledge, 1965);

W. G. Hoskins, *Fieldwork in Local History* (London, Faber, rev. edn, 1982) is the classic guide.

M. Reed (ed.), *Discovering Past Landscapes* (London, Croom Helm, 1984) is an excellent introduction using the 'retrogressive method'.

M. Pasquinucci, F. Trement (eds), *Non-Destructive Techniques applied to Landscape Archaeology* (Oxford, Oxbow, 1999).

Amateurs are urged not to engage in excavation except in an emergency; their well-meaning efforts may well destroy evidence that professionals would have understood.

For various elements in the historic landscape, see

A. Fleming, R. Hingley (eds), *Prehistoric and Roman Landscapes* (Oxford, Windgather 2007);

R. Morris, *Churches in the Landscape* (London, Dent, 1989);

J. H. Bettey, *Estates in the English Landscape* (London, Batsford, 1993);

T. Rowley, *Villages in the Landscape* (London, Orion, rev. edn, 1994);

M. W. Beresford, *History on the Ground* (Stroud, Sutton, rev. edn, 1996);

C. Taylor, *Fields in the English Landscape* (Stroud, Sutton, rev. edn, 2000);

R. Muir, *The New Reading the Landscape: fieldwork in landscape history* (Exeter, Exeter UP, 2nd edn, 2000);

T. Rowley, *The English Landscape in the Twentieth Century* (London, Hambledon, 2006). There are numerous studies of regional landscapes.

For up-to-date assessments of the archaeological evidence for pre-Norman settlement, see

S. James, *Exploring the World of the Celts* (London, Thames & Hudson, 1993, repr. 2002);

D. O'hOgain, *The Celts: a history* (Woodbridge, Boydell, 2002);

B. Jones and D. Mattingly, *An Atlas of Roman Britain* (Oxford, Blackwell, 1990);

N. Christie and P. Stamper (eds), *Medieval Rural Settlement: Britain and Ireland, AD 800–1600* (Oxford, Windgather P, 2012) and

H. Hamerow, *Rural Settlements and Society in Anglo-Saxon England* (Oxford, OUP, 2012).

C. Dyer *et al.* (eds), *New Directions in Local Hitory since Hoskins* (Hatfield, Hertfordshire UP, 2011) is a useful review of recent developments in local history.

4. Domesday England

4 *(i) Sources*

The easiest to use and cheapest text of Domesday Book is that edited by John Morris and colleagues and printed in county volumes by Phillimore (Chichester, 1974–86). It has some oddities, notably the translation of *miles* as 'man-at-arms' rather than 'knight', but its reference-system does enable the user to refer to individual entries quickly and easily.

There is no up-to-date introduction to the Domesday survey or its 'satellites':

R. W. Finn, *Domesday Book: a guide* (London, Phillimore, 1973), now needs revision;

R. Smith (ed.), *Domesday: 900 years of England's Heritage* (London, Manorial Society of Great Britain, 1986), contains several useful articles, as does

P. Sawyer (ed.), *Domesday Book: a re-assessment* (London, Arnold, 1985),

J. Holt (ed.), *Domesday Studies* (Woodbridge, Boydell, 1986), and

R. W. H. Erskine and A. Williams, *The Story of Domesday Book* (Chichester, Phillimore, 2003).

E. M. Hallam, *Domesday Book through Nine Centuries* (London, Thames & Hudson, 1986), deals with the later history of Domesday Book.

4 *(ii) Countryside*

R. Lennard, *Rural England, 1086–1135* (Oxford, OUP, 1959) is a masterly survey of the Anglo-Norman countryside.

For the Domesday landscape, see

H. C. Darby (ed.), *The Domesday Geography of Eastern England* (Cambridge, CUP, 3rd edn, 1971);

H. C. Darby and I. B. Terrett (eds), *The Domesday Geography of Midland England* (Cambridge, CUP, 2nd edn, 1971);

H. C. Darby and E. M. J. Campbell (eds), *The Domesday Geography of south-east England* (Cambridge, CUP, 1962);

H. C. Darby and I. S. Maxwell (eds), *The Domesday Geography of Northern England* (Cambridge, CUP, 1962);

H. C. Darby and R. W. Finn (eds), *The Domesday Geography of South-west England* (Cambridge, CUP, 1967).

H. C. Darby, *Domesday England* (Cambridge, CUP, 1977).

For a minority often overlooked, see

J. S. Moore, 'Domesday Slavery' (*Anglo-Norman Studies* XI (1989), 191–220).

4 *(iii) Towns*

Towns were not included in the original instructions for DB and most were awkwardly inserted at the beginning of each county section. Notable absentees include London, Bristol and Winchester. The DB record needs to be augmented by the evidence for local mints and their coinage, any available archaeological evidence for towns and their trade, and any available 'satellites'.

A. Ballard, *The Domesday Boroughs* (Oxford, OUP, 1904);

A. Ballard (ed.), *British Borough Charters, 1042–1216* (Cambridge, CUP, 1913);

A. Ballard, *The English Borough in the Twelfth Century* (Cambridge, CUP, 1914);

J. Tait, *The Medieval English Borough* (Manchester, UP, 1936);

J. Munby, 'The Domesday Boroughs revisited', *Anglo-Norman Studies* 23 (2011), 127–49.

4 *(iv) Population*

J. S. Moore, '"*Quot homines?*" The population of Domesday England', *Anglo-Norman Studies* 19 (1997), 307–34.

4 *(v) Economic and social developments*

A. Williams, *The English and the Norman Conquest* (Woodbridge, Boydell, 1995) is by far the best study of the native English after the Norman Conquest.

For the evolution of the parochial system, beginning in the Anglo-Saxon period and continuing into the later medieval period, see

G. W. O. Addleshaw, *The Beginnings of the Parochial System* (London, St Anthony's P, 1952);

G. W. O. Addleshaw, *The Development of the Parochial System from Charlemagne (768–814) to Urban II (1088–1099)* (London, St Anthony's P, 1954);

G. W. O. Addleshaw, *Rectors, Vicars and Patrons in Twelfth- and Early Thirteenth-century Canon Law* (London, St Anthony's P, 1956);

J. W. Blair (ed.), *Minsters and Parish Churches: the local church in transition, 900–1200* (Oxford, Oxford University Committee for Archaeology, 1988);

J. W. Blair, *The Church in Anglo-Saxon Society* (Oxford, OUP, 2005), is now the standard work on the subject;

5 Medieval England, 1135–c. 1525

R. Horrox and W. M. Ormerod (eds), *A Social History of England, 1200–1500* (Cambridge, CUP, 2006) is a good modern introduction.

5 (i) 1. General Sources

The Chancery Enrolments of the Charter, Patent, Close, Liberate and Fine Rolls are of great value to both rural and urban history: they contain grants of privilege, lands, offices, and payments for these. In the thirteenth and fourteenth centuries government orders were also enrolled on the Close Rolls, though their main content became enrolled private deeds, which were the sole matter recorded after 1500.

The charter rolls are calendared in T. D. Hardy (ed.), *Rotuli Chartarum ... 1199–1216* (London, Rec. Comm., 1837) and *Calendar of Charter Rolls* (London, HMSO, 6 vols, 1903–27). For earlier royal charters see D. Bates (ed.), *Regesta Requm Anglo-Normannorum: the acta of William I (1066–1087)* (Oxford, OUP, 1998); H. W. C. Davis *et al.* (eds), *Regesta Regum Anglo-Normannorum, 1066–1154* (Oxford, OU, 3 vols, 1913, 1956, 1968). The *Acta* of Henry II and Richard I are being calendared at Cambridge University.

The Patent Rolls are calendared in T. D. Hardy (ed.), *Rotuli Litterarum Patentium ... 1201–1216* (London, Rec. Comm., 1835) and *Calendar of Patent Rolls* [1216–1509, 1547–97] (London, HMSO, 79 vols, 1903–82; *List and Index Society Series*, vols 272, 282, 286–7, 293–7, 300–2, 305, 309–11, 317, 322–3; 2010–12, in progress; for Henry VIII's reign (1509–47), the patent rolls are included in J. Brewer *et al.* (eds), *Letters and Papers ... Henry VIII* (London, HMSO, 16 vols in 37 pts, 1864–1932).

The Close Rolls are calendared in T. D. Hardy (ed.), *Rotuli Litterarium Clausarum* (London, Rec. Comm., 2 vols, 1833–44), and *Calendar of Close Rolls* [1227–1509] (London, HMSO, 62 vols, 1902–63).

The fine rolls of King John are printed in T. D. Hardy (ed.), *Rotuli de Oblatis et finibus* (London, Rec. Comm., 1835); the fine rolls of Henry III's reign, inadequately calendared in C. Roberts (ed.), *Excerpta e Rotulis Finium* (London, Rec. Comm., 2 vols, 1835–6), are being replaced by a new and full edition: D. Carpenter, P. Dryburgh and B. Hartland (eds), *Calendar of Fine Rolls, Henry III, 1216–72* (Woodbridge, Boydell, 3 vols, 2007–11, in progress). For the present, contact the Fine Rolls web-site www.finerollshenry3.org.uk/home.html. The Fine Rolls from 1272 to 1509 are calendared in *Calendar of the Fine Rolls* (London, HMSO, 22 vols, 1911–63).

The Liberate rolls are printed in T. D. Hardy (ed.), *Rotuli de Liberate ...* [1199–1216] (London, Rec. Comm., 1844), and *Calendar of Liberate Rolls* [1220–72] (London, HMSO, 6 vols, 1917–64).

The Exchequer enrolled accounts (Pipe Rolls) survive from 1130 and from 1155 in an almost continuous series: those for 1130, 1155–8 and 1189–90, J. Hunter (ed.), *Magnum rotulum scaccarii* were printed by the Rec. Comm. (3 vols, 1833, 1844); the rest are being printed by the *Pipe Roll Society*, currently to 1224.

5 *(i) 2. Records of Feudal Tenure*

The Book of Fees (London, HMSO, 3 vols. 1921–31) and

Feudal Aids (London, HMSO, 6 vols, 1899–1921) are the two most important 'feodaries' (returns of knight service) for the medieval period.

For the *cartae baronum* of '1166' [*recte* 1165], see

H. Hall (ed.), *The Red Book of the Exchequer* (London, Rolls Series 99, 3 pts, 1897), at pt. i, 186–445), a poor edition which is overdue for replacement.

5 *(i) 3. Judicial records*

These are also relevant to urban as well as rural history. TNA, Research Guides Legal Ser., 12–14, 20, 36 are useful for the *Curia Regis* and Assize Records; the Curia Regis rolls are now in print down to 1250:

F. Palgrave (ed.), *Rotuli Curiae Regis* (London, Rec. Comm., 2 vols, 1835);

F. W. Maitland (ed.), 'The rolls of the King's court in the reign of King Richard the First, AD 1194–5' (*Pipe Roll Society* 14, 1891);

R. A. Brown (ed.), '... the Curia Regis Rolls of Hilary 7 Richard I, 1196, and Easter, 9 Richard I, 1198' (*Pipe Roll Society* 69, 1956);

D. M. Stenton (ed.). 'Pleas before the King or his Justices, 1198–1212' (*Selden Soc.* 67–8 and 83–4, 1952–3 and 1967);

Curia Regis Rolls, (London, HMSO and Woodbridge, Boydell, 20 vols, 1923–2006, in progress).

W. C. Bolland (ed.), *Select Bills in Eyre, A.D. 1292–1333* (*Selden Soc.* 130, 1914).

5 *(i) 4. Local Assize/Eyre rolls in print*

G. H. Fowler (ed.), '... Roll of the justices in Eyre at Bedford, 1202' (*Bedfordshire Hist. Rec. Soc.* 1, 1913);

G. H. Fowler (ed.), 'Roll of the justices in eyre at Bedford, 1227' (*Bedfordshire Hist. Rec. Soc.* 3, 1916);

G. H. Fowler (ed.), '... Roll of the justices in eyre, 1240' (*Bedfordshire Hist. Rec. Soc.*10, 1925);

G. H. Fowler (ed.), 'Calendar of the roll of the justices in eyre, 1247' (*Bedfordshire Hist. Rec. Soc.* 21, 1939);

M. T. Clanchy (ed.), 'The Roll and Writ file of the Berkshire Eyre of 1248' (*Selden Soc.* 90, 1973);

J. G. Jenkins (ed.), 'Calendar of the Roll of the Justices on Eyre, 1227' (*Buckinghamshire Rec. Soc.* 6, 1945);

L. Boatwright (ed.), 'The Buckinghamshire Eyre of 1286' (*Buckinghamshire Rec. Soc.* 34, 2006);

A. M. Hopkinson (ed.), 'The Rolls of the 1281 Derbyshire Eyre' (*Derbyshire Rec. Soc.* 27, 2000);

H. R. T. Summerson (ed.), 'Crown Pleas of the Devon Eyre of 1238' (*Devon and Cornwall Rec. Soc.* 27, 1984);

K. E. Bayley (ed.), 'Two thirteenth-century Assize Rolls for the County of Durham' (*Surtees Soc.* 127, 1916);

F. W. Maitland (ed.), *Pleas of the Crown for the County of Gloucester ... 1221* (London, Macmillan, 1884);

D. M. Stenton (ed.), 'Rolls of the justices in eyre ... for Gloucestershire, Warwickshire and [Shropshire], 1221–1222' (*Selden Soc.*, 59, 1940);

[For Kent, see under Surrey]

J. Parker (ed.), 'A Calendar of the Lancashire assize rolls ... [1241–85]' (*Lancashire and Cheshire Rec. Soc.*, 47 and 49, 1904–5);

D. M. Stenton (ed.), 'The earliest Lincolnshire assize rolls, AD 1202–1209' (*Selden Soc.* 22, 1926);

D. M. Stenton (ed.), 'Rolls of the justices in eyre ... Lincolnshire, 1218–9, and Worcestershire, 1221' (*Selden Soc.*53, 1934);

W. S. Thomson (ed.), 'A Lincolnshire assize roll for 1298' (*Lincoln Rec. Soc.* 36, 1944);

H. M. Chew and M. Weinbaum (eds) 'The London eyre of 1244' (*London Rec. Soc.* 6, 1970);

M. Weinbaum (ed.), 'The London Eyre of 1276' (*London Rec. Soc.*12, 1976);

D. M. Sutherland (ed.), 'The Eyre of Northamptonshire, 3–4 Edward III, AD 1329–30' (*Selden Soc.* 97–8, 1981–3);

A. H. Thompson (ed.), 'Northumbrian Pleas from the De Banco Rolls, 1–19 (1–8 Ed.I)' (*Surtees Soc.* 158–9, 1943–4);

C. M. Fraser (ed.), 'The Northumberland Eyre Roll for 1293' (*Surtees Soc.* 211, 2007);

J. Cooper (ed.), 'The Oxfordshire eyre, 1241' (*Oxfordshire Rec. Ser.* 56, 1989);

A. Harding (ed.), 'The Roll of the Shropshire Eyre of 1256' (*Selden Soc.* 96, 1981);

C. E. H. Chadwyck-Healey (ed.), 'Somerset pleas, civil and criminal, from the rolls of the itinerant justices, close of 12th century – 41 Henry III' (*Somerset Rec. Soc.* 11, 1897);

L. Landon (ed.), 'Somersetshire pleas from the rolls of the itinerant justices, vol. II: 41 Henry III to the end of the reign' (*Somerset Rec. Soc.* 36, 1923);

L. Landon (ed.), 'Somersetshire pleas from the rolls of the itinerant justices, vol. III: For the years 1 to 7 of the reign of Edward I' (*Somerset Rec. Soc.* 41, 1926);

L. Landon (ed.), 'Somersetshire pleas from the rolls of the itinerant justices, vol. IV: For the 8th year of the reign of Edward I (*Somerset Rec. Soc.* 44, 1929);

E. J. Gallagher (ed.), 'The Civil Pleas of the Suffolk Eyre of 1240' (*Suffolk Rec. Soc.* 52, 2009);

C. A. F. Meekings and D. Crook (eds), 'The 1235 Surrey eyre' (*Surrey Rec. Soc.* 31–2 and 37, 1979, 1993, 2002);

A. H. Hershey (ed.), 'The 1258–9 Special Eyre of Surrey and Kent' (*Surrey Rec. Soc.* 38, 2004);

S. Stewart (ed.), 'The 1263 Surrey Eyre' (*Surrey Rec. Soc.* 40, 2006);

C. A. F. Meekings (ed.), 'Crown Pleas of the Wiltshire Eyre, 1249' (*Wiltshire Rec. Soc.* 16, 1963);

M. T. Clanchy (ed.), 'Civil Pleas of the Wiltshire Eyre, 1249' (*Wiltshire Rec. Soc.* 24, 1970);

[For Worcestershire, see under Lincolnshire]

J. Rohrkasten (ed.), 'The Worcestershire Eyre of 1275' (*Worcestershire Hist. Soc.* NS 22, 2008);

D. M. Stenton (ed.), 'Rolls of the justices in eyre ... for Yorkshire in 3 Hen. III, 1218–9' (*Selden Soc.* 56, 1937);

C. T. Clay (ed.), 'Three Yorkshire assize rolls for the reigns of King John and King Henry III' (*Yorkshire Arch. Soc., Rec. Ser.* 44, 1911);

W. T. Lancaster (ed.), '... Extracts from a Yorkshire assize roll, 3 Hen.III, 1219' (*Yorkshire Arch. Soc., Rec. Ser.* 61, 1920);

Several *ad hoc* enquiries were instituted by Edward I's government; for the hundred rolls, partly printed in

W. Illingworth and J. Caley (eds), *Rotuli Hundredorum* (London, Rec. Comm., 2 vols, 1812–18); see also

S. Raban, *A Second Domesday? The Hundred Rolls of 1279–80* (Oxford, OUP, 2004); additional rolls are printed in

E. Stone and P. Hyde (eds), 'Oxfordshire hundred rolls of 1279' (*Oxfordshire Rec. Ser.* 46. 1969), and

T. John (ed.), *The Warwickshire Hundred Rolls of 1279–80: Stoneleigh and Kineton hundreds* (Oxford, OUP, 2002).

For the *quo warranto* proceedings, printed in

W. Illingworth and J. Caley (eds), *Rotuli de Quo Warranto* (London, Rec. Comm., 1818); see also

D. W. Sutherland, *Quo Warranto Proceedings in the reign of Edward I, 1278–94* (Oxford, OUP, 1963).

5 (i) 5 Deeds and Charters

Many deeds still survive in local muniment rooms (see the National Register of Archives, part of TNA) or in local record offices (see details on the A2A online network) or in the National Archives and national and university libraries: see their websites. For a good guide, now in need of updating, see

N. W. Alcock, *Old Title Deeds* (Chichester, Phillimore, 1986).

Many medieval deeds were copied into registers known as cartularies; an excellent guide to surviving cartularies and printed editions of them is

G. R. C. Davis, *Medieval Cartularies of Great Britain and Ireland* (London, British Library, 2nd edn, 2010).

5 *(ii) Countryside*

5 *(ii) 1. The manor and its records*

N. J. Hone, *The Manor and Manorial Records* (London, Methuen, 1906), pt. II;

D. Stuart, *Manorial Records* (Chichester, Phillimore, 1992);

M. Ellis, *Using Manorial Records* (London, 2nd edn, PRO, 1997);

P. D. A. Harvey, *Manorial Records* (London, 2nd edn, British Rec. Association, 1999).

P. D. A. Harvey, (ed.), 'Manorial Records of Cuxham (Oxfordshire), *c.* 1200–1359' (*Oxfordshire Rec. Soc.* 50, 1975) is a model edition.

T. H. Aston, 'The origins of the manor' (*Trans. Roy. Hist. Soc.*, 5th ser. 8 (1958), 59–83), fruitfully explored a difficult topic.

L. R. Poos and L. Bonfield (eds), 'Select cases in Manorial Courts, 1250–1550' (*Selden Soc.* 114, 1998).

5 *(ii) 2. Surveys, custumals, extents, rentals (ecclesiastical)*

R. Scargill Bird (ed.), 'Custumals of Battle Abbey ... 1283–1312' (*Camden Soc.*, NS 41, 1887);

M. Chibnall (ed.), *Charters and Custumals of the Abbey of Holy Trinity Caen* (Oxford, OUP, 1982);

W. D. Peckham (ed.), 'Thirteen Custumals of the Sussex manors of the bishop of Chichester' (*Sussex Rec. Soc.* 31, 1925);

N. E. Stacy (ed.), *Surveys of the Estates of Glastonbury Abbey, c.1135–1201* (Oxford, OUP, 2001);

C. I. Elton *et al.* (eds), 'Rentalia et Custumaria Michaelis de Ambresbury (1235–52) et Rogeri de Ford (1252–61) Abbatum Monasterii Beatae Mariae Glastonie' (*Somerset Rec. Soc.* 5, 1891);

A. T. Bannister (ed.), 'A transcript of the Red Book [of the Bishop of Hereford]' (*Camden Soc.*, 3rd ser. 41, 1929);

J. Lister (ed.), 'Chapter House Records' (*Thoresby Soc.* 33, 1935);

R. Richmond (ed.), 'Three records of the alien priory of Gore and the manor of Leighton Buzzard' (*Bedfordshire Rec. Soc.* 8, 1924);

W. H. Hale (ed.), 'The domesday of St Pauls' (*Camden Soc.*, OS 69, 1858);

M. W. Barley (ed.), 'Documents relating to the manor and soke of Newark-on-Trent' (*Thoroton Soc.* 16, 1956);

T. Stapleton (ed.), 'Chronicon Petroburgense' (*Camden Soc.*, OS 47, 1849, 157–83). [Peterborough abbey estates in 1125].

P. A. Lyons (eds), 'Cartularium monasterii de Rameseia' (*Rolls Ser.* 79, 3 pts, 1884–4) (contains extents for *c.* 1135, *c.* 1160, *c.* 1195 and *c.* 1250);

N. E. Stacy (ed.), *Charters and Custumals of Shaftesbury Abbey, 1089–1216* (Oxford, OUP, 2006);

B. A. Lees (ed.), *Records of the Templars in the twelfth century: the inquest of 1185* (Oxford, OUP, 1935);

T. A. M. Bishop (ed.), 'Extents of the prebends of York' (*Yorkshire Arch. Soc., Rec. Ser.* 79, 1937);

B. C. Redwood and A. E. Wilson (eds), 'Custumals of the Sussex manors of the archbishop of Canterbury' (*Sussex Rec. Soc.* 59, 1958);

B. F. Harvey (ed.), 'Custumal (1391) ... of the manor of Islip' (*Oxfordshire Rec. Soc.* 40, 1959);

W. H. Hart and A. H. Denny (ed.), 'The Sibton Abbey estates' (*Suffolk Rec. Soc.* 2, 1960);

R. H. Hilton (ed.), 'The Stoneleigh leger book' (*Dugdale Soc.* 24, 1960);

P. M. Barnes and W. R. Powell (eds), 'Interdict Documents' (*Pipe Roll Soc.*, NS 34, 1960);

C. L. S. Williams (ed.), 'A rental of the manor of East Malling, 1410' (*Kent Records* 21 (1979), 22–79).

5 *(ii) 3. Surveys, custumals, extents, rentals (secular)*

F. B. Stitt (ed.), 'A Kempston estate in 1341' (*Bedfordshire Rec. Soc.*, vol. 32 (1952), pp. 71–91);

J. Harland (ed.), 'Mamecestre, pt. 2' (*Chetham Soc.*, OS 56, 1861);

S. J. Madge *et al.* (eds), 'Abstracts of *inquisitones post mortem* for Gloucestershire ... 1236–1413' (*Index Library* 30 (1903), 40 (1910), 47 (1914).) [includes extents]

J. Harland (ed.), 'Three Lancashire Documents of the fourteenth and fifteenth centuries' (*Chetham Soc.*, OS 74, 1868);

W. Farrer (ed.), 'Lancashire inquests, extents and feudal aids, 1205–1355' (*Lancashire and Cheshire Rec. Soc,*, vols. 48, 54, 70, 1903–15);

J. Harrop *et al.* (eds), 'Extent of the lordship of Longdendale, 1360' (*Lancashire and Cheshire Rec. Soc.* 140, 2005);

C. L. Kingsford (ed.), 'The Stonor Letters and Papers, 1290–1483, pt. ii' (*Camden Soc.*, 3rd ser30, 1919);

N. Neilson (ed.), *A Terrier of Fleet, Lincolnshire* (Oxford, OUP, 1920);

V. W. Walker (ed.), 'An extent of Upton, 1431', *Thoroton Soc.* 14 (1951), 27–38;

A. Chinnery (ed.), 'The Oakham Survey, 1305' (*Rutland Occasional Publications* 2, 1988);

A. E. Wilson (ed.), 'Custumals of the manors of Laughton, Willingdon and Goring' (*Sussex Rec. Soc.* 61, 1962);

M. Clough (ed.), 'Two estate surveys of the Fitzalan earls of Arundel' (*Sussex Rec. Soc.* 67, 1969);

E. A. Fry and E. Stokes (eds), 'Abstracts of Wiltshire *inquisitions post mortem* ... 1242–1377' (*Index Library*, 37 (1908), 47 (1914).). [includes extents]

F. S. Colman, 'A History of the parish of Barwick-on-Elmet' (*Thoresby Soc.* 17, 1908);

J. Lister (ed.), 'The extent or survey of the graveships of Raistrick, Hipperholme and Sowerby, 1309' (*Halifax Antiq. Soc., Rec. Ser.* 2, 1914).

Calendar of Inquisitions post mortem (London, HMSO, 1–20, 1904–95; 21–7, Woodbridge, Boydell, 2002–10, in progress), mentions the existence of extents but does not print them before 1422. This is also true of

J. Caley and J Bayley (eds), *Calendarium Inquisitionum Post Mortem* 4 (London, Rec. Comm., 1829) for the period 1448–85.

Calendar of Miscellaneous Inquisitions (London, HMSO, 7 vols, 1916–69), also contain extents, often described as 'inquisitions', but does not print them.

M. Hicks (ed.), *The Fifteenth-Century Inquisitions Post Mortem. A Companion* (Woodbridge, Boydell, 2012), despite its title is a valuable guide to inquisitions post mortem and their extents in the period 1235–1509.

For surveys in TNA, see

'List of Rentals and Surveys' (*PRO List and Index*, 25, 1908) and

'List of Rentals and Surveys. Addenda and Index' (*Supplementary List and Index*, 14, 1968).

Similar surveys also occur as 'extents and inquisitions' (TNA E 143) and 'extents for debts' (TNA C 131, C 239); C 131 is now fully listed in TNA: a model edition is

A. Conyers (ed.), 'Wiltshire Extents for Debts, Edward I – Elizabeth I' (*Wiltshire Rec. Soc.* 28, 1973).

Those for the London area are listed in

M. Carlin (ed.), *London and Southwark inventories, 1316–1650* (London, Centre for Metropolitan History, 1997).

5 *(ii) 4. Accounts*

J. Le Patourel (ed.), 'Documents relating to the manor and borough of Leeds, 1066–1400' (*Thoresby Soc.* 45, 1957);

M. W. Farr (ed.), 'Accounts and Surveys of the Wiltshire lands of Adam de Stratton' (*Wiltshire Rec. Soc.* 14, 1959);

H. E. Boulton (ed.), 'The Sherwood Forest Book' (*Thoroton Soc.* 23, 1965).

P. H. W. Booth (ed.), 'The financial administration of the lordship and county of Chester, 1272–1337' (*Chetham Soc.*, 3rd ser. 28, 1981).

Most manorial account-rolls in TNA are listed in 'List of Ministers' Accounts' (Public Record Office List and Index, 5 and 8, 1894, 1898) and 'List of Ministers' Accounts, Ed.VI–Charles I' (Public Record Office List and Index, Supplementary Series 2, 1967).

5 *(ii) 5. Court-rolls*

F. W. Maitland (ed.), 'Select pleas in manorial and other seigneurial courts' (*Selden Soc.* 2, 1889), is a classic introduction;

R. Lock (ed.), 'The Court Rolls of Walsham le Willows, 1303–1399' (*Suffolk Rec. Soc.*41, 45, 1998–2002), is a good modern edition.

Some but not all court-rolls in TNA are listed in *List and Index of Court Rolls* VI, (London, PRO, 1896). Most but not all manorial records not in TNA will be found in local record offices or libraries: consult the Manorial Documents Register at TNA; less than half the lists for English counties are computerized and available on-line; for the remainder a postal or email enquiry is necessary.

5 *(ii) 6. Feet of Fines (final concords)*

The first six entries cover several counties:

J. Hunter (ed.), *Fines sive pedes finium sive finales concordiae in curia domini regis ... AD 1195 – AD 1214* (London, Rec. Comm., 2 vols, 1835–44 [Bedfordshire–Dorset only];

'Feet of fines of the reign of the seventh and eighth years of the reign of Richard I, AD 1182 – to AD 1196' (*Pipe Roll Soc.* 17, 1894);

'Feet of fines of the seventh and eighth years of the reign of Richard I, AD 1196 to AD 1197' (*Pipe Roll Soc.* 20, 1896);

'Feet of fines of the seventh and eighth years of the reign of Richard I, AD 1196 to AD 1197' (*Pipe Roll Soc.* 20, 1896);

'Feet of fines for the ninth year of the reign of Richard I, AD 1197 to AD 1198' (*Pipe Roll Soc.* 23, 1898);

'Feet of fines of the tenth year of the reign of King Richard I' (*Pipe Roll Soc.* 24, 1900) [excluding those printed by Hunter];

G. H. Fowler (ed.), 'A calendar of the feet of fines for Bedfordshire' [1195–1307] (*Bedfordshire Rec. Soc.* 6 and 12, 1919, 1928);

L. J. A. Pike (ed.), 'Feet of Fines for Berkshire' (*Berkshire, Buckinghamshire, Oxfordshire Arch. Journal*, NS 14–17, 19–20, 1908–11, 1913–14);

M. W. Hughes (ed.), 'A calendar of the feet of fines for the county of Buckingham, 7 Richard I to 44 Henry III' (*Buckinghamshire Rec. Soc.*4, 1942);

A. Travers (ed.), 'A Calendar of the Feet of fines for Buckinghamshire, 1259–1307' (*Buckinghamshire Rec. Soc.* 25, 1989).

W. Rye (ed.), *Pedes Finium* relating to the county of Cambridge [1195–1485]' (*Cambridge Antiq. Soc.,* 1891);

J. H. Rowe (ed.), 'Cornwall Feet of Fines [1195–1461]' (*Devon and Cornwall Rec. Soc.* 8, 2 pts, 1914–50);

W. H. Hart and C. Kerry (eds), 'A Calendar of the Fines in the County of Derby, 1196–1324', *Derbyshire Arch. and Natural Hist. Soc. Journal* 7 (1885), 195–207; 8 (1886), 15–64; 9 (1887), 84–93; 10 (1888), 151–8; 11 (1889), 93–106; 12 (1890), 23–42; 13 (1891), 9–31; 14 (1892), 1–15; 15 (1893), 1–19; 17 (1895), 95–113; 18 (1896), 1–17);

C. Rawcliffe (ed.), 'Derbyshire Feet of Fines, 1323–1546' (*Derbyshire Rec. Soc.* 11, 1985};

O. J. Reichel *et al.* (eds), 'Devon Feet of Fines [1196–1309]' (*Devon and Cornwall Rec. Soc.*6, 2 pts, 1912–39;

E. A. Fry and G. S. Fry (eds), 'Full abstracts of Feet of Fines relating to the County of Dorset [1195–1485]' (*Dorset Records* 5 and 10, 1896, 1910);

R. E. G. Kirk *et al.* (eds), 'Feet of Fines for Essex [1182–1547]' (*Essex Arch. Soc.*, 4 vols, 1899–1964);

C. R. Elrington (ed.), 'Abstracts of Feet of Fines relating to Gloucestershire [1199–1359]' (*Gloucestershire Rec. Ser.* 16 and 20, 2003, 2006);

G. J. Turner (ed.), 'A Calendar of the Feet of Fines relating to the County of Huntingdon ... 1194–1603' (*Cambridge Antiq. Soc.*, Octavo ser. 37, 1913);

I. J. Churchill *et al.* (eds), 'Calendar of Kent feet of fines [1196–1272]' (*Kent Arch. Soc., Rec. Branch* 15, 1956);

M. Zell (ed.), 'Kent Feet of Fines: Henry VIII' (*Kent Arch. Soc., Kent Rec.* NS 1–5, 1995–6);

W. Farrer (ed.), 'Final Concords of the county of Lancaster [1196–1558]' (*Lancashire and Cheshire Rec. Soc.* 39, 46, 50, 60, 1899–1916);

W. O. Massingberd (ed.), *Lincolnshire Records, Abstracts of Final Concords* [1196–1242] (London: no publisher, 1896);

M. S. Walker (ed.), 'Feet of Fines for the county of Lincoln for the reign of King John, 1199–1216' (*Pipe Roll Soc.*, NS 29, 1954);

C. W. Foster (ed.), 'Final concords of the county of Lincoln ... AD 1242–1272' (*Lincoln Rec. Soc.* 17, 1920);

W. J. Hardy and W. Page (eds), *A Calendar of Feet of Fines for London and Middlesex* [1195–1570] (London, Hardy and Page, 2 vols, 1892–3);

B. Dodwell (ed.), 'Feet of Fines for the county of Norfolk ... 1198–1202' (*Pipe Roll Soc.*, NS 27, 1952);

B. Dodwell (ed.), 'Feet of Fines for the county of Norfolk ... 1201–1215; for the county of Suffolk, 1199–1214' (*Pipe Roll Soc.*, NS 32, 1958);

H. E. Salter (ed.), 'The feet of fines for Oxfordshire, 1195–1291' (*Oxfordshire Rec. Soc.* 12, 1930);

W. K. Boyd and W. G. D. Fletcher (eds), 'Shropshire Feet of Fines [1196–1248]' (*Shropshire Arch. and Natural Hist. Trans.,* 2nd ser. 10 (1898), 307–30; 3rd ser. 6 (1906), 167–78; 7 (1907), 379–89; 4th ser. 1 (1911), 385–401);

E. Green (ed.), '*Pedes finium*, commonly called Feet of Fines, for the county of Somerset [1196–1470]' (*Somerset Rec. Soc.* 6, 12, 17, 22, 1892–1906);

G. Wrottesley and W. Boyd (eds), 'Calendar of final concords [1196–1547' (*Staffordshire Rec. Soc.* 3–4, 11–18, 1882–97);

[For Suffolk, see Norfolk]

F. B. Lewis (ed.), '*Pedes Finium* or fines relating to Surrey [1195–1509]' (*Surrey Arch. Soc.,* 1894);

L. F. Salzmann (ed.), 'An abstract of feet of fines ... [1196–1509]' (*Sussex Rec. Soc.*, vols. 2, 7, 23, 1903–1916);

F. C. Wellstood *et al.* (eds), 'Warwickshire feet of fines [1195–1509]' (*Dugdale Soc.*, vols. 11, 15, 18, 1932–43);

E. A. Fry *et al.* (eds), 'Calendar of the Feet of Fines [1195–1509]' (*Wiltshire Arch. and Natural Hist. Soc.*, OS 7; NS 1, 29, 41, 1930–9, 1974, 1986);

W. Brown (ed.), 'Pedes finium Ebor. [1191–1214]' (*Yorkshire Arch. and*

Topographical Association Journal 11 (1891), 174–88; *Surtees Soc.* 94, 1897);

J. Parker *et al.* (eds), 'Feet of Fines for the county of York [1218–1377] (*Yorkshire Arch. Soc., Rec. Ser.* 62, 67, 82, 121, 127, 1921–65).

Feet of fines continue until 1833: there are indexes of persons and places available in TNA.

5 *(ii) 7. Lay Subsidy Rolls*

H. Jenkinson (ed.), '... An early Bedfordshire Taxation [1237]' (*Bedfordshire Hist. Rec. Soc.* 2, 1914);

A. T. Gaydon (ed.), 'The taxation of 1297' (*Bedfordshire Hist. Rec. Soc.* 39, 1959);

A. C. Chibnall (ed.), 'Early Taxation returns: taxation of personal property in 1332' (*Buckinghamshire Rec. Soc.* 14, 1966).

'Rolls of the Fifteenth of the ninth year of Henry III for Cambridgeshire, Lincolnshire and Wiltshire; and rolls of the fortieth of the seventeenth year of Henry III for Kent' (*Pipe Roll Soc.* 83, 1983);

A. M. Erskine (ed.), 'The Devonshire lay subsidy of 1332' (*Devon and Cornwall Rec. Soc.* 14, 1969);

A. R. Rumble (ed.), 'The Dorset lay subsidy roll of 1327' (*Dorset Rec. Soc.* 6, 1980);

A. D. Mills (ed.), 'The Dorset lay subsidy roll of 1332' (*Dorset Rec. Soc.* 4, 1971);

P. Franklin (ed.), *The Taxpayers of Medieval Gloucestershire ... the 1327 Lay Subsidy Roll* (Stroud, Sutton, 1993);

J. Brooker and S. Flood (eds), 'Lay Subsidy Rolls for Hertfordshire, 1307–8 and 1334' (*Hertfordshire Rec. Soc.* 14, 1999);

[For Kent, see under Cambridgeshire]

J. A. C. Vincent (ed.), 'Lancashire Lay Subsidies ... Henry III to Edward I' (*Lancashire and Cheshire Rec. Soc.* 27, 1903);

J. P. Rylands (ed.) 'The Exchequer lay subsidy roll ... in the county of Lancaster, AD 1332' (*Lancashire and Cheshire Rec. Soc.* 33, 1896);

[For Lincolnshire, see under Cambridgeshire]

C. M. Fraser (ed.), 'The Northumberland lay subsidy roll 1296' (*Soc. Antiq. Newcastle upon Tyne, Rec. Ser.* 1, 1968);

F. H. Dickinson (ed.), '... Exchequer Lay Subsidies 169/5 ... for Somerset of the first year of Edward the 3rd' (*Somerset Rec. Soc.* 2, 1889);

G. Wrottesley (ed.), '... The Exchequer subsidy roll of AD 1327 [Staffordshire]' (*William Salt Arch. Soc.* 9, pt.1, 1886);

G. Wrottesley (ed.), '... The subsidy roll of 6 Edward III, 1332–33' (*William Salt Arch. Soc.* 10, pt.1, 1889);

J. F. Willard and H.C. Johnson (eds), 'Surrey taxation returns. Fifteenths and Tenths. Being the 1332 assessments ...' (*Surrey Rec. Soc.* 11, 1922);

W. Hudson (ed.), 'The three earliest subsidies for the county of Sussex in the years 1296, 1327, 1332' (*Sussex Rec. Soc.* 10, 1910);

W. F. Carter *et al.* (eds), 'The lay subsidy for Warwickshire of 6 Ed. III, 1332' (*Dugdale Soc.* 6, 1928);

[Fog Wiltshire, see under Cambridgeshire]

J. W. Willis Bund *et al.* (eds), 'Lay Subsidy Roll for the County of Worcester, ca. 1280' (*Worcestershire Hist. Soc.* 1, 1893);

F. J. Eld (ed.), 'Lay subsidy roll for the county of Worcester, 1 Edward III [1327]' (*Worcestershire Hist. Soc.* 4, 1895);

J. Amphlett (ed.), 'Lay subsidy roll, AD 1332 ... for the county of Worcester' (*Worcestershire Hist. Soc.* 10, 1899);

W. Brown (ed.), 'Yorkshire Lay Subsidy ... 25 Ed.I, 1297' (*Yorkshire Arch. Soc., Rec. Ser.* 16, 1894);

W. Brown (ed.), 'Yorkshire Lay Subsidy ... 30 Edward I, 1301' (*Yorkshire Arch. Soc., Rec. Ser.* 21, 1897).

J. Parker (ed.), '... Lay Subsidy Rolls, 1 Ed.III [1327], N[orth] R[iding] and the City of York' (*Yorkshire Arch. Soc., Rec. Ser.* 74, 1929).

P. Franklin, 'Gloucestershire Medieval Taxpayers' (*LPS* 54 (1955), 16–27) investigates the relationship between taxpayers and heads of household.

Subsidy lists of taxpayers generally cease in 1332, after which the collectors account only for a fixed sum which is usually the sum-total of the individual assessments in 1332. Most subsidies are found in TNA E 179, a series recently re-catalogued which is available on the TNA web-site in the Discovery online catalogue.

5 *(ii)* 8. Castles

R. A. Brown, *English Castles* (London, Batsford, 3rd edn, 1976);

D. J. C. King, *Castellarium Anglicanum: an index and bibliography of the castles of England, Wales* (Millwood (USA), Kraus, 2 vols, 1982);

D. J. C. King, *The Castle in England and Wales: an interpretative history* (London, Croom Helm, 1988);

C. Coulson, *Castles in Medieval Society: fortifications in England, France and Ireland in the central Middle Ages* (Oxford, OUP, 2003);

R. Liddiard, *Castles in Context: power, symbolism and landscape, 1066–1500* (Macclesfield, Windgather P, 2005);

J. R. Kenyon, *Castles, town defences and artillery fortifications in the United Kingdom and Ireland: a bibliography, 1945–2006* (Donington, Tyas, 3rd edn, 2008).

For a stimulating view of the role of the upper classes, see

D. Crouch, *The Image of Aristocracy in Britain, 100–1300* (London, Routledge, 1992);

F. M. Stenton, *The First Century of English Feudalism, 1066-1166* (Oxford, OUP, 2nd edn, 1961);

C. Given-Wilson, *The English Nobility in the Later Middle Ages* (London, Routledge, 1987).

For identifying barons and baronies, see

I. Sanders, *English Baronies: their origin and descent, 1086–1327* (Oxford, OUP, 1960), and

V. Gibbs and G.E. Cokayne (eds), *The Complete Peerage of England, Scotland, Ireland, Great Britain and the United Kingdom* (London, St Catherine's P, rev. edn., 14 vols, 1910–59).

5 *(ii) 9. The peasantry*

R. Faith, *The English Peasantry and the Growth of Lordship* (Leicester, Leicester UP, 1997) is excellent;

G. C. Homans, *English Villagers in the Thirteenth Century* (Cambridge (USA), Harvard UP, 1942, repr. 1960) and

E. A. Kosminsky, *Studies in the Agrarian History of England in the Thirteenth Century* (Oxford, Blackwell, 1956) provide contrasting views.

J. Z. Titow, *English Rural Society, 1200–1350* (London, Allen & Unwin, 1969).

H. E. Hallam (ed.), *The Agrarian History of England and Wales, II. 1042–1350* (Cambridge, CUP, 1988) and

E. Miller (ed.) *The Agrarian History of England and Wales, III. 1350–1500* (Cambridge, CUP, 1991) are both standard authorities; both have regional sections.

For late medieval developments, see

M. W. Beresford, *The Lost Villages of England* (London, Lutterworth, 1954, repr. Gloucester, Sutton, 1983):

M. W. Beresford and J. G. Hurst, *Deserted Medieval Villages: Studies* (Gloucester, Sutton, 2nd edn, 1989);

C. Dyer and R. Jones (eds), *Deserted Villages Revisited* (Hertford, Hertfordshire UP, 2010).

Evidence of arable contraction is to be found in

G. Vanderzee (ed.), *Nonarum inquisitions in Curia Scaccarii* (London, Rec. Comm., 1807).

5 *(ii) 10. Agrarian discontent*
This became particularly evident after the Black Death lowered prices and raised wages, movements opposed in vain by the ruling classes which led to the Peasants' Revolt of 1381 and later rebellions.

C. Oman, *The Great Revolt of 1381* (London, Greenhill, 3rd edn, 1969);

R. H. Hilton, *Bond Men made Free: Medieval Peasant Movements and the English Rising of 1381* (London, Methuen, 1973, repr. 1977), and

R. H. Hilton, *The English Peasantry in the later Middle Ages* (Oxford, OUP, 1975) provide a Marxist analysis.

R. B. Dobson, *The Peasants' Revolt of 1381* (London, Macmillan, 2nd edn, 1983);

T. H. Aston and R.H. Hilton (eds), *The English Rising of 1381* (Cambridge, CUP, 1984);

I. M. W. Harvey, *Jack Cade's Rebellion of 1450* (Oxford, OUP, 1991).

Revolts and riots, especially food-riots, continued into the earlier nineteenth century. See sections 6 (v) 1 and 7 (v) 9.

5 *(ii) 11. The church*
Episcopal records relating to individual parishes will be found in D. M. Smith *et al.* (eds), *English Episcopal Acta* (Oxford, OUP, 40 vols, 1980–2012, in progress), and in the bishops' registers listed in

D. M. Smith (ed.), *Guide to the Bishops' Registers of England and Wales* (London, Roy. Hist. Soci., 1981) and D. M. Smith, 'Supplement to the Guide to Bishops' Registers' (*Canterbury and York Soc.*, extra vol., 2003).

For mortmain legislation, requiring most acquisitions of property by the church after 1279 to be recorded in royal sources, see

S. Raban, *Mortmain Legislation and the English Church, 1279–1500* (Cambridge, CUP, 1982).

R. N. Swanson, *Church and Society in Late Medieval Rnhlsnf* (Oxford, Blackwell, 1989), and

K. L.. French *et al.*, eds *The Parish in English Life, 1400–1600*, Manchester, MUP, 1997), are good general guides.

The main directory of English medieval parishes and ecclesiastical property is in

S. Ayscough and J. Caley (eds), *Taxatio Ecclesiastica Angliae et Walliae auctoritatae Papae Nicholai IV* (London, Rec. Comm., 1803); the earlier survey of 1254 is incomplete:

W. E. Lunt (ed.), *The Valuation of Norwich* (Oxford, OUP, 1926).

The best information on church property at the end of the Middle Ages is

J. Caley and J. Hunter (eds), *Valor Ecclesiasticus temp. Henrici VIII* (London, Rec. Comm., 7 vols, 1810–34); the 'List of Lands of Dissolved Religious Houses' (*Supplementary Lists and Indexes* 3, 7 pts, 1964) has now been superseded by

M. Jurkowski and N. Ramsay (eds), 'English Monastic Estates, 1066–1540: a list of manors, churches and chapels', *List and Index Society*, Supplementary Series 40–42, 2007; see also

TNA Research Guides, Domestic Ser. 12, 14.

5 *(ii) 12. Landscape*

G. White, *The Medieval English Landscape, 1000–1540* (London, Bloomsbury, 2012) is an up-to-date survey using both historical and archaeological sources. For some good examples see

M. Gardiner, S. Rippon (eds), *Medieval Landscapes* (Oxford, Windather, 2007).

R. Liddiard (ed.), *The Medieval Park: New Perspectives* (Oxford, Windgather, 2007) is a useful introduction to a frequent element in the medieval landscape

5 *(iii) Medieval Towns, 1135–c. 1525*

M. W. Beresford and H. P. R. Finberg, *English Medieval Boroughs: a handlist* (Newton Abbot, David & Charles, 1973), is the most up-to-date list of medieval towns;

C. Platt, *The English Medieval Town* (London, Secker & Warburg, 1976), and

S. Reynolds, *An Introduction to the History of English Medieval Towns* (Oxford, OUP, 1977) are both good introductions.

R. Holt and G. Rosser (eds), *The Medieval Town: a reader in English urban history, 1200–1540* (London, Longman, 2nd edn, 1995) and

P. Corfield and D. Keene (eds), *Work in Towns, 850–1950* (Leicester, Leicester UP, 1990) are stimulating.

D. Palliser (ed.), *The Cambridge Urban History of Britain, I: 600–1540* (Cambridge, CUP, 2000) is the standard survey.

For London, always the largest town in medieval and early modern England, see

C. N. L. Brooke, *London, 800–1216. The Shaping of a City* (London, Secker & Warburg, 1975);

G. A. Williams, *Medieval London from Commune to Capital* (London, Athlone P, 1963);

C. Barron, *London in the Later Middle Ages* (Oxford, OUP, 2004).

For linguistic evidence of industrial and commercial specialisation, see

G. Fransson, *Middle English Surnames of occupation, 1100–1350* (Lund (Sweden), Gleerup, 1935).

5 *(iv) Medieval population, 1135–c. 1525*

J. C. Russell, *British Medieval Population*, Albuquerque (USA), New Mexico UP, 1948. A pioneer work, badly arranged, which argued for a 'small' average medieval household of 3.5.

J. Krause, 'The medieval household: large or small?', *Econ. Hist. Rev.*, 2nd ser. 9 (1957), 420–32, demolished Russell's argument for a household 'multiplier' of 3.5.

H. E. Hallam, 'Some thirteenth-century censuses', *Econ. Hist. Rev.*, 2nd ser. 10 (1958), 340–61, provides empirical evidence for an average medieval household of 4.5–5 persons.

T. H. Hollingsworth, *Historical Demography* (London, Hodder & Stoughton, 1969) reworks Russell's data from *inquisitions post mortem*, and compares the results with Russell's calculations.

J. Z. Titow, 'Some evidence of the thirteenth-century population increase', *Econ. Hist. Rev*, 2nd ser. 14 (1961), 231–51). The pioneering study of hundred pennies as a demographic source.

M. Ecclestone, 'Mortality of Rural Landless men before the Black Death; the Glastonbury Head-Tax lists', *LPS* 63 (1999), 6–29;

T. John, 'Population change in medieval Warwickshire: Domesday Book to the hundred rolls of 1279–80', *LPS* 59 (1997), 41–53;

D. Postles, 'Demographic change in Kibworth Harcourt in the Later Middle Ages', *LPS* 48 (1992), 41–8;

The Black Death was traditionally seen as an outbreak of Bubonic plague (*Yersinia pestis*); this is now in doubt though there is no general agreement on the precise disease involved.

G. Twigg, *The Black Death: biological reappraisal* (London, Batsford, 1984);

G. Twigg, 'The Black Death: a problem of population-wide infection', *LPS*71 (2003), 40–52;

S. Scott and C. J. Duncan, *Biology of Plagues: evidence from historical populations* (Cambridge, CUP, 2001)

R. Poos, *A Rural Society after the Black Death: Essex, 1350–1525* (Cambridge, CUP, 1991), 89–110;

P. Schofield, 'Frankpledge Lists as indices of migration and mortality: some evidence from Essex lists', *LPS* 52 (1994), 32–9;

W. A. Champion, 'The Frankpledge population of Shrewsbury, 1500–1720', *LPS* 41 (1988), 51–60;

S. L. Thrupp, 'The problem of replacement-rates in late medieval England', *Econ. Hist. Rev.*, 2nd ser. 18 (1965), 101–19;

R. S. Gottfried, *Epidemic Disease in Fifteenth-Century England* (New Brunswick (USA), Rutgers UP, 1978);

W. G. Hoskins, 'The population of an English village, 1086–1801', in his *Provincial England* (London, Macmillan, 1963), 182–3, 186, is a model study, as is

Z. Razi, *Life, Marriage and Death in a Medieval Parish: Halesowen, 1270–1400* (Cambridge, CUP, 1980), using manorial court-rolls.

For the size of noble households, see

K. Mertes, *The English Noble Household, 1250–1600* (Oxford, Blackwell, 1988) and

C. M. Woolgar (ed.), *Household Accounts from Medieval England* (Oxford, OUP, 2 vols, 1992–3).

5 (v) Economic and social developments

J. C. Drummond and A. Wilbraham, *The Englishman's Food. A History of Five Centuries of English Diet* (London, Cape, 2nd edn, 1958);

C. A. Wilson, *Food and Drink in Britain from the Stone Age to Recent Times* (London, Constable, 1973);

C. C. Dyer, *Standards of Living in the Later Middle Ages. Social change in England, c. 1200–1520* (New Haven (USA), Yale UP, 1989);

C. C. Dyer, *Everyday Life in Medieval England* (London, Hambledon, 1994).

6. Early modern England, *c.* 1525–*c.* 1750

There are two good studies of England in this period:

C. G. A. Clay, *Economic Expansion and Social Change* (Cambridge, CUP, 2 vols, 1984);

J. A. Sharpe, *Early Modern England. A social history, 1550–1750* (London, Arnold, 2nd edn, 1997).

6 (i) Sources

For sources in the National Archives and elsewhere, see

TNA, Research Guides, Domestic Ser. 86;

Guide to the Contents of the Public Record Office (London, HMSO, 2 vols, 1963);

W. E. Tate, *A Domesday of English Enclosure Acts and Awards* (Reading, University Library, 1978).

6 (ii) Countryside

J. Thirsk (ed.), *The Agrarian History of England and Wales, IV. 1500–1640* (Cambridge, CUP, 1967);

J. Thirsk (ed.), *The Agrarian History of England and Wales, V. 1640–1750* (Cambridge, CUP, 2 vols, 1984–5); both have regional sections.

A. Kussmaul, *A General View of the Rural Economy of England, 1538–1840* (Cambridge, CUP, 1990), is excellent.

For the enclosure movement, see

M. W. Beresford, *The Lost Villages of England* (London, Lutterworth, 1954, repr. Gloucester, Sutton, 1983);
M. W. Beresford and J. G. Hurst, *Deserted Medieval Villages: Studies* (Woking, 1971, repr. Gloucester, 1989);
E. Kerridge, *The Agricultural Revolution* (London, Allen and Unwin, 1967);
J. A. Yelling, *Common Field and Enclosure in England, 1450–1850* (London, Macmillan, 1977);
J. R. Wordie, 'The chronology of English enclosure, 1500–1914', *Econ. Hist. Rev*, 2nd ser. 36 (1983), 483–505).

These showed that 'depopulation', leading to 'deserted' or 'shrunken' villages, was increasingly evident from the Black Death of 1348–9 onwards but had passed its peak by 1485; Wordie demonstrated that by 1500 more than half England's agricultural land was already 'enclosed', i.e. no longer in any type of 'common' or 'open' field-system nor in common pasture.

The older views exemplified by

R. H. Tawney, *The Agrarian Problem in the Sixteenth Century* (London, Longmams, 1912, repr. London, Harper and Row, 1967), and
W. E. Tate, *The English Village Community and the enclosure movements* (London, Gollancz, 1967)

can thus be largely discounted.

It is also clear that there were at least two major periods of agricultural improvement or 'revolution', one in the period *c.* 1480–*c.* 1640, the other from *c.* 1750–*c.* 1870; in addition to Kerridge above, see:

R. A. Butlin, *The Transformation of Rural England, c.1580–1800* (Oxford, OUP, 1982);
E. L. Jones (ed.), *Agriculture and Economic Growth, 1650–1815* (London, Methuen, 1967);
G. E. Mingay (ed.), *The Agricultural Revolution: changes in agriculture, 1650–1880* (London, Black, 1977);
J. D. Chambers and G. E. Mingay, *The Agricultural Revolution, 1750–1880* (London, Batsford, 1966).

6 *(iii)* *The early modern town, c. 1525–c. 1750*

P. Clark, *English Towns in Transition, 1500–1700* (Oxford, OUP, 1976);

P. Clark (ed.), *The Early Modern Town: a reader* (London, Longman, 1976);

P. Clark (ed.), *County Towns in Pre-Industrial England* (Leicester, Leicester UP, 1981);

J. Barry (ed.), *The Tudor and Stuart Town. A Reader in English Urban History, 1530–1688* (Harlow, Longman, 1990);

P. Borsay (ed.), *The Eighteenth-Century Town. A Reader in English Urban History, 1688–1820* (London, Longman, 1990);

P. Clark (ed.), *The Cambridge Urban History of Britain, 1540–1840* (Cambridge, CUP, 2000) is the standard work on the subject.

6 *(iv)* *Early modern population, c. 1525–c. 1750*

6 *(iv)* *1. Parish registers*

E. A. Wrigley (ed.), *Introduction to English Historical Demography* (London, Weidenfeld and Nicolson, 1966): an excellent work in its time, but now in need of updating, particularly in regard to computer studies;

E. A. Wrigley and R. S. Schofield, *The Population History of England, 1541–1871* (London, Arnold, 1981, repr. Cambridge, CUP, 1989), and

E. A. Wrigley *et al.*, *English Population History from Family Reconstitution, 1580–1837* (Cambridge, CUP, 1997), are the standard authorities.

J. Hatcher, 'Understanding the population history of England, 1450–1750', *Past and Present*, 180 (2003), 83–130 criticises much of Wrigley and Schofield's methodology and underlying assumptions. For earlier criticisms see

D. Reher and R. S. Schofield (eds), *Old and New Methods in Historical Demography* (Oxford, OUP, 1993), chaps 1–5. For earlier criticisms see

The best lists of parish registers are the *National Index of Parish Registers* series published by the Society of Genealogists and those in C. Humphery-Smith (ed.), *The Phillimore Atlas and Index of Parish Registers* (Andover, Phillimore, 3rd edn, 2010). Each Record Office will have an up-to-date list of registers in their custody and their covering dates.

J. C. Cox, *The Parish Registers of England* (London, Methuen, 1910), is still the best guide to parish registers.

The effects of delayed baptism on local population are considered in

B. M. Berry and R. S. Schofield, 'Age at baptism in pre-industrial England' (*Population Studies* 25 (1971), 453–63), and

E. A. Wrigley, 'Births and baptisms: the use of Anglican registers as a source of information about the numbers of births in England before the beginning of civil registration' (*Population Studies* 31 (1977), 281–312), deals with allowances to be made for delayed baptism, mostly after 1660. The causes and effects of suicide are considered in

P. E. H. Hair, 'A note on the incidence of Tudor suicide', *LPS* 5 (1970), 36–43;

P. E. H. Hair, 'Deaths from violence in Britain: a tentative secular survey', *Population Studies* 25 (1971), 5–24, esp. 15–16;

M. Zell, 'Suicide in pre-industrial England', *Social History* 11 (1986), 303–17;

S. J. Stevenson, 'The rise of suicide verdicts in south-east England, 1530–1590: the legal process', *Continuity and Change* 2 (1987), 38–76;

S. J. Stevenson, 'Social and economic contributions to the pattern of 'suicide' in south-east England, 1530–1590', *Continuity and Change*, 2 (1987), 232–30;

M. Macdonald and T. R. Murphy, *Sleepless souls. Suicide in early modern England* (Oxford, OUP, 1990).

(iv) 2. 'Listings'

J. S. W. Gibson and M. Medlycott, *Local Census Listings, 1522–1930: holdings in the British Isles* (Birmingham, Federation of Family History Societies, 1992) is the most usefully arranged list of these documents.

C. R. Chapman, *Pre-1841 Censuses and Population Listings* (Dursley, Lochin, 4th edn, 1994) is slightly more up-to-date.

R. Wall and M. Woollard, 'Pre-1841 population schedules and lists', *LPS* 74 (2009), 84–93).

D. A. Gatley *et al.* (eds), 'The Stoke-upon-Trent Parish Listing, 1701', *Collections for a History of Staffordshire*, 4th ser. 16 (1994), 171–225, and separately (Stafford, Staffordshire Record Office, 1995) is a good example.

6 *(iv) 3. Subsidy Rolls and Muster Rolls*

The following list is the result of my own researches into early modern population; it includes several privately printed volumes not to be found in most bibliographies. The classic study of English population in the 1522 'Military Survey is

J. Cornwall, 'English Population in the Early Sixteenth Century', *Econ. Hist. Rev.* 2nd ser 23 (1970), 32–44.

For editions of the 'military survey' and the resulting 1524-5 lay subsidy, see

A. C. Chibnall (ed.), 'The certificate of musters for Buckinghamshire in 1522' (*Buckinghamshire Rec. Soc.* 17, 1973);

A. C. Chibnall and A.V. Woodman (eds), 'Subsidy Roll for the county of Buckingham, anno 1524' (*Buckinghamshire Rec. Soc.* 8, 1950);

T. L. Stoate (ed.), *Cornwall Subsidies in the reign of Henry VIII, 1524 and 1543* (Almondsbury, Stoate, 1985);

T. L. Stoate (ed.), *Devon Subsidy Rolls, 1524–7* (Almondsbury, Stoate, 1979);

T. L. Stoate (ed.), *Devon Subsidy Rolls, 1543–5* (Almondsbury, Stoate, 1986);

T. L. Stoate (ed.), *Dorset Tudor Subsidies granted in 1523, 1543, 1593* (Almondsbury, Stoate, 1982);

R. W. Hoyle (ed.), 'The military survey of Gloucestershire, 1522' (*Gloucestershire Rec. Ser.* 6, 1993);

M. A. Faraday (ed.), 'The Bristol and Gloucestershire Lay Subsidy of 1523–1527' (*Gloucestershire Rec. Ser.* 23, 2009);

J. Smith (ed.), *Men and Armour for Gloucestershire in 1608* (London, Sotheran, 1902, repr. Gloucester, Sutton, 1980) is a rare full muster list annotated with occupational and physical details by the steward of the Berkeley estates;

M. A. Faraday (ed.), 'Herefordshire taxes in the Reign of Henry VIII' (*Woolhope Club*, 2005);

J. Tait (ed.), 'Taxation in Salford Hundred, 1524–1802' (*Chetham Soc.*, NS 83, 1924);

J. Cornwall (ed.), 'The County Community under Henry VIII: the military survey, 1522, and lay subsidy, 1524–5' (*Rutland Rec. Soc.* 1, 1980);

M. A. Faraday (ed.), 'The Lay Subsidy for Shropshire, 1524–7' (*Shropshire Rec. Ser.* 3, 1999);

J. Pound (ed.), 'The military survey of 1522 for Babergh Hundred' (*Suffolk Rec. Soc.* 28, 1956);

J. Cornwall (ed.), 'The lay subsidy rolls for the county of Sussex, 1524–5' (*Sussex Rec. Soc.* 56, 1957).

M. A. Faraday (ed.), 'Worcestershire taxes in the 1520s: the military survey and forced loans of 1522–3 and the Lay Subsidy of 1524–7' (*Worcestershire Hist. Soc.*, NS 19, 2003).

The 1524–5 subsidy for London has not survived, but a return for the 1530s has been found:

J. Oldland, 'The allocation of mercantile capital in early Tudor London', (*Econ. Hist. Rev.* 63 (2010), 1058–80).

6 (iv) 4. Chantry certificates

A. Kreider, *English Chantries: the road to dissolution* (Cambridge (USA), Harvard UP, 1979), lists all printed editions of chantry certificates to 1978, to which should now be added

C. J. Kitching (ed.), 'London and Middlesex Chantry certificate, 1548' (*London Rec. Soc.* 16, 1980).

6 (iv) 5. Protestation Returns

J. Gibson (ed.), 'Oxfordshire and North Berkshire Protestation Returns, 1641–2' (*Oxfordshire Rec. Soc.* 59, 1994);

J. Wilson (ed.), 'Buckinghamshire Contributions for Ireland, 1642 ...' (*Buckinghamshire Rec. Soc.* 21, 1983);

T. L. Stoate (ed.), *Cornwall Protestation Returns, 1641* (Bristol, Stoate, 1974);

W. F. Webster (ed.), *Protestation Returns, Notts/Derby, 1641–2* (Nottingham, Webster, 1980);

A. J. Howard and T. L. Stoate (eds), *Devon Protestation Returns, 1641* (Pinner, Howard, 2 vols, 1973);

E. A. Fry (ed.), 'Protestation Returns ... 1641–2' (*Dorset Records*, 1912);

H. M. Wood (ed.), 'Durham Protestation Returns' (*Surtees Soc.* 135, 1922) [these include Berwick-on-Tweed and Morpeth now in Northumberland];

Becontree Hundred, Essex: *East Anglian Miscellany*, 1922, 81;

Dunmow Hundred, Essex: *Essex Rev.*, 25 (1916), 55–64;

Chelmsford Hundred, Essex: *Manchester Genealogist*, Winter 1970, 11–12;

Chafford Hundred, Essex: *Essex Rev.* 26 (1917), 93;

Dengie Hundred, Essex: *Essex Rev.* 32 (1923), 34–5);

G. Proby (ed.), 'The Protestation Returns for Huntingdonshire' (*Trans. of the Cambridgeshire and Huntingdonshire Arch. Soc.* 5, 1937);

W. F. Webster (ed.), *Protestation Returns, Lincolnshire, 1641/2* (Nottingham, Technical Print Services, 1984);

A. J. C. Gumraens (ed.), 'London and Middlesex [Protestation Returns]' (supplement to *British Archivist* 1 (1913–20) and *Miscellanea Genealogica et Heraldica*, 1921); S. A. J. McVeigh (ed.), 'The protestation returns for West Drayton and Harmondsworth' (*West Drayton and District Historian* 31 (1969), 5–9; Hampton: B. Garside (ed.), *People and Homes in Hampton-on-Thames in the 16th and 17th centuries* (Hampton, Garside, 1956); R. Chapman (ed.), '"As far as I lawfully may": the Protestation Returns of 1641' (*West Middlesex Family History Soc. Journal* 12, pt. 1, 1964);

[For Nottinghamshire, see Derbyshire above]

[For Oxfordshire, see Berkshire above]

A. J. Howard and T. L. Stoate (eds), 'Somerset Protestation Returns and Lay Subsidy Rolls, 1641–2' (Bristol, Stoate, 1975);

H. Carter (ed.), 'The Surrey Protestation Returns, 1641–2', *Surrey Arch. Collections* 59 (1962), 35–68, 97–104;

R. G. Rice (ed.), 'West Sussex Protestation Returns, 1641–2' (*Sussex Rec. Soc.* 5, 1906); only four East Sussex parishes have returns, of which Brighton is printed in *Sussex Family Historian* 2 (1975), 84–9.

M. A. Faraday (ed.), 'Westmorland Protestation Returns, 1641–2' (*Cumberland and Westmorland Antiq. and Arch. Soc.*, Tract Ser. 17, 1971);

E. A. Fry (ed.), 'The Wiltshire Protestation Returns of 1641–2' (*Wiltshire Notes and Queries* 7, 1913);

C. T. Clay (ed.), '[Protestation Returns for] Morley Wapentake' (*Halifax Antiq. Soc. Trans.* 16 (1919), 105–15).

For an evaluation of these Returns as demographic sources, see A. Whiteman, V. Russell, 'The Protestation Returns of 1641–42', LPS 55 (1995), 14–27; 56 (1996), 17–29.

J. Gibson and A. Dell, *The Protestation Returns, 1641–42 and other Contemporary Listings* (Birmingham, Federation of Family History

Socs, 1995) is an up-to-date list of the contemporary subsidies and other listings as well as the returns themselves.

For the little known Commonwealth return of 1650, see

J. Houston, *Catalogue of Ecclesiastical Records of the Commonwealth, 1643–1660, in the Lambeth Palace Library* (Farnborough, Gregg, 1968), 81–181.

6 *(iv) 6. Hearth Tax rolls*

Volumes have so far been published in the British Rec. Soc. series for Cambridgeshire, 1664, Durham 1666, Kent, 1664, Warwickshire, 1670, with Coventry, 1666, Westmorland, 1670–5, and Yorkshire, West Riding, 1672. Volumes in preparation in this series include Essex, 1672–3, and London, 1666.

Previously, local record societies had printed editions for many counties:

L. M. Marshall (ed.), 'The rural population of Bedfordshire' (*Bedfordshire Rec. Soc.* 16, 1934);

F. C. Beazley (ed.), 'Miscellanies relating to Lancashire and Cheshire' (*Lancashire Rec. Soc.* 52, 1906) [Chester, 1664–5];

D. G. Edwards (ed.), 'Derbyshire hearth tax assessments, 1662–70' (*Derbyshire Rec. Soc.* 7, 1982).

W. G. Hoskins (ed.), 'Exeter in the seventeenth century' (*Devon and Cornwall Rec. Soc.*, NS 2, 1957);

E. Hughes and P. White (eds), 'The Hampshire hearth tax, 1665, with the Southampton assessments for 1662 and 1670' (*Hampshire Record Ser.* 11, 1991);

P. P. D. Russell (ed.), 'Hearth Tax returns for the Isle of Wight, 1664–74' (*Isle of Wight Rec. Soc.* 1, 1981);

J. Tait (ed.), 'Taxation in Salford hundred, 1524–1802' (*Chetham Soc.*, NS 83, 1924) [1666];

W. F. Webster (ed.), 'Nottinghamshire Hearth Tax, 1664, 1674' (*Thoroton Soc., Rec. Ser.* 37, 1988);

J. E. T. Rogers (ed.), 'Oxford City Documents ... 1268–1665' (*Oxford Hist. Soc.* 18, 1891) [1665], re-edited in H. E. Salter (ed.), 'Surveys and tokens' (*Oxford Hist. Soc.* 75, 1923) [1665];

M. W. B. Weinstock (ed.), 'Hearth Returns, Oxfordshire, 1665' (*Oxfordshire Rec. Soc.* 21, 1940);

J. Bourne and A. Goode (eds), 'The Rutland Hearth Tax, 1665' (*Rutland Occasional Papers* 3, 1991);

Anon (ed.), 'The Staffordshire Hearth Tax [1666]' (*Staffordshire Rec. Soc.* 45 (1921), 42–173; 47, (1923), 47–256; 49 (1925), 155–242; 51 (1927), 1–79);

Anon (ed.), 'Hearth Tax for Lichfield [1662]' (*Staffordshire Rec. Soc.* 60, 1936);

C. A. F. Meekings (ed.), 'Surrey Hearth Tax, 1664' (*Surrey Rec. Soc.* 17, 1940): note that this is 'an alphabetical list of entries' which needs to be re-arranged under places for demographic purposes;

T. Arkell (ed.), 'Warwickshire Hearth Tax returns, Michaelmas 1670, with Coventry, Lady Day 1666' (*Dugdale Soc. Publications* 43, 2010).

T. Arkell, 'Multiplying Factors for estimating population totals from the Hearth Tax', *LPS* 28 (1982), 51–7 is valuable.

See *TNA, Research Guide*, Domestic Ser. 10.

6 *(iv)* 7. *Visitation Returns*

J. Gairdner (ed.), 'Bishop Hooper's Visitation of Gloucester Diocese', *English Hist. Rev.* 19 (1904), 98–121; see analysis in

J. S. Moore, 'Episcopal Visitations and the demography of Tudor Gloucestershire', *Southern Hist.* 22 (2000), 72–130.

L. E. Whatmore (ed.), 'Archdeacon Harpsfield's Visitation, 1557' (*Catholic Rec. Soc.* 45–6, 1950-1); see analysis in

J. S. Moore, 'Canterbury Visitations and the Demography of Mid-Tudor Kent', *Southern Hist.* 15 (1993), 36–85.

A. D. Dyer and D. M. Palliser (eds), *The Diocesan Population Returns for 1563 and 1603* (Oxford, OUP, 2005);

A. O. Whiteman (ed.), *The Compton Census of 1676: a critical edition* (Oxford, OUP, 1986);

P. Bell (ed.), 'Episcopal Visitations in Bedfordshire, 1706–20' (*Bedfordshire Hist. Rec. Soc.* 81, 2002); [1706, 1709, 1712, 1717, 1720]

J. Broad (ed.), 'Buckinghamshire Dissent and Parish Life, 1669–1712' (*Buckinghamshire Rec. Soc.* 28, 1993); [1706, 1709, 1712]

F. R. Raines (ed.), 'Notitia Cestrensis, or historical notices of the diocese of Chester' (*Chetham Soc.*, OS 8, 19, 21–22, 1845–50). [1714–25: only a few scattered entries for Cheshire and Lancashire];

L. A. S. Butler (ed.), 'The Cumbria parishes, 1714–25, from Bishop Gastrell's Notitia with additions by Bishop Porteous, 1778–1779' (*Cumberland*

and Westmorland Antiq. and Arch. Soc., Rec. Ser NS 12, 1998). [1714–25: only a few scattered entries; 1778–9: houses or families recorded for most entries]

J. V. Beckett *et al.* (eds), 'Visitation Returns from the archdeaconry of Derby, 1718–1824' (*Derbyshire Rec. Soc.* 29, 2003). [1718, 1751, 1772]

J. Fendley (ed.), 'Bishop Benson's survey of the diocese of Gloucester, 1735–50' (*Gloucestershire Rec. Ser.* 13, 2000);

E. Ralph (ed.), 'Bishop Secker's "Diocese Book"' (*Bristol Rec. Soc.* 38 (1985), 23–67). [1735, 1766, 1784];

W. B. Ward (ed.), 'Parson and church in eighteenth-century Hampshire: replies to bishops' visitations' (*Hampshire Rec. Ser.* 13, 1995). [1717–88]

J. Gregory (ed.), 'The Speculum of Archbishop Secker' (*Church of England Rec. Soc.* 2, 1995). [Kent, 1758–61]

R. E. G. Cole (ed.), 'Speculum diocesis Lincolniensis sub episcopis Gu. Wake et Edmund Simpson, AD 1705–1723' (*Lincoln Rec. Soc.* 4, 1913). [1706, 1718, 1721]

H. A. L. Jukes (ed.), 'Articles of Enquiry addressed to the clergy of the diocese of Oxford at the primary visitation of the diocese of Oxford at the primary visitation of Dr Thomas Secker, 1738' (*Oxfordshire Rec. Soc.* 38, 1957);

S. Watts (ed.), 'The Visitation Returns of Archdeacon Joseph Plymley, 1782–1808' (*Shropshire Rec. Ser.* 11–12, 2010–11).

M. Ransome (ed.), 'Wiltshire Returns to the bishops' visitation enquiries, 1783' (*Wiltshire Rec. Soc.* 27, 1972);

M. Ransome (ed.), 'The State of the bishopric of Worcester, 1782–1808' (*Worcestershire Hist. Soc.* 49, 1968); [1782]

L. A. S. Butler (ed.), 'The Archdeaconry of Richmond in the Eighteenth Century: Bishop Gastrell's Notitia: the Yorkshire parishes, 1714–1725' (*Yorkshire Arch. Soc., Rec. Ser.* 146, 1990) [Very few entries of 'families']

S. L. Ollard and P. C. Walter (eds), 'Archbishop Herring's Visitation Returns, 1743' (*Yorkshire Arch. Soc. Rec. Ser.* 71–2, 75, 77, 1928–30);

C. Annesley and P. M. Hoskin (eds), 'Archbishop Drummond's Visitation Returns, 1764' (*Borthwick Texts and Calendars*, 22–3, 26, 1997–2001).

6 *(iv) 8. Wills and Probate Inventories*

There are two good guides to locating pre-1858 probate jurisdictions and their records; Camp is better than Gibson:

A. J. Camp, *Wills and their Whereabouts* (London, Camp, 4th edn, 1974), and

J. S. W Gibson, *Wills and Where to Find Them* (Chichester, Phillimore, 1974).

The best guide to using all pre-1858 probate documents is

T. Arkell *et al.* (eds), *When Death do us Part: understanding and interpreting the Probate Records of early modern England* (Oxford, Leopard's Head P, 2000).

M. Overton, *A Bibliography of British Probate Inventories* (Newcastle upon Tyne, University of Newcastle, 1983), lists all inventories printed to 1982. Later editions will be found in the 'Original Documents' section of the annual bibliographies in the *Econ. Hist. Rev.*

6 *(iv) 9. Civil parish records*

Still the best guide to civil parish records, though now in need of updating, is

W. E. Tate, *The Parish Chest: a study of the records of parochial administration* (Cambridge, CUP, 3rd edn, 1969, repr. Chichester, Phillimore, 1983, pt. 2); also useful is

E. Trotter, *Seventeenth-Century Life in the Country Parish, with special reference to Local Government* (Cambridge, CUP, 1919, repr. New York (USA) Barnes & Noble, 1968).

Still the starting-point for the history of local government is

S. Webb and B. Webb, *English Local Government* (London, Longmans, 11 vols, 1906–29, repr. London, Cass, 1963).

6 *(iv) 10. Land Tax*

Land Tax assessments rarely survive before the 1780s and their value as a historical source for landholding is disputed:

W. R. Ward, *The English Land Tax in the Eighteenth Century* (Oxford, OUP, 1953);

M. Turner and D. Mills (eds), *Land and Property: the English Land Tax, 1692–1832* (Gloucester, Sutton, 1986);

D. E. Ginter, *A Measure of Wealth. The English Land Tax in Historical Analysis* (London, Hambledon, 1992).

For the records themselves, see

J. S. W. Gibson *et al.*, *Land and Window Tax Assessments* (Birmingham, Federation of Family History Socs, 2nd edn, 1998).

6 *(iv) 11. Methods*

T. H. Hollingsworth, *Historical Demography* (London, Hodder & Stoughton, 1969);

N. Goose and A. Hinde, 'Estimating population size at fixed points in time', *LPS* 77 (2006), 66–74; 78 (2007), 74–88;

A. Hinde, 'Calculating crude birth- and death rates for local populations during the "parish register" era', *LPS* 79 (2007), 90–6;

C. Galley, 'Infant mortality', *LPS* 82 (2009), 71–7;

A. Hinde, 'A review of methods for identifying mortality "crises" using parish register data', *LPS* 84 (2010), 82–92;

6 *(v) Economic and social developments*

6 *(v) 1. Law and order*

J. R. Kent, *The English Village Constable, 1580–1642* (Oxford, OUP, 1986);

J. H. Gleason, *The Justices of the Peace in England, 1558–1640* (Oxford, OUP, 1969);

E. A. L. Moir, *The Justice of the Peace* (Harmonsworth, Penguin, 1969);

J. S. Cockburn (ed.), *Crime in England, 1550–1800* (London, Methuen, 1977);

M. Beloff, *Public Order and Popular Disturbances, 1660–1714* (Oxford, OUP, 2nd edn, 1963);

J. Brewer and J. Styles (eds), *An Ungovernable People. The English and their law in the seventeenth and eighteenth Centuries* (London, Hutchinson, 1979);

J. A. Sharpe, *Crime in Early Modern England, 1550–1750* (London, Longman, 2nd edn, 1999).

6 *(v) 2. Landscape*

B. P. Hindle, *Maps for Local History* (London, Batsford, 1988);

D. Smith, *Maps and Plans for the Local Historian and Collector* (London, Batsford, 1998) and

B. P. Hindle, *Maps for Historians* (Chichester, Phillimore, 1998)

are the best introductory guides; for specific types of map, see the following:

J. B. Harley and C.W. Phillips, *The Historians' Guide to Ordnance Survey Maps* (London, Standing Conference for Local History, 1964);

J. B. Harley, *The Ordnance Survey and Land-use Mapping: parish books of reference and the county series 1:2500 maps, 1855–1918* (Norwich, Geographical Abstracts, 1979);

R. Oliver, *Ordnance Survey Maps: a concise guide for historians* (London, Charles Close Soc., 1993);

W. Foot, *Maps for Family History: a guide to the records of the Tithe, Valuation Office and national farm surveys of England and Wales* (London, PRO, 1994);

R. J. P. Kain and R. Oliver (eds), *The Tithe Maps of England and Wales* (Cambridge, CUP, 1995);

R. J. P. Kain *et al.*, *The Enclosure Maps of England and Wales, 1595–1918* (Cambridge, CUP, 2004);

S. Hollowell, *Enclosure Records for Historians* (Chichester, Phillimore, 2000). For maps in the National Archives, see

TNA, Research Guides, Domestic Ser. 41, 46, 72, 132.

P. S. Barnwell and M. Palmer (eds), *Post medieval Landscapes* (Oxford, Windgather, 2007).

6 *(v) 3. Migration*

J. Patten, *Rural-Urban Migration in Pre-Industrial England* (Oxford, School of Geography, 1973);

D. A. Souden and P. Clark, *Migration and Society in Early Modern England* (London, Hutchinson, 1987);

I. D. Whyte, *Migration and Society in Britain, 1550–1850* (Basingstoke, Macmillan, 2000).

N. Goose and L. Luu (eds), *Immigrants in Tudor and Early Stuart England* (Falmer, Sussex Academic P, 2005);

E. Rich, 'The population of Elizabethan England', *Econ. Hist. Rev.*, 2nd ser.

3 (1950), 247–65). Rich was a pioneer in recognising the importance of local migration in England.

For the major foreign immigrants, see

I. Scoloudi (ed.), *Huguenots in Britain and their French Background, 1550–1800* (Basingstoke, Macmillan, 1987);

R. D. Gwynn, *Huguenot Heritage: the history and contribution of the Huguenots in Britain* (Brighton, Sussex Academic P, 2nd edn, 2001);

C. Roth, *A History of the Jews in England* (Oxford, OUP, 1941);

For apprenticeship, a major cause of migration until the nineteenth century, see

J. Lane, *Apprenticeship in England, 1600–1914* (London, UCL Press, 1996).

(v) 4. The clergy

A. T. Hart, *The Country Priest in English History* (London, Pheonix, 1959);

P. Heath, *The English Parish Clergy on the Eve of the Reformation* (London, Routledge, 1969);

F. Heal and R. O'Day, *Continuity and Change. Personnel and Administration of a Profession, 1558–1642* (Leicester, Leicester UP, 1976);

R. O'Day, *The English Clergy. The Emergence and Consolidation of a Profession, 1558–1642* (Leicester, Leicester UP, 1979);

R. O'Day, *The Professions in Early Modern England, 1450–1700* (Harlow, Longman, 2000), pt. 2.

(v) 5. Leisure

T. Burke, *The English Inn* (London, Batsford, 3rd edn, 1981);

P. Clark, *The English Alehouse, 1200–1830* (Harlow, Longman, 1983);

R. V. Lennard (ed.), *Englishmen at Rest and Play: some phasas of English leisure, 1558–1714* (Oxford, OUP, 1931);

(v) 6. Housing

M. W. Barley, *The English Farmhouse and Cottage* (London, Routledge, 1961);

P. M. Eden, *Small Houses in England, 1520–1820* (London, Hist. Association, 1969);

W. G. Hoskins, *Provincial England* (London, Macmillan, 1963), chap. 7;

A. Clifton-Taylor, *The Pattern of English Building* (London, Faber, 4th edn, 1987);

D. Tredale, *This Old House* (Aylesbury, Shire, 3rd edn, 1986);

O. Cook, *The English Home through Seven Centuries* (Harmondsworth, Penguin, 2nd edn, 1984) are classica studies:

for the proliferation of regional studies, see the journal *Vernacular Architecture*.

For one local study, see

J. S. Moore, 'Rural Housing in the North Bristol region, 1600–1850', in M. Baulant *et al.* (eds), *Inventaires après deces et ventes de meubles. Apparts a une histoire de la vie economique et quotidienne (XIVe–XIXe siecles* (Louvain (Belgium), Academia, 1988, 197–209).

6 (v) 7. The family

M. Anderson, *Approaches to the History of the Western Family* (Cambridge, CUP, 2nd edn, 1995);

P. Laslett and R. Wall (eds), *Household and Family in Past Time* (Cambridge, CUP, 1972);

R. Houlbrooke, *The English Family, 1450–1700* (London, Longman, 1984).

For the church courts, see

A. Tarver, *Church Court Records* (Chichester, Phillimore, 1995);

M. Ingram, *Church Courts, Ssex and Marriage in England, 1570–1640* (Cambridge, CUP, 1987);

L. Stone, *The Family, Sex and Marriage in England, 1500–1800* (London, Weidenfeld and Nicholson, 1977);

R. M. Smith (ed.), *Land, Kinship and Life-Cycle* (Cambridge, CUP, 1985);

A. Capp, *When Gossips Meet: family and neighbourhood in early modern England* (Oxford, OUP, 2003).

B. Hill, *Women Alone: spinsters in early modern England* (New Haven (USA), Yale UP, 2001);

A. M. Froide, *Never Married: singlewomen on Early Modern England* (Oxford, OUP, 2005);

P. Laslett, *Family Life and Illicit Love in Earlier Generations* (Cambridge, CUP, 1977);

P. Laslett *et al.* (eds), *Bastardy and its Comparative History* (London, Arnold, 1980), and

M. Levene *et al.* (eds), *Illegitimacy in Britain, 1700–1920* (Basingstoke, Palgrave, 2005),

deal with bastardy and its effects on the family. For bridal pregnancy, see

P. E. H. Hair, 'Bridal pregnancy in rural England in earlier centuries', *Population Studies* 20 (1966), 233–43 and

P. E. H. Hair, 'Bridal pregnancy in earlier rural England re-examined', *Population Studies* 24 (1970), 59–70 are the standard guides to this subject.

D. Cressy, *Birth, Marriage and Death. Ritual, religion and the Life-Cycle in Tudor and Stuart England* (Oxford, OUP, 1997) and

C. Dyer (ed.), *The Self-contained Village? The Social History of Rural Communities, 1250–1900* (Hertford, Hertfordshire UP, 2007) are good up-to-date guides.

A. Fletcher, *Growing up in England. The Experience of Childhood, 1600–1914* (New Haven (USA), Yale UP, 2008);

R. C. Richardson, *Household Servants in Early Modern England* (Manchester, Manchester UP, 2010).

For clandestine marriage the standard survey is now

R. B. Outhwaite, *Clandestine Marriage in England, 1500–1850* (London, Hambledon, 1995).

7. Modern England, *c.* 1750–2012

E. Royle, *Modern Britain: A Social History, 1750–1985* (London, Arnold, 1987) is a good introduction.

7 *(i) Sources*

For the nineteenth century, see

E. A. Wrigley (ed.), *Nineteenth-Century Society. Essays in the Use of Quantitative Methods for the Study of Social Data* (Cambridge, CUP, 1972),

and for the twentieth century, see

E. Lord, *Investigating the Twentieth Century: sources for local historians* (Stroud, Tempus, 1999), which is invaluable, as is

M. Drake *et al.*, *Sources and Methods for Family and Community History* (Cambridge, CUP, 2nd edn, 1997).

For increasing official numeracy and data-collection, see

E. Higgs, *The Information State in England* (Basingstoke, Palgrave, 2004).

For the 'New Poor Law', see

A. Brundage, *The Making of the New Poor Law ... 1832–8* (Ann Arbor (USA), Michigan UP, 2nd edn, 1999) and

D. Fraser (ed.), *The New Poor Law in the Nineteenth Century* (London, Macmillan, 1976).

For changes in local government areas and boundaries, see V. D. Lipman, *Local Government areas, 1834–1945* (Oxford, Blackwell, 1949), which now needs considerable updating to include the many later changes.

The essential guide to 'Blue Books' is

W. R. Powell, *Local History from Blue Books: a select list of the sessional papers of the House of Commons* (London, Historical Association, 1962).

For the archives of Parliament, see

M. F. Bond, *Guide to the records of Parliament* (London, HMSO, 1971) and

M. F. Bond, *Select List of Classes of Records in the House of Lords Record Office* (London, House of Lords Record Office, 1973).

7 *(ii)* *The modern countryside, c. 1750–2011*

G. E. Mingay (ed.), *The Agrarian History of England and Wales. VI. 1750–1850* (Cambridge, CUP, 1989);

E. J. T. Collins (ed.), *The Agrarian History of England and Wales. VII. 1850–1914* (Cambridge, CUP, 2000);

E. H. Whetham (ed.), *The Agrarian History of England and Wales. VIII. 1914–39* (Cambridge, CUP, 1978); all have regional sections.

T. Rowley, *The English Landscape in the Twentieth Centre* (London, Hambledon, 2006), and

B. A. Holderness, *British Agriculture since 1945* (Manchester, Manchester UP, 1985), between them cover the entire period.

Changes in rural society are considered in

H. A. Clemenson, *English Country Houses and Landed Estates* (London, Croom Helm, 1982);

M. Beard, *English Landed Society in the Twentieth Century* (London, Routledge, 1989);

H. J. Habakkuk, *Marriage, Debt and the Estates System: English Landownership, 1650–1950* (Oxford, OUP, 1994).

7 *(iii) Modern towns, c. 1750–2011*

M. J. Daunton (ed.), *The Cambridge Urban History of Britain, 1840–1950* (Cambridge, CUP, 2000) is the standard work on the subject.

P. J. Corfield, *The Impact of English Towns, 1700–1800* (Oxford, OUP, 1982);

A. Briggs, *Victorian Cities* (Harmondsworth, 2nd edn, 1968);

J. Brown, *The English Market Town. A Social and Economic History, 1750–1914* (Marlborough, Crowood, 1986) and

J. R. Kellett, *The Impact of Railways on Victorian Cities* (London, Routledge, 1969)

deal with various aspects of Victorian towns. Those working on individual towns should consult Richardson's *Bibliography* and the larger *Bibliography of British History* series in addition to Daunton above.

7 *(iv) Modern population, c. 1750–2011*

7 *(iv) 1. Censuses, 1801–2011*

S. Lumas, *Making Use of the Census* (London, TNA, 4th edn, 2002);

E. Higgs, *Making Sense of the Census: the manuscript returns for England and Wales, 1801–1901* (London, TNA, 2nd edn, 2005);

E. Higgs, *A Clearer Sense of the Census: the Victorian censuses and historical research* (London, HMSO, 1996);

E. Higgs, *Making Sense of the Census Revisited* (London, Institute of Hist. Studies, 2005);

TNA, Research Guide, Domestic Ser. 99.

R. Woods, *The Demography of Victorian England and Wales* (Cambridge, CUP, 2000);

H. Southall, 'A Vision of Britain through time: making sense of 200 years of Census Reports', *LPS* 76 (2006), 76–89.

7 *(iv)* 2. *Parish Registers*

The books in section 6 (iv) 1 remain relevant for the modern period.

7 *(iv)* 3. *Migration*

A. Redford, *Labour Migration in England, 1800–1850* (Manchester, Manchester UP, 1976);

D. Friedlander, *Internal Migration in England and Wales, 1851–1951* (London, Centre for Urban Studies, 1966);

D. Baines, *Migration in a Mature Economy: emigration and internal migration in England and Wales, 1861–1900* (Cambridge, CUP, 1985).

For the major foreign immigrants in this period, see

V. D. Lipman, *Social History of the Jews in England, 1850–1950* (London, Watts, 1954);

H. Pollins, *Economic History of the Jews in England* (London, Associated UP, 1982);

V. D. Lipman, *A History of the Jews in England since 1858* (Leicester, Leicester UP, 1990).

J. A. Jackson, *The Irish in Britain* (London, Routledge, 1963);

R. Swift and S. Gilley, *The Irish in Britain, 1815–1939* (London, Pinter, 1989);

R. Swift, *The Irish in Britain, 1815–1914* (London, Historical Association, 1990).

G. Davis, *The Irish in Britain, 1815–1914* (Dublin (Eire), Gill and Macmillan, 1991);

R. Swift and S. Gilley (eds), *The Irish in Victorian Britain: the local dimension* (Dublin (Eire), Four Courts P, 1999);

R. Swift, *Irish Migrants in Britain, 1815–1914: documentary history* (Cork (Eire), Cork UP, 2002);

R. Ballard *et al.* (eds), *Desh Pardesh: the South Asian presence in Britain* (London, Hurst, 1994);

R. Panayi and K. Burrell, *Histories and Memories: migrants and their history in Britain* (London, Tauris, 2006);

K. Panayi, *An Immigration History of Britain: multicultural racism since 1800* (London, Routledge, 2006).

For alien immigrants see also TNA, *Research Guides*, Domestic Ser. 50.

7 *(v) Economic and social developments*

7 *(v) 1. Roads and road-transport*

For the development of turnpike roads, see

W. Albert, *The Turnpike Road System in England, 1663–1840* (Cambridge, CUP, 1971), and

E. Pawson, *Transport and Economy. The Turnpike Roads of Eighteenth-Century Britain* (London, Academic P, 1977).

For the country carriers, see

G. L. Turnbull, 'Provincial road carrying in the eighteenth century', *Journal of Transport History* NS 4 (1977), 17–39;

A. M. Everitt, 'Country carriers in the nineteenth century', *Journal of Transport History* NS 3 (1976), 179–202, and a model local study,

K. O. Morgan, *Country Carriers in the Bristol Region in the Nineteenth Century* (Bristol, Hist Association, 1988).

For the revival of road-transport in the twentieth century, see

D. H. Aldcroft, *British Transport since 1914: an economic history* (Newton Abbot, David & Charles, 2nd edn, 1975)

J. Hibbs, *The History of British Bus Services* (Newton Abbot, David & Charles, 2nd edn, 1989);

J. Hibbs, *The Bus and Coach Industry: its economics and organization* (London, Dent, 1975);

T. C. Barker, *The Rise and Rise of Road Transport, 1700–1990* (Basingstoke, Macmillan, 1993);

T. C. Barker (ed.), *The Economic and Social Effects of the Spread of Motor Vehicles* (Basingstoke, Macmillan, 1986);

K. Richardson, *The British Motor Industry, 1896–1939* (London, Macmillan, 1977);

R. Church, *The Rise and Decline of the British Motor Industry* (Basingstoke, Macmillan, 1994);

J. Foreman-Peck *et al.*, *The British Motor Industry* (Manchester, Manchester UP, 1995).

7 *(v) 2. Canals*

L. T. C. Rolt, *The Inland Waterways of England* (London, Allen & Unwin, 1950);

C. Hadfield, *The Canals of South-West England* (Newton Abbot, David & Charles, 1967);

C. Hadfield, *The Canals of South Wales and the Border* (Newton Abbot, David & Charles, 2nd edn, 1967);

C. Hadfield, *The Canals of South and South-east England* (Newton Abbot, David & Charles, 1969);

C. Hadfield, *The Canals of the West Midlands* (Newton Abbot, David & Charles, 2nd edn, 1969);

C. Hadfield and G. Biddle, *The Canals of North-West England* (Newton Abbot, David & Charles, 2 vols, 1970);

C. Hadfield, *The Canals of the East Midlands* (Newton Abbot, David & Charles, 2nd edn, 1970);

C. Hadfield, *The Canals of Yorkshire and North-East England* (Newton Abbot, David & Charles, 2 vols, 1972–3);

Local historians should check the volume(s) for their region.

7 *(v) 3. Railways*
The best available bibliography is

G. Ottley, *A Bibliography of British Railway History* (London, HMSO, 2nd edn, 1983).

For the national history, see

J. Simmons, *The Railway in Town and Country, 1830–1914* (Newton Abbot, David & Charles, 1986);

T. R. Gourvish, *Railways and the British Economy, 1830–1914* (Cambridge, CUP, 1980);

D. H. Aldcroft, *British Railways in Transition: the economic problems since 1914* (London, Macmillan, 1968);

R. Bell, *History of the British Railways during the War, 1939–45* (London, Railway Gazette, 1946);

T. R. Gourvish, *British Railways, 1948–73: a business history* (Cambridge, CUP, 1986).

The most detailed survey is

C. H. Ellis, *British Railway History: An Outline from the accession of William IV to the Nationalization of Railways* (London, Allen & Unwin, 2 vols, 1954–9).

For pre-steam railways, see

A. Baxter, *Stone Blocks and Iron Rails* (Newton Abbot, David & Charles, 1966);

M. J. T. Lewis, *Early Wooden Railways* (London, Routledge, 1970, repr. 1974); and

C. F. D. Marshall, *A History of British Railways Down to the Year 1830* (Oxford, OUP, 2nd edn, 1971).

Local historians should check the existence of regional or local railways in their region and consult any county or regional bibliographies for their area. The easiest way to trace the existence of local railways is to scan the appropriate sheets of the first and second editions of the large-scale (6 in or 25 in) Ordnance Survey maps or to consult M. Freeman and D. Aldcroft, *The Atlas of British Railway History* (London, Croom Helm, 1986). Many regional studies are written by or for train-spotters and need to be used with caution.

7 *(v) 4. Industry*

There was a very wide range of industries in England from the medieval period onwards, both in town and country. In the modern period, their presence can be detected in a wide range of maps (Estate and inclosure maps, tithe maps and first and second editions of the large-scale Ordnance Survey), in detailed Census returns from 1841 onwards which record individual occupations and usually the number of people employed on farms or in factories, and in local directories. This will provide a foundation on which you can build as you progress back to earlier periods: Richardson's Bibliography will then guide you to appropriate books and articles. Whether industrialisation created a north–south divide is considered in

A. R. H. Baker and M. Billinge (eds), *Geographies of England. The North–South Divide, Imagined and Material* (Cambridge, CUP, 2004).

J. Tann, *The Development of the Factory* (London, Cornmarket P, 1970);

P. Joyce, *Work, Society and Politics. The Culture of the Factory in late Victorian England* (Aldershot, Gregg Revivals, repr. 1991) deal with the classic factory system.

The population-growth under industrialisation accentuated some social developments, notably the growth of child labour and of the aged poor:

P. Kirby, *Child Labour in Britain, 1750–1870* (Basingstoke, Palgrave, 2003);

S. R. Ottaway, *The Decline of Life: old age in eighteenth-century England* (Oxford, OUP, 2000);

N. Goose (ed.), *Women's Work in Industrial England. Regional and Local Perspectives* (Hertford, Local Population Studies, 2007).

More positive reactions were the rise of friendly societies and later trade unions.

P. H. J. H. Gosden, *The Friendly Societies in England, 1815–75* (Aldershot, Gregg Revivals, repr. 1993);

P. H. J. H. Gosden, *Self-Help: Voluntary Associations in the Nineteenth Century* (London, Batsford, 1973);

S. Cordery, *British Friendly Societies, 1750–1914* (Basingstoke, Palgrave Macmillan, 2003);

C. R. Dobson, *Masters and Journeymen. A pre-history of Industrial Conflict, 1717–1800* (London, Croom Helm, 1980);

J. Rule (ed.), *British Trade Unionism, 1750–1850* (Harlow, Longmans, 1988);

A. E. Musson, *British Trade Unions, 1800–1875* (London, Macmillan, 1972);

J. Lovell, *British Trade Unions, 1875–1933* (Basingstoke, Macmillan, 1990);

S. Mason, *Trade Unions and Social Change, 1750–1980* (Oxford, Blackwell, 1987).

7 *(v)* 5. Shopping

A. Adburgham, *Shops and Shopping, 1800–1914* (London, Allen & Unwin, 1964);

D. Davis, *A History of Shopping* (London, Routledge, 1966);

H.-C. Mui and L. H. Mui, *Shops and Shopkeeping in Eighteenth-Century England* (London, Routledge, 1989);

J. Benson and G. Shaw, (eds), *The Evolution of Retail Systems, c. 1800–1914* (Leicester, Leicester UP, 1992);

K. Morrison, *English Shops and Shopping: an architectural history* (New Haven (USA), Yale UP, 2003).

7 *(v)* 6. Religion and society

There is an enormous literature on modern religion, much of it being sectarian and biased: the social role of religion since the eighteenth century is studied in the following selection by historians:

W. R. Ward, *Religion and Society in England, 1790–1850* (London, Batsford, 1972);

A. Armstrong, *The Church of England, the Methodists and Society, 1700–1850* (London, London UP, 1973);

E. R. Norman, *Church and Society in England, 1770–1970; a historical study* (Oxford, OUP, 1972);

K. S. Inglis, *Churches and the Working Classes in Victorian England* (London, Routledge, 1963);

D. H. MacLeod, *Class and Religion in the Late Victorian City* (London, Croom Helm, 1974);

H. MacLeod, *Religion and the Working Classes in Nineteenth-Century Britain* (London, Macmillan, 1984);

A. D. Gilbert, *Religion and Society in Industrial England. Church, Chapel and Social Change, 1740–1914* (London, Longman, 1976).

7 (v) 7 Housing

J. N. Tarn, *Working-Class Housing in Nineteenth-Century Britain* (London, Architectural Association, 1971);

E. M. Gauldie, *Cruel Habitations: a history of working-class housing, 1780–1914* (London, Allen & Unwin, 1974);

D. Rubinstein (ed.), *Victorian Homes* (Newton Abbot, David & Charles, 1974);

M. J. Daunton, *House and Home in the Victorian City. Working Class Housing, 1850–1914* (London, Arnold, 1983);

M. J. Daunton, *Housing the Workers. A Comparative History, 1850–1914* (Leicester, Leicester UP, 1990);

M. A. Simpson and T. Lloyd (eds), *Middle Class Housing in Britain* (Newton Abbot, David & Charles, 1976);

W. V. Noble, *Trends in Population, Housing and Occupancy Rates, 1861–1961* (London, HMSO, 1971);

M. J. Daunton (ed.), *Councillors and Tenants: local authority housing, 1919–1939* (Leicester, Leicester UP, 1984);

J. Burnett, *A Social History of Housing, 1815–1985* (London, Methuen, 2nd edn, 1986);

A. J. Cornford, *The Market for Owned Houses in England and Wales since 1945* (Farnborough, Saxon House, 1979);

J. McEwan and P. Sharpe (eds), *Accommodating Poverty: the housing and living arrangements of the English Poor, 1600–1850* (Basingstoke, Palgrave, 2010).

7 (v) 8. Literacy and education

R. S. Schofield, 'The Measurement of Literacy in pre-industrial England', in J. Goody (ed.), *Literacy in Traditional Societies* (Cambridge, CUP, 2nd edn, 1981), 311–25;

D. W. Galenson, 'Literacy and age in pre-industrial England. Quantitative evidence and implications', *Economic Development and Social Change* 29 (1981), 813–31);

D. Cressy, *Education in Tudor and Stuart England* (London, Arnold, 1975);

D. Cressy, *Literacy and the Social Order. Reading and Writing in Tudor and Stuart England* (Cambridge, CUP, 1980);

M. G. Jones, *The Charity School Movement* (Cambridge, CUP, 1938, repr. London, Cass, 1964);

J. W. A. Smith, *The Birth of Modern Education: the contribution of the Dissenting Academies, 1660–1800* (London, Independant P, 1954);

H. McLachlan, *English Education under the Test Acts* [1663–1820] (Manchester, Manchester UP, 1931);

B. Simon, *Studies in the History of Education* [1780–1940] (London, Lawrence and Wishart, 3 vols, 1960–74);

B. Simon, *Education and the Social Order, 1940–1990* (London, Lawrence and Wishart, 1991);

H. Silver, *Education as History: interpreting nineteenth- and twentieth-century education* (London, Methuen, 1983);

D. Wardle, *English Popular Education, 1780–1970* (Cambridge, CUP, 2nd edn, 1976);

J. Lawson and H. Silver, *A Social History of Education in England* (London, Methuen, 2nd edn, 1984).

For the Post Office and postal service, see

J. H. Robinson, *The British Post Office* (Princeton (USA), Princeton UP, 1948) and

M. J. Daunton, *Royal Mail. The Post Office since 1840* (London, Athlone P, 1985).

7 *(v)* 9. *Law and order*

F. O. Darvall, *Popular Disturbances and Public Order in Regency England* (Oxford, OUP, 2nd edn, 1969);

G. Armitage, *The History of the Bow Street Runners, 1729–1829* (London, Wishart, 1935);

D. J. Cox, '*A Certain Share of Low Cunning'. A History of the Bow Street Runners, 1792–1839* (Cullompton, Willan, 2010).

J. M. Beattie, *The First English Detectives: The Bow Street Runners and the Policing of London, 1750–1840* (Oxford, OUP, 2012).

D. Foster, *The Rural Constabulary Act, 1839: national legislation and the problems of enforcement* (London, Standing Conference for Local History, 1982);

D. Taylor, *The New Police in Nineteenth-century England. Crime, Conflict and Control* (Manchester, Manchester UP, 1997);

S. H. Palmer, *Police and Protest in England and Ireland, 1780–1850* (Cambridge, CUP, 1988);

J. Morgan, *Conflict and Order: the police and labour disputes in England and Wales, 1900–1939* (Oxford, OUP, 1987);

D. T. Brett, *The Police of England and Wales: a bibliography* (Bramshill, Police Staff College, 3rd edn, 1979);

J. J. Tobias, *Crime and Justice in England, 1700–1900* (Dublin (Eire), Gill and Macmillan, 1979);

J. M. Hart, *The British Police* (London, Allen & Unwin, 1951);

T. A. Critchley, *A History of Police in England and Wales* (London, Constable, 2nd edn, 1978);

J. P. Marlin, *The police: a study in manpower; the evolution of the service in England and Wales, 1829–1965* (London, Heinemann, 1969);

S. Holdaway (ed.), *The British Police* (London, Arnold, 1979).

J. J. Tobias, *Crime and Industrial Society in the Nineteenth Century* (Harmondsworth, Penguin, 1972);

D. W. James (ed.), *Crime and Punishment in Nineteenth-Century England* (London, Arnold, 1975);

W. R. Cornish (ed.), *Crime and Law in Nineteenth-Century Britain* (Dublin, Irish UP, 1979);

V. Bailey (ed.), *Policing and Punishment in Nineteenth-Century Britain* (London, Croom Helm, 1981);

A. Evans, *Victorian Law and Order* (London, Batsford, 1988).

R. Wells, I*nsurrection. The British Experience, 1795–1803* (Gloucester, Sutton, 1984);

S. Palmer, *Police and Protest in England and Ireland, 1780–1850* (Cambridge, CUP, 1988);

D. C. Richter, *Riotous Victorians* (Athens (USA), Ohio UP, 1981);

R. Geary, *Policing Industrial Disputes, 1895–1985* (Cambridge, CUP, 1985);

J. Morgan, *Conflict and Order. The Police and Labour Disputes in England and Wales, 1900–1939* (Oxford, OUP, 1987).

Poaching presented special problems because of widespread popular support:

E. P. Thompson, *Whigs and Hunters. The Origins of the Black Act* (London, Allen Lane, 1975);

D. Hay *et al.*, *Albion's Fatal Tree. Crime and Society in Eighteenth-Century England* (London, Allen Lane, 1976);

P. B. Munsche, *Gentlemen and Poachers. The English Game Laws, 1671–1831* (Cambridge, CUP, 1981);

H. Hopkins, *The Long Affray. The Poaching Wars, 1760–1914* (London, Secker & Warburg, 1985);

J. G. Rule (ed.), *Outside the Law. Studies in Crime and Order, 1650–1850* (Exeter, Exeter UP, 1992).

7 (v) 10. Leisure

P. Mathias, *The Brewing Industry in Britain, 1700–1830* (Cambridge, CUP, 1959);

T. R. Gourvish, *The British Brewing Industry, 1830–1980* (Cambridge, CUP, 1994).

H. Cunningham, *Leisure in the Industrial Revolution, c.1780–c.1880* (London, Croom Helm, 1980);

J. H. Plumb, *The Commercialisation of Leisure in Eighteenth-Century England* (Reading, University of Reading, 1973);

R. W. Malcolmson, *Popular recreations in English Society, 1700–1850* (Cambridge, CUP, 1973);

J. Walton and J. Walvin (eds), *Leisure in Britain, 1780–1939* (Manchester, Manchester UP, 1983);

J. Walvin, *Leisure and Society, 1830–1950* (London, Longman, 1978);

J. A. R. Pimlott, *The Englishman's Holiday* (Hassocks, Harvester P, 1976).

7 (v) 11. Travellers' Reports

G. E. Fussell, *The Exploration of England. A Select Bibliography of Travel and Topography, 1570–1815* (London, Mitre, 1935) is the only bibliography, now in need of updating.

T. Platter (ed.), *The Journals of Two Travellers in Elizabethan and Early Stuart England* (London, Caliban, 1995);

A. Hadfield, *Literature, Travel and Colonial Writing in the English Renaissance, 1548–1625* (Oxford, OUP, 1998);

A. McRae, *Literature and Domestic Travel in Early Modern England* (Cambridge, CUP, 2009);

C. Lancaster, *Seeing England: Antiquaries, Travellers, Naturalists* (Stroud, History Press, 2008).

R. Bayne-Powell, *Travellers in Eighteenth-Century England* (London, Murray, 1951, repr. London, Blom, 1972);

R. Le Claire, *Three American Travellers in England* (Westport (USA), Greenwood, 1978);

L. Simond, *An American in Regency England: the journal of a tour in 1810–11* (London, Maxwell, 1968);

T. Mitchell, *Gleanings from travels in England* (Belfast, Smyth, *c.* 1880);

M. Brayshay (ed.), *Topographical Writings in south-west England* (Exeter, Exeter UP, 1996).

The *Gentleman's Magazie* ran from 1731 to 1922 and should be available in major libraries, as should the indexes in

G. L. Gomme (ed.), *The Gentleman's Magazine, being a classified collection of the chief contents of the Gentleman's Magazine from 1731 to 1868. Indexes: Topographical History* (London, Elliott Stock, 11 vols, 1891–1904).

G. E. Mingay, *Arthur Young and his times* (London, Macmillan, 1975).

P. Horn, *William Marshall (1745–1818) and the Georgian Countryside* (Abingdon, Beacon Publications, 1982).

G. Spater, *William Cobbett: The Poor Man's Friend* (Cambridge, CUP, 2 vols, 1982).

R. Jefferies, *Hodge and his Masters* (London, Smith Elder, 1880; repr. Stroud, Sutton, 1992).

Much topographical information will be found in diaries and auto-biographies:

W. Matthews, *British Diaries: An annotated Bibliography of British Diaries written between 1442 and 1942*, Cambridge, CUP, 1950;

W. Matthews, *British Autobiographies: An annotated Bibliography of British Autobiographies Published or Written before 1951*, Berkeley (USA), California UP, 1955;

A. Smyth, *Autobiography in Early Modern England* (Cambridge, CUP, 2010).

A. Ponsonby, *English Diaries from the 16th to the 20th Century*, London, Methuen, 1923;

A. Ponsonby, *More English Diaries*, London, Methuen, 1927.

For foreigners' views of England, see Richardson, *Bibliography*, 54, 113, and P. E. Kruger, *German Travellers in England* (n.p., Kruger, 2008).

7 (v) 12. Newspapers

Mitchell's *The Newspaper Press Directory and Advertiser* [1846–1907];

J. S. North, (ed.), *The Waterloo Directory of English Newspapers and Periodicals, 1800–1900* (Waterloo (Canada), North Waterloo Academic P, 30 vols, 1996, 2003);

D. Linton and R. Boston, *The Newspaper Press in Britain: an annotated bibliography* (London, Mansell, 1987);

D. Linton, *The Twentieth-century Press in Britain: an annotated bibliography* (London, Mansell, 1994).

7 (v) 13. Directories

The making of directories, initially of tradesmen and merchants from the later seventeenth century in London, proliferated in the next two centuries and finally covered every county and most towns. By the early twentieth century Kelly's Directories had a virtual monopoly of comprehensive directories covering every householder, though specialist directories of particular professions are still produced. For London, see

P. J. Atkins, *The Directories of London, 1677–1977* (London, Mansell, 1980).

For the rest of England, consult

J. E. Norton, *Guide to the National and Provincial Directories of England and Wales (excluding London)* (London, Roy. Hist. Soc., 1950) and

G. Shaw and A. Tipper, *British Directories: a bibliography and guide to directories published in England and Wales (1850–1950) and Scotland (1773–1950)* (Leicester, Leicester UP, 1988).

7 *(v) 14. Oral history*

Despite many people's doubts about the veracity of oral tradition, it is perhaps worth exploring since the elderly, once dead, cannot be re-interrogated.

G. E. Evans, *Ask the Fellows who Cut the Hay* (London, Faber, 1956);

G. E. Evans, *Where Beards Wag All: the relevance of the oral tradition* (London, Faber, 1970);

E. Roberts, *A Woman's Place: an oral history of working class women, 1890–1940* (Oxford, Blackwell, 1984);

J. M. Vansina, *Oral Tradition in History* (London, Currey, 1985);

G. E. Evans, *Spoken History* (London, Faber, 1987);

T. Lummis, *Listening to History: the authenticity of oral evidence* (London, Hutchinson, 1987);

E. Roberts, *Women and Families: an oral history, 1940–1970* (Oxford, Blackwell, 1995);

S. Humphries, *Hooligans or Rebels? An oral history of working-class childhood, 1880–1939* (Oxford, Blackwell, 2nd edn, 1995);

R. Perks, *Oral History: talking about the past* (London, Hist. Association, 2nd edn, 1995);

P. R. Thompson, *The Voice of the Past* (Oxford, OUP, 3rd edn, 2000);

R. Perks and A. Thomson (eds), *The Oral History Reader* (London, Routledge, 2nd edn, 2006).

Updating

As I said at the beginning, all bibliographies are out-of-date as soon as they have been completed. Updating is therefore a necessity. You may find some new items using a general search on the internet, but you will not usually find an assessment of quality. Do not fall into the trap of assuming that everything you find on the internet is correct, anymore than you would assume that every book or article is necessarily complete and correct.

For printed primary sources, the two volumes of E. L. C. Mullins, *Texts and Calendars* are continued on a free web-site maintained and updated by the Royal Historical Society:

www.royalhistoricalsociety.org/textsandcalendars.htm

At present, this site has no indexes and no SEARCH function.

For books and articles, the Royal Historical Society's *Bibliography of British and Irish History* is only available to subscribers: it is worthwhile enquiring if your local reference library is a subscriber. If not, the best substitute is the 'Annual List of Publications' in the Econ. Hist. Rev., which should be available in most reference and all university libraries.

Good luck with your research!

Index

Academies, Dissenting, 85
Accounts, farm and household 21, 102–3, 124
   manor 37, 40, 42, 73
   Tithe 73
Act, George Rose's Registration (1812) 93
   Highways (1555) 2, 83
   Lord Hardwicke's Marriage (1753) 93
   Marriage Duty Act (1695), widely disregarded 93
   Mines (1842) 129
   Rural Constabulary Act (1839) 123
   Toleration (1689) 31, 38, 98
Acts, Settlement 85, 106
Acton, Iron (Gloucs), manor of 55; fig.1
   John de, lord of Iron Acton manor (1321) 55; fig. 1
   Sir Nicholas Poyntz,
   lord of Iron Acton manor (1547) 55; fig. 3
'Addition', occupation or status 23
Administration, probate series, as indicator of
   trends in mortality 72
Advowson, the right to present a suitable clerk to the bishop for induction 44, 93
   normally first belonged to the manorial lord 44
Aerial photography 7
Agriculture,
   arable, employs less labour now than in the past 4
   more labour-intensive than pastoral agriculture 3–4
     produces more basic foodstuffs 4
   as by-occupation 19

Board of, *County Reports* 130
   common or open fields 72, 104
   dairy 4
   demesnes, land-use in 72
     size of 72
   Home Office Returns 109
   mechanization of, in modern period 4
   pastoral, less labour-intensive 4
   pasture, both common and 'several' 72
   peasant farms, size of 72
   primary occupation in
   medieval countryside 72
   rotation fallow of common field 72
   specialization in modern period 4
   still important in early modern period
     as employer of labour and supplier of foodstuffs and industrial raw materials 102–3
   surpluses, regional and international 4
   tenure 'in severalty' 72
   waste, common 72
America, North, transportation of criminals to 84
   See also USA
Analysis, aggregative 84, 139
   comparative static 27
Anglia, East, supplied food to London 5
Ancient Order of Foresters 122
Apprenticeship 85
   by poor law officers 101
Arable farming, labour requirements of 3–4
Archaeology, evidence for period
   before the Norman Conquest 7, 76

field-walking 73–4
Archdeaconry records 23
  Visitations 67, 107
Archives, episcopal, few printed cata-
    logues 99
  family, often deposited in record
    offices 17
  National Register of 18
  The National (TNA) 18, 29, 64–5
Areas, Local Government, radical
    changes in,
  in and after 1973 117
  mainly agricultural, often depressed
    in 18th and 19th centuries 103
  new industrial, often had poor living
    conditions but high wages 103
Argentina, supplied beef to Britain 5
Agricultural Returns 126
Aristocracy, Anglo-Saxon,
    disappearance of after Norman
      Conquest 51, 75
  importance of in local society 16–17
  misleading view of 25
Army, regular, helped to suppress riots
    123
Articles for training barristers, attorneys,
    solicitors and accountants 85
'As(h)ton', possible meanings of 7, 77
Assizes 54
Associations, Employers', records of 129
Atlases 25
Augustus Caesar 7
Australia, transportation of criminals
    to 84
Autobiographies, useful source 109
A2A website (local record office holdings)
    18

Baptism *See* Christening
Baptists, effects of their rise
    on christenings 87–8
Basildon (Essex), new town 120
Bastardy, legal and social disabilities of 88

rate 88
Beaufort, Dukes of 125
Beddingham (Sx), Beddingham manor
    in 15
  partly in Laughton manor 15
Bedfordshire, poor coverage of 1524–5
    Lay Subsidy 33
'Beerocracy', the 128
Bench, King's, Court of, non-return of
    Coroner' inquests 90
Beresford, Maurice, historian 67
Bibliography 163
Billinghay (Lincs), Dogdyke in 35
Birmingham Central Library 18
Birth-rate, crude 29, 34
Births, interval between and Christening/
    baptism 29, 89
  Marriages, Deaths, 1837– 9, 117–8
    Registers, access to, denied to
      historical demographers 118
    Registrar-General's Reports xi, 9, 118,
      145
  proxies or substitutes for 70–1
Bishops, registers of 44, 67
  English Episcopal Acta 67
  estates, most survived until they were
    transferred to the Ecclesiastical
    Commissioners 62
  visitations 67, 107
Bloggston (a typical manor) 62, 64
Blue Books *See* Parliament, Records of
Board of Health,
  Central 128
  Trade, regulation of
    canals and coalmining 129
Bodleian Library, Oxford, deposited
    records in 18, 61, 66
Book of Fees (London, 3 vols, 1921–31) 62
Boroughs, 'Pocket' 6
Botesdale in Redgrave (Suff) 35
Bournville, Birmingham, Cadbury's
    factory at 121
Bow Street Runners 123

Bread, white, eaten by English labourers in eighteenth century 4
Breaks, need for frequent 146
Bridal pregnancy 88
Bridges, County, rates to maintain 3
Bristol, diocese, catalogue of records 99
  disappearance of most medieval records 75
  growth in population 74
  Incorporation of the Poor 108
  major slave port in C18 128
  new town of *c.* 1000 AD 5
  no full entry in *DB* 53
  non-return of Coroner' inquests at 90
  parishes in, number of 11
  rates levied in 75
  regional capital with corporate government 74
  University of, Department of Historical Studies vii
Britain, Great, only great power with a strong representative assembly 108–9
  created by union of England and Scotland in 1707 116
  Roman, economic collapse after end of 5
British Economic and Social History. A bibliographical Guide, ed. Richardson 138
British Library, London 18
British Record Society 29
Budgets, family, rarity of 106
Building, speculative 121
Burghley, Lord, Treasurer, previously Sir William Cecil, a quantifier 116
  proposal for national copies of parish registers abortive 94
Burial rate, misleading nature of 29
Burials as source for deaths 39, 88–90
  declining parochial registration of 89
  of bastards 88
  of excommunicants and suicides 90

series, interpolation in incomplete 91
Burton, William, antiquary 60
Bus services 120, 122
Business Archives Council 104
  history 129
  records 102
Butter and cheese, making of 4

Cadbury's, chocolate manufacturers at Bournville 121
Cade, Jack, rebellion of (1450) 2
Caird, Edward, agricultural writer, author of *English Agriculture in 1851* 131
Calculator, electronic 139
Calendar of Inquisitions Post Mortem 58
Calendar of Miscellaneous Inquisitions 59
Calendars, Public Record Office 60
Cambridge University, after 1660 clergy mostly graduates of 11
  Library, deposited records in 18
Cambridgeshire, Inquest (*ICC*) 52
  includes slaves omitted from *DB* 54
  unprinted Hundred Rolls (1279–80) 59
Camera, electronic or digital, desirable 143
Canal boats 122
Companies 108, 110
  records 129
Canterbury, Prerogative Court of 39, 101
Car ownership, expanding after 1945 120
Carriers, country 119, 122
Cartae Baronum (feudal returns), 1165 61
Cartularies 66
Castles 54–5
  about 500 built by 1087 55
  centres of baronies 54
  garrisons of, omitted from *DB* 53–4
  under 50 in *DB* 55
Cathedrals, Chapter estates, history and records of 62
Catholics ('Papists'), Anglican fear of 38
  expanding numbers in C19–C20

linked to Irish immigration 121
survival of, especially in North 87
Cause and effect, not obvious to
    contemporaries 137
Census, Biblical reference to Roman 7
    Bishop Compton's (1676) 31, 38, 67,
        98
    British decennial xi, 8, 16, 23, 27, 37,
        117, 145
        ages in 8
        birthplaces in 8
        employment 24–5, 119
        enumerators' schedules, 1841–2011
            8, 24, 29, 117–9
            available in TNA 8
            and online 119
        enable local family reconstitution
            and recovery of kinship net-
            works 119
        gender in 8
        increasing detail 8
        local population in 27, 91
        margins of error in 10
        marital status in 8, 119
        names in 8
        occupations in 8, 119
        rooms, number of 8, 119
        size of local farms and businesses
            119
        Reports 9
    diocesan, of 1563 and 1603 31, 36, 67,
        94, 98
    German and Italian 8
    National, more plentiful from seven-
        teenth and eighteenth centuries 8
    regular 8
    See also Commonwealth Church
        Survey
Certificates, Settlement 106
Chancery records 23
Change, natural, totals of christenings
    less burials 84
Chantries, dissolution of 23, 31

Chantry certificates 31, 34, 44, 67
    estimates of 'houseling people' in
        31, 44
    chapel, in parish church or churchyard
        44
    purpose of 44
    recorded in various sources 44
    Commissioners of 1546, Suffolk 35
    Gloucestershire 44
Charities, local 107
Charters, Anglo-Saxon 7, 75
    non-random selection, preserved in
        ecclesiastical archives 75
    medieval 7
Cheshire, under-tenants and demesne
    lessees generally mentioned in *DB* 54
Chester diocese, Archdeaconry of
    Richmond, Western deaneries, some
    wills lost in mid-eighteenth century 101
Chichester diocese, catalogue of records
    99
Chiddingly (Sx), Chiddingly manor in 15
    partly in Laughton manor 15
Christenings, as source for births 28
    birth-baptism gap 29, 89–90
    effects of delayed baptisms 29
    mass 29
    of bastards 87
    rate, misleading nature of 29
    series, interpolation in incomplete 91
Chronicle, Anglo-Saxon 53, 75
Chronology 137
Church in England,
    courts 24
        jurisdiction included defamation,
            probate matters and slander
            24
        jurisdiction over tithes shared
            with equity and common-law
            courts 24
        division of, between 'high' (Anglo-
            Catholic) and 'low' (Evangelical)
            factions 120

fear of Catholicism 38
fear of nonconformity 38
major landholder in medieval England 55
visitation returns 38, 107
Cicero, Roman orator and lawyer 137
Cinque Ports, exempt from Tudor subsidy 33
Cistercians, lands given to, meant to be free of lay tenants, and worked by monks and lay brothers 64
Clandestine marriage 88–9
Class, middle, expansion of 12
Clergy *See* Parish, clergy *and* Parish, priests
Cloth, migration of clothmaking to countryside 73
trade in 73
Clubs, Conservative and Liberal 122
Coal Board, National 129
Commission 129
mines, inspection of 128–9
Mines Reorganization Committee 129
supplied to London from Newcastle-upon-Tyne 5
Cobbett, William, propagandist, author of *Political Register* and *Rural Rides* 130–1
Comment, contemporary, on local events 130–1
Commission, Charity 107
Coal 129
on Historical Manuscripts, Royal, *Records of British Business and Industry* 104
Commissioners, Improvement 108
Common Pleas, Court of 64–5
Commons, House of 33
Commonwealth Church Survey 38, 98
Communicants 14–15, 27, 31
lists of 28
numbers of, affected by changing age

of first communion 27, 31
See also houseling people
Communion, Holy, age of first 27, 31
taking once a year compulsory until 1689, enforced by both church and state 31
Company records, among Chancery Masters' exhibits 129
former railways 129
Complete Peerage, ed. G. E. Cokayne, V. Gibbs (London, 15 vols, 1910–59, 1998) 61
Compton Berwick (Sx), partly in Laughton manor 15
Compton Census of 1676 31, 38, 67
probably under-estimated dissenters 31
Computer, lap-top or notebook 139, 141–3
advantages of using 139–40
applications should be mutually compatible 140–1
camera (digital or electronic) useful 143
data-base 139
files, need to backup frequently to external source 140–1
lap-top batteries to be fully charged each day 141
personal (PC), desktop or office xi, 139–43
printer, inkjet or laser? 142
processor, single or dual-core? 142
programs, multi-word filenames 146
rigid spelling requirements 92, 102
specification 141–2
spreadsheet 139
'Windows', e.g. Microsoft Office 140–1
word-processing 140
Computer Shopper 142
Convents, monks and nuns omitted from *DB* 53

Cornwall, Duchy of, records of **63**
 Julian, historian **32**
 probate records of, destroyed in 1942
  101
'Coronation Street', back yards of **20**
Correspondence, private **14–15, 21, 101, 109**
Cottage gardens **19–20**
Council houses, building of **4, 20**
 sale of **20**
Council, Privy, letters and registers **124, 128**
Councils, Borough **6, 107, 110**
 County **20, 129**
 District **20, 129**
  some records lost after 1973 **129**
 Parish **20, 129**
  records liable to loss **129–30**
Counties, changes in areas (1834–1973) **118**
 (1973–) **129**
Counting, importance of **1–2**
 margins of error **2**
 misleading precision **2**
 what is to be counted **18–19**
County, again important administrative
 unit after 1889 **117**
County Histories, value of **60, 99**
Court hand, generally used in manorial
 records until c.1600 **43**
 superseded by italic hand **43**
Courts, local, of itinerant justices and
 assize judges **54**
 See also manorial courts, probate
  courts
Coventry (Warws), divided lordship in **75**
Cox, J. C., antiquary **83**
Crafts and trades, new **12**
 rural **73**
Crawley (Sussex), new town **120**
Crises, demographic, 1315–16, 1348–50,
 1550s, 1590s, 1646–9 **3**
 caused by epidemic disease or starvation **42**

decrease of after 1750 **3**
 indicated by many deaths in court
  rolls **41**
 indicated by many wills proved in
  short period **39**
 indicated by rapidly rising cereal
  prices **42**
 regional, Cumberland and Westmorland, 1590s **3**
Cromwell, Oliver, Lord Protector **123**
 re-admitted Jews to England **121**
Cromwell, Thomas, Secretary of State
 67, 82, 86
 Injunctions of **86**
Crop Returns **23, 109**
Crouch, David, historian **1**
Crown, the, estates, records of **63**
 fiscal needs of **50**
 interests of as sovereign, landlord and
  ultimate feudal superior **50**
 knight service due to **58**
 lands held directly from, 'in chief'
  58
 military needs of **50**
 'regalian right' over church estates on
  death of a bishop or abbot **58**
Cumberland, chantry certificates, no
 data for houseling people **36**
 exempt from Tudor subsidy **33**
 in Scotland until 1092 **52, 118**
 regional crisis in 1690s **3**
Curia Regis rolls **54**
Custumals (often called extents, rentals or
 surveys) **14, 23, 37, 39–42, 50, 55, 72**

Danelaw (area settled by Danes), **37**
 northern **53**
Dates, Handbook of **137**
Datestones, significance of **105**
Dating by church festivals **137**
 regnal years **137**
Death duties **127**
 Black, 1348–50 **50**

Deaths, causes of, better recorded after c.1860 118
  clustering of, indicative of prevalent disease 85–6
  proxies or substitutes for 71
Debts, extents for 55
Deeds, in cartularies 66
  Ancient, in TNA 64
  enrolled, in TNA 65
  private, in TNA 65
  private, in libraries and record offices 66
  source for field- and place-names 76, 103
    for land-use 103
    for occupations 73
Defoe, Daniel, writer 108, 130
Democracy, house-owning 20
Demography, modern, facilitated by regular Censuses and efficient registration 10
Depopulation 67
De Rochefoucald, Duc, traveller 108
Derbyshire, gaps in *DB* coverage 52
  lay subsidy poorly assessed and collected in 1524–5 33
Devon, probate records of, destroyed in 1942 101
  South Hams of 11
Diaries, may reveal friendship 101
  useful source 100
Diet, differences between classes 4
  foreigners' observations of 4
Diocesan censuses of 1563 and 1603, returns for many dioceses missing 36
  court records 23
  deposition books 100–1
  visitation records, often included population details 98–9
    variety of possible names 99
    Canterbury diocese (1557) 36, 38, 98
    Gloucester diocese (1551) 38, 99

Directories 130
  advertisements in 130
Dissenters, numbers under-estimated in Compton Census of 1676 31
Dissenting Academies 85
Districts, new ecclesiastical 120
Docks and Inland Waterways Executive 129
Dogdyke, in Billinghay (Lincs) 35
Domesday Geography series 118
Domesday Book, Survey, 1086 xi, 37, 41, 50–5, 61
  14,000 manors recorded 13
  churches and priests frequently omitted 60
  Durham and Northumberland omitted 52, 118
  enumeration of heads of household 52
  Great or Exchequer or *DB I* 51
  Lancashire, coverage scrappy 52
  Little or *DB II* 51
  name from day of doom 51
  omissions from 13, 53
  original returns or 'satellites' 51
  population enumerated for 1066 and 1086 in *DB II* 53
    mainly for 1086 in *DB I* 53
  priests often included among 'villagers' 60
  reasons for compilation 51–2
  second, Hundred Rolls (1279) 59
  slaves in, marital status unclear 53
  'survey of the whole of England' 51
  terms of reference 52
    no mention of boroughs or burgesses in 53
  thoroughness of 52–3
  unit of recording the manor 53
Dominabus, Rotuli de, 1185 50
Du Boulay, Professor Robin, historian 25
Durham [County], exempt from Tudor subsidy 33

omitted from Domesday **52**, **118**

Durham (Durh), Cathedral priory, estates of **68**
liber vitae of **70**

Dyer, Christopher, historian **67–8**

East, Middle, migrants from **12**

Ecclesiastical Commissioners, transfer of bishops' and cathedral estate records to **62**
Visitation Returns **38**

Eckington manor, in Ripe (Sx) **15**

Economics, London School of, Library **127**

Education, primary, **20**, **122**
compulsory and free after 1880s **122**, **130**

Ely Inquest (*IE*), includes slaves omitted from *DB* **54**

Enclosure awards **23**, **103**
'by agreement' **23**, **103**
maps **23**, **103**
Parliamentary **23**, **103**, **124**
progress of **103**
riots **124**

Encyclopaedias as a source **104**

England, a collection of different regions **9**, **35**
half of, enclosed by 1500 **103**
pre-industrial, comparable with modern Third World **11**
replacement of English by Norman aristocracy after 1066 **52**, **75**
Union with Scotland (1707) **116**

English Place-names Society, publications of **77**

Epidemics, cholera **3**
influenza (1556–60) **36**, **71**
smallpox **3**
'Spanish 'flu' **3**

Equipment, necessary **139–40**

Erosion, coastal, caused loss of towns and villages **64**

Error, margins of **2**, **10**, **27**, **35**

Escheators, royal **55**

Essex, hundred penny payments from **39**, **71**

Estates, break-up of large **20**
records of **14–15**, **63**
source for upper-class life **22**
ecclesiastical, records of **58**

European Union, migrants from **12**

Extents (also called custumals, rentals or surveys) **14**, **23**, **37**, **39–42**, **50**, **55**, **72**
and Inquisitions **58**
described the lord's demesne and listed free and customary tenants and their holdings with rents and services due **55**
Domesday Book a national extent **37**
for Debts (Series I and II) **58**
included manors not held in chief **58**
less plentiful for ecclesiastical estates **55**, **58**
made less frequently after c.1350 **58**
not printed in *Calendar of Inquisitions Post Mortem* before 1422 **58**
relating to Crown Debtors **58**
roughly at 30 year intervals for secular estates assumed to be held from the Crown in chief **58**

Factory records **24**, **102**, **104**

Families, data on number of **14**
reconstituted an atypical minority **84**, **92**
from court rolls **17**, **39**
from parish registers **16–17**, **84**, **92**, **139**
from wills **17**

Family life, new strains on, in C20–21 **122**

Famine, great European, 1315–17 **50**

Farm records **21**, **24**

Farming, significant supplier of foodstuffs and industrial raw materials **103** still major early modern occupation 103

Farm sizes 103

Fee, lay 43, 45

Fees, Book of (London, 3 vols, 1921–31) 62

Feudal Aids (London, 6 vols, 1899–1921) 62

Fields, common or open 41, 72, 137
    in Frampton Cotterell 45

Fielding, Sir John, magistrate 123

Fieldwork 73–4, 76
    precise location of, on maps 76

Fiennes, Lady Celia, traveller 108

Filton (Gloucs), industrialized village after 1900 120

Finberg, H.P.R., historian 76

Fines, feet of (final concords) 64–5, 103
    useful source for land-use 73, 103

Fish, Simon, Tudor pamphleteer, author of *A supplicacyon for the Beggars* (1529) 32

Fisher, F.J., historian 71

Food crises, decreasing 4

Foodstuffs, basic, for lower orders 4
    processed 24

Forest, royal 40–1

Fornication, legal and social disabilities of 88

Fox, Sir Stephen, financier 128

Frampton Cotterell (Gloucs) xii
    and District Local History Society vii, x
    coal and stone tiles titheable in 45
    expanding population after 1950 120
    extent of 1321 55; fig.1
    glebe terriers 45
    immigrants in 1930s questioned about religious affiliation 121
    interlocking parish boundaries 76
    late medieval long-house in 105
    lordship of Winterbourne and Frampton, included Stoke Gifford 76

medieval 'long house' in 107
    new residents from 1930s on mostly skilled workers in aero-engineering at Filton 120
    open fields enclosed by 1390, hence scattered glebe land in glebe terriers 45
    parish church, chantry in Gastelin chapel in 44
    survey of 1547 55; fig. 3
    tithes of coal and stone roof-tiles 45

Freemasons 122

Friendly Societies, local 119, 122
    new national 122

Friendship as found in wills 101

Fry's, chocolate manufacturers at Keynsham 121

Garrisons, castle, omitted from *DB* 53–4

Gazette (official newspaper) 120

Gazetteers 25

Geld (land-tax), assessments out-of-date and unrealistic by 1086 52

Genealogy, development into 'Family History' xii

Gentleman's Magazine, useful source 109

Gentry, importance of in local society 16–17, 25
    misleading view of 25

George, Lloyd, Chancellor of the Exchequer, ordered detailed survey of land 126–7
    records of 127

Giffard family, lords of Stoke Gifford 76

Glebe terriers 45, 125
    field-systems in 45
    local topography in 45
    natural resources in 45

Gloucester, diocesan records, catalogue of 99
    Roman origin of 5
    Vale of 118

Gloucestershire, chantry certificates for 44

Forest of Dean in 11
marriage registers after 1754, 50% give groom's occupation or status 93
Protestation not circulated in 38
Godolphins, army contractors 128
Gomme, G. L., indexer 109
Gottfried, R. S., historian 71
Government, central, growth of its powers 116–7
concerned with the 'condition of the people' 117
fears of rioting and disorder 117
reports to Parliament 117
Guide-books 104
Guilds 6

Haggard, H. R., writer, author of *Rural England ... 1901 and 1902* 131
Halesowen (Worcs) 40–1
Hall *See* Manor house
Handlist, Revised Medieval Latin 137
Handwriting, court hand 43
italic 43
old, deciphering, help with 43, 136–7
Harlow (Essex), new town 120
Harrison, Tom, pollster 130
Health, Central Board of Health 128
Hearth Taxes 29, 31–2, 38, 45, 100
compared with Compton Census 38, 100
Gloucestershire, 1672 29
fairly reliable 29, 33
lists must include 'exempt hearths' 29
Heathfield (Sx), partly in Laughton manor 15
Henry VIII, King of England 29
Hereford, bishop of, Robert of Losinga 52
Herefordshire, Protestation not circulated in 38
Hertfordshire, poor coverage of 1524–5 Lay Subsidy 33
Highways, diversion of 76

Historian, The Local 138
History, Local, area of study, agricultural type in 6
boundaries of 6
industries in 6
population of 6–7
regional economy and 6
urbanization of 6
usually a parish 12, 14
History by Numbers 143
Midland 138
Northern 138
Southern 138
oral (spoken opinion) 14, 131
Hoares, bankers 128
Hoathly, East (Sx), partly in Laughton manor 11
Hollingsworth, T.H., historian 72
mortality statistics from inquisitions post mortem 72
Home, drinking at, more common in and after C20 119
Home Counties, supplied food to London 5
Home Office, agricultural Returns 126
inspection and regulation of coal mines 128–9
Papers 124, 128
Hoskins, W. G, historian 32, 51, 76
Hours, decline in working after mid-nineteenth century 21
House, great *See* Manor
three bedroom becoming the norm after 1918 21
ownership, increasing from mid-C19 121
Household accounts 21
Comptroller of Royal Household 63
Householders, heads of household 27–8
lists of 28
Households, aristocratic, usually 50–100 after 1660 30–1
average size of 28–30, 54, 68–70

baronial, omitted from *DB* 53
data on number of 14
larger in towns 29
lords', omitted from *DB* 53
manorial lords', if resident 30, 53–4
    include domestic servants 30
    much larger than average; often
      over 100 in size 30, 37, 59
  of major barons, whether secular or
    ecclesiastic, will include knights,
    men-at-arms and clerks 30
    lost military members after 1660
    30, 59
  reconstruction of, from census
    enumerators' schedules 119
  royal, omitted from *DB* 53
  servants, apprentices, lodgers in
    urban households 29
  under-tenants and demesne lessees
    omitted except in Cheshire and
    Shrophire 54
Houseling people 35–6, 44
See also communicants
Houses, country, many built or rebuilt,
  c. 1500–1914 30
Housing, adapted to accommodate
  looms and machinery 21, 73–4
  built by paternalist employers 121
  central heating in 22
  demand for new 21, 121
  effects on landowners 122
  effects of life-cycle on 21, 105
  evidence of datestones often
    misleading 105
  evidence of surviving buildings 105
    often obliterated by 'improvement'
    105
  fixed site within a plot 104
  improved after both World Wars 21
  layout of 105
  modern improvements 21–2
  municipal, increasing from c.1880,
    decreasing after 1980s 121–2

  numbers of, in Census *Reports* 122
  number of storeys 104–5
  -ownership, growing since the
    Industrial Revolution 121
  overcrowding of 21, 105
  private building of 20
  probate inventories a major source
    for 21, 104–5
  speculative house-building increasing
    in C19 and C20 121
Huguenots, persecuted by Louis XIV,
  fled to England 121
Hundred, regional unit of administration
  37, 71
  accounts 42
  court-rolls 42
  -penny 42, 71
  Rolls, 1254–5 54, 62
  Rolls, 1279–80 37, 41, 50, 54, 59, 61
    a second Domesday 59
    copy of lost roll in Nichols' *History
      of Leicestershire* 61, 99
    coverage of, patchy 59
    unprinted returns for Cambridge-
      shire, Huntingdonshire,
      London, Norfolk, Oxford-
      shire, Rutland and Shropshire
      59
Huntingdonshire , unprinted Hundred
  Rolls (1279–80) 59
Hyde (Hants), Abbey, *liber vitae* of 70

Illegitimacy, stigma of 88
Immigrants, from European Union 12
  from Indian sub-continent 12, 121
  from 'New Commonwealth' 12, 121
  Irish 121
Improvement Commissioners 108
Indexes, of places, incomplete for small
  areas 118
  of subjects, fallibility of 117–8
Indian sub-continent, migrants from
  12, 121

Indies, West, transportation of criminals to 85
migrants from 12, 121
Industrialization, effects on labour 20, 128
higher living standards 102
major creator of wealth 128
rural, apparent by later Middle Ages 68
Industrial processes more complex in and after C19 128
regulation in C19 not well coordinated 128
Industry, coal, major wealth-producer 128
decline of heavy, 20
extractive (mining and quarrying) 73
iron, major wealth-producer 128
local effects of 4, 20, 103
migration of, into countryside 68, 73
records 104, 126
results in long-term better housing and standards of living 103
rise of tertiary services 20
rural 19, 68, 73–4
state-regulation of, divided between several bodies 128
textiles, major wealth-producer 128
wages in, higher than in agriculture 103
woollen textiles 73
Infants, unbaptised 28
interval between birth and baptism of 28–9
misleading burial rate of 29
Inns and taverns, more in C19 than before or since 119
reduction in numbers after 1918 119
tied houses 119
Inns of Chancery and Court 85
Inquisitions, miscellaneous 50
post mortem 23, 50, 62
mortality data from 72
Interest, agricultural 128

commercial 128
East India 128
West India 128
Internet, check for equipment prices 142
Interpolation in incomplete register series 90
Invasion Returns 125
Inventories *See* Probate
Ireland, destruction of central government and church records x
Iron, trade in 73

Jacobite invasions, 1715, 1745 38
Jefferies, Richard, author of *Hodge and his masters* 131
Jews as refugees 12
fleeing from Tsarist pogroms in C19 121
Nazi persecution in 1930s 121
re-admitted to England by Oliver Cromwell 121
Justices, itinerant 54
Justices of the Peace, main local law-enforcers, C16–C18 123

Keele (Staffs) xii, 88, 104, 137
'East Field' and 'Hall Field' in 104
Kent, poor coverage of 1524–5 Lay Subsidy 33
supplied food to London 5
Weald of 11
Keynsham (Som), Fry's factory at 121
Kinship in parish registers and wills 101
network, can be reconstructed from Census enumerators' schedules 119
Knights, Hospitallers 63, 104
Templars 63
Korea, South, supplies computer components to Britain 5

Labour, forced, 'servile work', services 2, 42

history **129**
Ministry of **129**
subdivision of **128**
Labourers, English, living standards of, noted by foreign travellers **109**
Lancashire, lay subsidy poorly assessed and collected in 1524–5 **33**
poor coverage in Domesday **52**, **118**
probate records partly lost in C18 **101**
Land-use, effects of changing **3–4**
sources for **72–3**, **103**
Landscape, simpler in past **137**
Land Utilisation Survey **127**
Landless inhabitants **40**
Landlords, income from rent and services **2**
Landscape, evidence of maps **7**, **76**
dispersed hamlets in **76**
field-walking **76**
nucleated villages in **76**
relict features in **7**, **73–4**
Land-Tax of 1695–6, **34**, **103**
assessments rarely survive before 1770s **34**
Land-use, effects of changes in **2**, **103**
Land Utilization Survey **23**, **127**
Landscape, earlier generally simpler **137**
Languages, medieval, help with **136**
Laslett, Peter, historian **29**, **88**
calculated low bastardy ratio **88**
suggested household 'multiplier' of 4.75 **33**
Last, Nella, reports to Mass Observation Survey **130**
Latin, medieval, generally used in all court records until 1733 **42**, **136**
guides to **43**, **137**
Laughton (Sx) **xii**, **15**
and Stockingham manors in **15**
parson of **131**
Law and order, enforced by musters in C16–C17 **123**
by Militia from 1660 **123**
by Regular army from 1658 **123**
records relating to **122–4**
Law Reports **25**
Lay fee **43**
Leicestershire, Gartree and Guthlaxton hundreds, 1279–80 Hundred Rolls for **60**
hundred penny payments from **39**, **71**
taxable population in **51**
Leland, John, traveller **108**
Length of books and articles **138**
Lever Bros, soap-manufacturers at Port Sunlight **121**
Library, Bodleian, Oxford, deposited records in **18**, **61**, **66**
British, London **18**, **66**
Cambridge University **66**
Libri vitae **68**, **70**
of Durham, Hyde and Thorney **70**
Life, quality of, sources for **21**
Life-cycle, effect on housing density **105**
Life-tables, Princeton North and West, level 7 **28**
Lincoln diocese, catalogue of records **99**
'Listings', local **9**, **29**, **33**, **69–71**
Literacy, low level amongst working classes **130**
more apparent earlier in towns than in countryside **102**
measurement of **20–1**, **74**, **100**
rise of **20–1**, **130**
effects of **20–1**
reasons for **102**, **130**
sources for, apprentice indentures **101**
bonds **100–1**
deeds (charters) **74**
ecclesiastical court depositions **100**
marriage registers after 1754 **21**, **100**
poor law documents **100**
probate inventories **74**, **100–1**
Protestation Returns **100**

Settlement records 101
  wills 74, 100–1
Liverpool (Lancs), a major slaving port
  in C18 128
Living, Standard of, sources for 21
London, corporate government 74
  extents for debts listed 59
  food-supply of 5
  fuel-supply of 5
  growth of, in area and population 74
  lay subsidy of 1524–5 missing 33
    for 1535–6 33
  no full entry in *DB* 53
  non-return of Coroner' inquests 90
  parishes in, number of 11
  prisons, 'marriage shops' attached to 89
  Roman origin of 5
  suburbs ('Metroland') 120
  unprinted Hundred Rolls (1279–80)
    59
  School of Economics, Library, archives
    of Land Utilisation Survey in 127
Lords, House of, Record Office,
  now Parliamentary Archives 23, 117
Lordship of Winterbourne and Frampton
  76
Losinga, Robert of, bishop of Hereford 52

Magazines as a source 25
Maitland, F. W., historian 76
Major Generals, rule of 123
Making History Count 143
Males, adult 28
Manor, accounts 37, 40, 42, 72
    field-names in 42, 76
    field-systems in 42, 74–6
  place-names in 76
  prices and wages in 42, 73
  and hundred 42
  and parish 37
  Anglo-Saxon charters, recorded in 53
  boundaries, and parish boundaries
    11–16, 37, 53

possible changes in, over time 60
centre, *caput manerii* 13, 53
  soke in the northern Danelaw 53
  of barony or substantial
    subtenancy 54
court-rolls 14–15, 37, 40–2, 54, 73
  may indicate landless squatters 40
  occupations in 41
  peasant land-market in 41–2
  place- and field-names in 75–6
  topographical information in 41,
    45
  could extend over more than one
    parish 53
courts 24
demesne (home farm) 40, 55, 72
    indicated by modern names
      Court, Hall, Home, Manor,
      Farm 40
    rarely more than one-third of
      manor's cultivated area 72
    size of 72
descent of 16, 60–2
    modern distaste for 16, 61
    relevance to local history 61
extents, rentals, surveys 14, 23, 37,
  39–40, 43, 55–6, 58–9, 62–3, 76
    place- and field-names in 76
    parish clergy normally not found
      in 43
fragmentation of 62–3
    by subinfeudation 62
    by grant to a religious institution
      62–3
    by division among co-heiresses 63
history of 15–16
house, often near parish church 14
identification of 64
identification of *DB* manor with later
  manor(s) 60–2
independent freeholders 40
land-use in 72, 126
    sources for 72–3

main unit of record in *DB* 53

not necessarily identical with parish of same name 53

outliers often called 'berewicks' 54

part usually of a larger estate 17

some not mentioned in Domesday 13, 54

still significant in much of England in the early twentieth century 53

tenants, enumerated in custumals, 'extents', rentals and surveys 14–15, 23, 39–40, 55

    of other lords in same area 40

    problem of landless 40

    under-tenants 40

    size of farms 72, 119

Manorial lords, changing policies towards labour services and peasants' personal status 68

usually founders of parish churches 44

households of, if located at an estate-centre 59

    may include domestic servants and military retainers 30, 59

often owned the advowson of the local parish church 44, 93

role of in contemporary society 17–18, 60

well above average household size 30, 59

visible in post-*DB* sources 54

records, source for upper-class life 22

Manors, 'reputed' 15

Manpower, military, Crown's need for 50

Maps, evidence of, for boundaries 7

    for landscape 7, 76

    Enclosure 23, 76

    Estate 41, 77

    Ordnance Survey, large scale 7, 41, 76, 126

'Parish Books' 126

Tithe 7, 24, 41, 77, 125–6

Marchant, R. A., historian 90

Markets, weekly, some still flourishing in C19 119

Marriage Act, Lord Hardwicke's (1753) 93

    Duty Act (1695) 93

    series, interpolation in incomplete 90

    'shops' 89

Marriages, clandestine 88–9

    of pregnant brides 88

Mass Observation Survey 130

Mathew, William, vicar of Tickenham (Som) 89

Meadow, scarcest land in Domesday England 76

Meat, mostly consumed in past by upper classes 4

Medicine, modern, facilitates explanation 10

Methodists, divisions in after John Wesley's death only reversed by re-union in the 1920s 120

'Metroland' (London suburbs near Metropolitan Underground lines) 120

Middlesex, extents for debts listed 59

Midlands, work in after 1750 better paid in 12

Migration 9, 11, 84–5, 92

    betterment 85

    desperation 84

    effects on family reconstitution 92

        on vital rates 85

    immigration better recorded in the C19 and C20 9, 118

        in times of crisis, often inaccurate record 118

    involuntary (removal) 84–5

    often under-recorded 9, 118–9

    occurred from Middle Ages onwards 9–10, 84

Military service, men fit for 14–15, 27

Survey, Tudor **xi**

Militia helped to suppress riots **123**
    records **23**

Milton Keynes (Bucks), new town **120**

Miners' strike (1984) **124**

Modus (payment in lieu of tithes) **125**

Monasteries, dissolution of **23**, **62**, **64**
    estates of, secularized after the disso-
        lution **62–4**
        ecclesiastical status of **66**
    lands given to **62–4**
    population of, omitted from *DB* **53–4**
    sources for, sparse **54**, **59**

Mortmain, royal licences to give land
    in **44**

Multipliers **27–8**, **31–2**, **34–6**, **49**, **51**,
    68
    at best a compromise **35**
    margins of error in **27**, **35**

Museum, British **25**

Musters **14–15**, **23**, **40**, **50**
    numbers problematic **32**, **35**
        vary widely from year to year **34–5**
    of men aged 15–60 **34**
    enforced public order in C16–C17,
        not very effectively **125**

Names, field- and place- **7**, **76–7**
    often in Anglo-Saxon charters and
        later sources with Old English
        elements but not in *DB* **54**
    map of, as source for local topography
        77
    sources for **76–7**, **103**

National Archives, The (TNA) **18**, **23**, **29**
    website, not infallible **18**

National Farm Survey (1941–3) **127**

National Register of Archives **18**

Newcastle-upon-Tyne, supplied coal to
    London **5**

Newspapers as a source **14**, **16**, **21**, **25**,
    104, **130**
    advertisements **104**, **130**

stamp duty on, reduced, then
    abolished **130**

'New Towns' **5**, **20**, **120**

Nichols, J, historian, author of *History
    and Antiquities of the County of
    Leicester* **61**, **99**

Ninths, inquisition of the, 1342 **73**

Noble titles, English, descended to eldest
    son **109**

Nonconformist Church records **17**

Nonconformity, fears of growing **38**, **98**

Norfolk Broads **11**
    churches 'appraised with the manors'
        in *DB* **60**
    unprinted Hundred Rolls (1279–80)
        59

North, harrying of the **52**
    work in after 1750 better paid in **12**

Northumberland exempt from Tudor
    subsidy **33**
    omitted from Domesday **52**, **118**

Norwich (Norf), non-return of Coroners'
    inquests **90**
    number of parishes **11**
    number of taxpayers, 1524–5 **32**
    Valuation of, 1254 **67**

Note-form outline of topics **143–5**

Nottinghamshire, Sherwood Forest in
    11, **118**

Numbering the people **2**

Numerals, roman, generally used in
    records until c.1600 **43**
    differences between classical
        and medieval numerals **43**

Observers, foreign, noticed improved
    labourers' diet in the eighteenth
    century **109**

Occupational surnames **41**

Occupations, range of local **41**, **77**
    sources for, apprentice indentures and
        registers **102**
        bonds **102**

christening registers from 1813 93
deeds 73, 102
ecclesiastical deposition books 100–2
marriage registers
after 1754 93
Oath rolls 102
parish registers 93, 102–4
poor law documents 102–4
probate inventories 73, 102–4
Sacrament Certificates 102
Settlement records 101–2
wills 73, 101–2
Occupiers, rates paid by 2
Oral history 14
Order, public, threats to 3
Orders, Lower, improvement of 3
Removal 106
Ordnance Survey maps, Parish Books 126
Orwell, George, satirist, author of *1984* 22
Oxbridge College, lands of 63
Oxford University, Library,
deposited records in 18, 61, 66
after 1660 clergy mostly graduates of 11, 116
Oxfordshire, unprinted Hundred Rolls (1279–80) 59

Papists, official requests for numbers 98
Parish, advowson 44
and manor 11–14, 53
as unit of study 14
boundaries 12–14
chantry, recorded in various sources 44
chapel 44
priest 44
chapelries 13
often become parishes later 13–14, 66–7
status of 67

charities in 107
church, appropriated 44
often had a chantry chapel 44
often near manor house 14
usually first built by the lord of the manor 44
rates to maintain 2
status acquired by *c.* 1100 66
churchwardens, accounts 107
civil supervisory powers 83, 106
original functions still remain 107
churchyard 45
civil 12–13, 83, 106, 117
loss of most civil powers in 1894 117
records 106–7
clerk 87
constable 125
in medieval period a manorial appointment 125
later elected by the parish vestry 125
Councils 20, 129
ecclesiastical 12
fees 45
glebe land 43
terriers 63, 75
householders, lists of 28
main unit of local administration 83
medieval, purely ecclesiastical unit 83
most common unit of study 12, 14
not an isolated unit 84
number of, in sixteenth century 13, 83
officers, identification and listing of 107
overseers of the poor 24, 83, 106
accounts 107
parsonage house 43
part of a deanery and a diocese 17
rector and rectory 43–4
Registers and Records Measure (1972) 17

Registers *See* Registers, Parish
surveyors of highways (waywardens)
    24, 83, 106
    accounts 107
tithes, great and small 43
tithing, unit of taxation 12
vestry 24, 83, 123
    minutes 107
    supervisory civil powers of 83
        lost in 1894 20
vicar and vicarage 43–4
Parish priest 43
    absent or careless 82
    at the centre of local society 116
    expelled during Civil War 82
    in *DB*, often included in villagers 60
    medieval, mostly illiterate 116
        often had co-resident assistant
            priest and housekeeper 44
        often married before *c.* 1250 44
        supposed to be celibate 44
        usually celibate after *c.* 1250 44
    mostly married graduates by 1600 85,
    116
    often a relative of the lord of the
        manor 14
    post-Reformation, usually married 44
    Puritan, ejected in 1662 82
    Rector and vicar 43–4
Parliament, Acts, Local and Personal 117
    Private 117
    authorized grant of powers to local
        authorities 110
    records of (Blue Books) 14, 16, 21, 25,
        110, 117
    records of evidence submitted and
        scrutinised by sub-committees 117
Parliamentary Archives, formerly House
    of Lords Record Office 23, 117
Pastoral farming, labour-requirements
    of 2, 19
Pauper children, apprenticing of 106
PC Advisor 142

PC Pro 142
Peasants' Revolt, 1381 2
Peculiar, Ecclesiastical, area exempt from
    diocesan control 39
Peasants, medieval, mainly visible in
    manorial records 54
'People, Numbering the' 2
Peterborough (Nhants), soke of 53
Peterloo (Lancs), riot at 123
Period, early modern 2, 8, 10–13, 31,
    34–6, 43
    medieval 2, 8, 10–13, 30, 35, 39, 42–4
    modern 1–2, 9, 11, 21, 53
    prehistoric, archaeological evidence
        for 76
    evidence of field-names 77
    Romano-British, evidence of field-
        names 77
Peterloo (Lancs) 123
Photographs, aerial 7
    topographical 7
Pipe Rolls (Exchequer accounts) 61
Place-names *See* Names, field- and place-
Plague 50
    See also Black Death
Poaching 124
Pocket boroughs 6
Police, British Transport 123
    County and Borough Forces 123
    Metropolitan Police Force 123
        records of, at New Scotland Yard
            and TNA 123
Political arithmetic 116
Poor, the, migration in search of work 12
    'non-settled' 106
    numbers of 3
    relief of, by civil parish 14–15, 24, 83,
        106
Poor houses 106
Poor Law, New (1834–1929) 117
    Old (1572–1834) 14–15, 24–5, 106
    records 14–15, 21
    Unions 117

basis of Highway, Sanitary and School Boards, and most Urban and Rural District Councils 117

Population, age-structure 19, 27–8
  in 1522–5, derived from Wrigley and Schofield's computer program 33
  changes in levels of, causes and effects still arguable 6–8, 116
  composition of 3, 19
  counts, direct 9, 27–8
    few for large areas 29
  crises 36, 91
  decline of, later medieval 50, 67–8
    caused mainly by epidemics of 'plague' 67
  estimates pre-1801 problematic 8, 27, 35
    1538–1841, derived from parish registers 8
    causes and effects of, still debateable 8–9
    for groups of parishes preferable to single parish 36
    margins of error in 27
  excessive, effects of 3
  family reconstitution and 16–17, 84, 92
  forecasting of, controversial 10
  government interest in number and condition of 116–7
    results of 117
  growth of, 1086–*c*. 1315 49–50
    c. 1315–*c*. 1450 50
    c. 1480–*c*. 1555 50
    effects of 4
  history, 'dark ages of' 9, 49, 82
    'direct' approach to 9, 16–17
    'indirect approach to 9, 16, 28–9, 49, 70–1
    sources for 28–9
    importance of 3
    main problems of x

  sources and methods xi
  interpolating missing events 91
  'listings' 9, 29, 69
  long-term trends in 6
  local, and local history 6–7
  interpolation between estimates hazardous 10
  medieval, problems with 49
    modern estimates 49–50
    sources for 50, 67–70
  migration and 9–11
  modern medical knowledge and 10
  monastic, omitted from *DB* and generally sparse 54
  multipliers 10, 27–8, 33, 35–6, 49, 71
    margins of error in 10, 27
  national, causes and effects still debateable 8
    course established by Censuses 8
    but not entirely accurate 10
  occupational structure 19–20
  overcrowding 6
  results of excess 4
  sex-ratio 19
  short-term fluctuations in 6
  size of, optimum 3
  social structure of 19–20
  sources, indirect 28, 50
  total 19
  trends, evidence of prices, wages and rents 70–1
    fluctuating and difficult to assess 6–7, 70–2
  urban, as part of total 74, 121
  village, nineteenth-century 20

Port Sunlight, Wirral (Chesh), Lever Bros' factory at 121

Ports, Cinque, exempt from Tudor subsidy 33

Postal service, cheap after 1840 122

Power, Ministry of 129

Poyntz chantry in Frampton Cotterell

church 44
Nicholas, Sir, lord of Iron Acton manor, in Frampton Cotterell survey of 1547 55; **fig. 3**
Robert, founder of the Poyntz chantry in Frampton Cotterell church 44
Pregnancy, bridal 88
Prerogative Court of Canterbury 39
Prices and wages, sources for 73
Prints and drawings 7
Prisons, development of modern system 124
Probate accounts 21
inventories 21, 24, 73–4, 100–1, 103–5
source for crops, furniture, housing, land-use, literacy, livestock, occupations, and tools 24, 73–4, 100–1
See also: Wills
Professions, recruits to ` 12
Programs *See* Computer, programs
Projection, back 28
general inverse 28
Protestation Returns of 1641–2 38, 100
not circulated in Gloucestershire or Herefordshire 38
mostly adult males or heads of household 38
Roylists often refused to sign 38
Public Record Office (now TNA) 25
Calendars 60
Publication, copyright 150–1
editing a text for 149–50
illustrations for 150
indexing a text 151–2
references 152–3
submitting a text 148–9, 153–5
Publishers of local history
Amberley of Stroud 153
Bredon of Derby 153
History Press of Stroud 153
Oxbow/Windgather of Oxford 153
Phillimores of Andover 153
Pucklechurch (Gloucs), ancient parish 67

chapelries of Westerleigh and Wick and Abson 67

Quakers, effects of their rise on christenings 87
good registration-system of 87
Quarter Sessions, judicial aspect of the county 117
records of 23
removal disputes settled 106–7
Quia Emptores (1290), statute ending subinfeudation 62
Quirinius, governor of Roman Syria 7
Quo Warranto proceedings 54, 62

Railway Companies 110, 129
Railways 122
Raleigh, Sir Walter, adventurer 33
Ramsay, Nigel, historian, author of *English Monastic Estates, 1066–1540* 63
Rank, social, sources for *See under* Occupations
Rate books 103
Rate-payers, number of 3
Rates, birth- and death-, difficult to calculate before parish registers begin in 1538 71
problems in calculating 85–6
reasons for changing 86
church 2
Commissions of Sewers 2
county bridges 2
highway 2
vital, changes in 85–6, 91
difficulties in estimating 91
effects of migration on 85–6
Ravenserodd (Yorks) 64
Rebellion, Jack Cade's (1450) 2
Records, family, often deposited in local record offices 17
legal 23
Records of British Business and Industry, 1760–1914 104

Rector and rectory, different from vicar and vicarage 43
Rectories, appropriated 44
Redgrave (Suff), Botesdale in 35
Refugees, Huguenot 121, 145
  Jewish 12
  Middle Eastern 12
  Protestant 12
Region, geographical, typicality of 17
  need to look at wider 17
  varying characteristics of 35
Regions, England and Wales a collection of 9
Register of Archives, National 18
Registers, bishops' 67
  Parish xi, 7–8, 14–15, 34, 82, 144–5
    additions by clergy 93–4
    aggregative analysis of 16–17, 84, 92–4, 139
    as parish memoranda books 93–4
    family reconstitution from 16, 84, 92, 139
    good source for christenings, marriages and deaths 82
    illegible through use of gall 83
    incomplete registration 86–7
    later gaps, especially during Civil War and Protectorate 82, 87
    little state interest in 93–4
    many lost or damaged 82–3, 87
    most start in 1558–60 82
    northern, generally start later and less complete 87
    number of, in seventeenth and eighteenth centuries 83
    occupations or status in 94
    only about 100 go back to 1538 82
    originally on paper 82
    places of residence in 94
    prominent notice of nobility or gentry frequently found 94
    reasons for losses 82–3
    recopied on parchment after 1597–8 82, 87
    registration not contentious issue 87
    start in 1538 82
    transcripts of (archdeacons', bishops') 83
    under-registration in 87–90
Religious adherence radically declined in C20 121
  institution, giving land to a 63
  motivation for new settlements 121
Removal of poor 85
Rent 2
Rentals (often called custumals, extents or surveys) 14, 23, 37, 39–42, 50, 55, 72
Research, aims of 138–9
  possible publication 138–9, 146–8
    book or articles 146–8
  where to start? 136–8, 143–6
Returns, Agricultural, 1866–1988 126
Revolt, Peasants' (1381) 2
Revolution, French, effects of 3
Ridge and furrow 74
Right, regalian, of Crown 58
Riots, enclosure (1760–1845) 124
  food (1780–1840) 124
Ripe (Sx), partly in Laughton manor 15
  Eckington and Ripe manors in 15
Roads, maintenance of, by civil parish 2–3, 24
Rolls, *Cartae Antiquae* 65
  Charter 65
  Close 63, 65
  Confirmation 65
  Curia Regis 66
  Fine 63
  Hundred, of 1254–5 54, 62
    of 1279–80 37, 50, 54, 59–60
  Patent 65
  Pipe 61, 63
  Plea, of Common Pleas 65

Rolls-Royce Ltd, aero-engine factory at Filton **120**

Rose, George, Registration Act (1812) **93**

Rotary Associations **122**

Rotuli de Dominabus, 1185 **50**, **68–70**

Round, J. H., historian **69**

Russell, J. C., historian **72**
  household multiplier of 3.5 **68**
  mortality statistics from inquisitions post mortem **72**
  Rutland, unprinted Hundred Rolls (1279–80) **59**

Sale particulars and plans **41**

Salesmen, travelling **119**

Salt, trade in **73**

Salt, Titus, factory-owner, built houses for employees **121**

Sanders, I.J., historian, author of *English Baronies, their origin and descent, 1086–1327* **61**

Sandringham (Norf) **63**

Schofield, Roger, historian **2**, **7**, **28**, **33**, **82**, **139**

Schools, Grammar **85**
  See also Academies, Dissenting

Scotland, Cumberland and Westmorland in until 1092 **52**
  different administrative records **x**
  Union with England (1707) **116**

Seebohm, Frederic, historian, author of *The English Village Community* **136**

Serf lists, Spalding **68**

Servants, domestic, many in lordly households **30**

Service, Military **2**
  See also Musters
  National Health **63**

Services, Labour **2**

Sessions, Quarter, heard appeals on settlement affairs **107**

Settlement [= Law] **85**, **101–2**, **106**

Settlements [= places], outlying, reasons for **14**

Severalty, meaning of **137**

Sherwood Forest **118**

Shops, Co-operative **119**
  town, faced more competition in C20 **119**
  village, more in C19 than before or after **119**
  records **24**

Shrewsbury (Salop), hundred penny payments from **39**

Shropshire, lay subsidy poorly assessed and collected in 1524–5 **33**
  under-tenants and demesne lessees generally mentioned in *DB* **54**
  unprinted Hundred Rolls (1279–80) **59**

Slater, William, vicar of Tickenham (Som) **90**

Slaves, female, probably unmarried servants in *DB* **53**
  male, probably heads of household in *DB* **53**
  often omitted from *DB* in E. Midlands but found in Cambridgeshire and Ely Inquests **54**

Slums, urban **20**

Sneyds of Keele, landowners, built new 'Keele Hall' **104**

Societies, Agricultural **131**
  early, generally simpler **137**
  most, hierarchical in structure with assumed Divine approval **22**

Society, a Local History **135**
  membership of **135**
    support of **135**
    talking to **146**
    possible publication by **138**
    starting **135**
    talking to **146**
    working as a team **135**
    British Record **29**

British School 130
National 130
Royal Agricultural, of England 131
Royal Bath and West of England 131
simpler in the past 137
Soils, character and quality of 68
Soke, a manorial centre in the northern
    Danelaw 53
of Peterborough 53
Soldiers, number of 3
Somerset, probate records of, destroyed
    in 1942 101
Sources, nature of 13
Spalding (Lincs), serf lists from 68
Specialization, commercial, increasing in
    and after C19 128
Spelling, variations in, reasons for 102
Squatters on waste 40
Staffordshire, gaps in Domesday coverage
    52
    lay subsidy probably poorly assessed
        and collected in 1524–5 33
Stamp, Sir Dudley, geographer 127
Standard of living difficult to assess 105
    evidence from budgets sparse 105
    periods of employment often
        unknown 105
State Papers, Domestic Series 123, 128
Statute *Quia Emptores* (1290) 62
Stevenage (Herts), new town 120
stoc, Old English meanings of 76
Stockingham manor, in Laughton (Sx)
    15
Stoke Gifford (Gloucs), also known as
    Winterbourne Giffard 76
    owned by the Dukes of Beaufort 125
    part of the lordship of Winterbourne
        and Frampton 76
    tithes restricted to a few fields 125
Stores, British Home 120
    chain 119
    department 120
Studies in British Business Archives 104

Local Population 138
Study, unit of 11–12
    parish as 14
Subinfeudation 62
Subsidies, Clerical 67
    Lay, 1290s – 1330s 33, 37, 49–50
        fairly reliable, but probably lists
            headed by lords and their
            stewards 34, 51, 54
        unsafe basis for estimating total
            population 33–4, 51
        useful for agriculture and industry
            73
    1524–45 fairly reliable xi, 33
    lists headed by lords and their
        stewards 54
        1524–5: tax-payers mostly adult
            male married householders 32,
            50
        exempt areas in sixteenth
            century Cumberland, Dur-
            ham, Northumberland, West-
            morland and the Cinque Ports
            33
    1544–5, fewer taxpayers than 1524–5,
        excluding labourers taxed in 1524–
        5 33–4
        comparison with chantry certifi-
            cates of 1546–8 34
        records did not survive as well as
            those of 1524–5 33
Suffolk, chantry commissioners of 1546
    35
Sugar, consumed by labourers in the
    eighteenth century 4
Suicide rate 90
Surnames, need to record variant forms
    and cross-reference to standard form
    92
Survey, Commonwealth Church, 1650
    38, 98
    National Farm Survey 127
'Survey, Military', 1522 xi, 50

Surveys (often called 'custumals', extents or rentals) 14, 23, 37, 39–42, 50, 55, 72
Survivals, pre-feudal 76
Sussex, University of, Library 130
    Weald of 11

Taiwan, supplies computer components to Britain 5
Taunton (Som), hundred penny payments 39, 42, 71
Taverns and inns, more in C19 than before or since 119
Tax, income 34
    Land of 1695–6 34
Tax-payers 14–15, 27–8
    numbers of, problematic 3, 32
    before 1334, doubtful guide to population 34
    in 1524–5 mostly adult male married householders 32
    in Norwich in 1524–5 32
Taxatio Papae Nicholai IV (1291) 67
Taxes,
    Direct 2, 32
        source for upper classes 22
        See also Subsidies, Lay, and Taxes, Hearth
    Hearth 3, 23, 29, 32, 34
        compared with Compton Census 31
        exempt hearths, need to include 29
        listed in exemption certificates 29
        generally reliable in 1660s and 1670s 33
        Gloucestershire, 1672 29
    Land, 1695, records rarely survive before c.1770 34
Telford (Salop), new town 120
Temperance movement 119
Tenterden (Kent), burial of suicide at 90
Thatcher, Mrs Margaret, prime minister, sale of council houses by 20

miners strike and, 124
Thornbury (Gloucs), vicar of 93
Thorney (Cambs), Abbey, *liber vitae* of 70
Thrupp, Sylvia, historian 71
Tickenham (Som), birth-christening gap 89–90
    vicars of, *see* Mathew, William, Slater, William
'Tied houses', in towns by C19 119
Tithe, accounts 73
    awards and Maps 23, 63, 125–6
    files 126
Tithe-free land, usually former monastic property 125
Tithes, great and small 43
Tithing, as unit of tax-collection 12, 14
    often the same area as parish or chapelry 13–14
TNA *See* National Archives
Tobacco, smoked by labourers in eighteenth century 4
Topography, historical sources for 7
Towns, borough councils in some 5–6, 74–5, 107
    better documentation 107–8
    churches and charities in 75, 107–8
    county 74
    'county in itself' 75
    commercial, financial and administrative services in 5, 75
    complexity of processes 128
    decline into 'rotten boroughs' 107
    finishing trades in 5
    greater density of population 4–5
    growth of 5–6
    guilds in 5, 75, 108
    hinterlands of 5
    imports sold in 5
    industries in 5, 20, 68, 128
    luxury crafts in 5
    market 75
    new 5, 20, 109

number of parishes in 11
origin of some 5
overcrowding in 6
Parliamentary constituency 75
population of, medieval, as share of
    total 74
    growth through immigration 6
    more than half of national
        population lived in towns by
        1851 121
rates levied on urban properties 75
reasons for growth of 5–6, 68
rents from urban property 5, 75
revenues from tolls at gates 75
revival of, in late Anglo-Saxon period
    5
roles of 5–6, 74
Roman 5
royal, self-governing 74–5
shops, more in Victorian times than
    before or since 119
specialization in 5, 128
supply-areas of, widening 5
tenure (burgage) 5, 68
unincorporated 75, 108
    evolved out of rural manor 75,
        108
    similar size to large villages with
        markets and fairs, but different
        in function 75
    unions of parishes for poor law
        purposes 108
    varying fortunes in early modern
        period 107
    walls 5, 75
    wider range of trades and industries
        in C19–20 than earlier 128
Trade, Board of, Mines Department 129
    coastal 5
    in coal, iron and salt 73
    long-distance 73
    Union branches, rise and decline of
        119, 122, 129

Transcripts of parish registers, Bishops
    or Archdeacons' 83, 94
    none during the Civil War or
        Interregnum (1642–60) 94
    some still being made after 1850 94
Transport, air- 4
    canals 4
    Companies 108
    improvements in, effects of 4
    Ministry of 129
    Railway Companies 110, 129
    River navigations 4
    Roads (Turnpike) 4
        Trusts 108, 110
Transportation of criminals 84–5, 124
Travellers' reports 108–10
    native and foreign 108
    varying interests of 108–9
Treasury Board Papers 124, 129
    Solicitor's records 124
Tunstall (Kent), birth-christening gap
    89–90
Turnpike Trusts 25, 108, 110
    records of 25
Typewriter, electric 139

Unemployment 106
Unit of study, possible choice of 11–12
    choice of, constrained by
        availability of sources 13
Units, administrative, boundaries of 7
University, Cambridge, post-Reformation
    clergy at 85
        students at 11
        University Library 18, 66
    Oxford, post-Reformation clergy at
        85
        students at 11
        Bodleian Library 18, 61, 66
Urbanization 5–6
USA, supplied wheat and beef to Britain 5
Using Computers in History 143

Valor Ecclesiasticus (1535) **44**, **58**, **63**, **67**

Valuation Office records **23**

Vernacular architecture, local tradition in **73**
    Journal **106**

Vicar and vicarage, different from rector and rectory **43**

Vicarage, 'ordination of' **43**

Victoria County History (*VCH*) **60–2**

VCH (Yorkshire, East Riding) **61**

Villagers' access to towns improved by bus services and increasing car ownership **120**

Villages, deserted **67**, **74**, **76**
    expanding after 1918, especially after 1945 **120**
    shops, more in Victorian times than before or since **119**

Visitation Returns, varying names of **99**

Wage-rates as substitute for money wages **105**

Wages, money **106**

Waldron (Sx), partly in Laughton manor **15**

Wapentake, regional unit in the Danelaw **37**, **71**

War, English Civil (1642–8) **31**, **82**, **92**
    period of poor registration **82**

Welwyn Garden (Herts) **121**

Westerleigh (Gloucs), chapelry of Pucklechurch **67**

Westmorland, chantry certificates, no data for houseling people **36**
    exempt from Tudor subsidy **33**
    in Scotland until 1092 **52**, **118**
    regional crisis in 1690s **3**

White, Sir George, 'Bristol' aircraft factory at Filton **120**

Whitfelde, John, suicide, buried at Tenterden (Kent) **90**

Wick and Abson (Gloucs), chapelry of Pucklechurch **67**

Wigston (Leics), estimated population of, in 1524–5 **32**

Will-counts, compared with burials **39**

William I, King, 'the Conqueror', and Domesday **51–2**

William II, King, 'Rufus', conquered Cumberland and Westmorland from Scotland in 1092 **52**

Wills, as proxy for burial or death series **39**, **71–2**
    compared with burials after 1538 **39**
    jurisdiction over, with church courts until 1858 **24**
    large increases in, indicate onset of epidemic disease **39**
    probate series of **24**, **71–2**
    source for chantry foundations **44**
    source for bequests, literacy, occupations, and personal relationships **24**, **71–3**, **100**, **102**

Wiltshire, extents for debts printed **59**
    hundred penny payments from **39**, **42**

Winchester (Hants), no full entry in *DB* **53**

Winterbourne (Gloucs),
    chantry land of Poyntz chantry in Frampton Cotterell in **44**
    in lordship of Winterbourne and Frampton **76**
    Giffard, alternative name for Stoke Gifford **76**

Woolworths **120**

Worcester, bishop of, estates of **68**
    John of, chronicler **52**
    William of, antiquarian **108**

Worcestershire, lay subsidy poorly assessed and collected in 1524–5 **33**

Word limits **138**, **147**

Work, after 1750 better paid in Midlands and North **12**

after 1900 most no longer home-based 21

place of, in home or outside 6

World, modern 'Third', comparable with pre-industrial England 11

Wrigley, E. A. (Sir Tony), historian 2, 7, 28, 33, 82, 139

Writer's and Author's Handbook 153

Writing a local history 146–55
    editing for publication 149–50
    endnotes or footnotes 152
    illustrations 150
    indexing 151–2
    need for a preliminary outline 147
    proof-reading 149–50
    publishing 153–5
        Conventions 153–4
    references 152–5
    releasing copyright 150–1
    royalties for a book 149
    submitting a text 148–9
    word-limits 138, 147–8

Year,
    New Style, beginning 1 January 137
    Old Style, starting 25 March 72, 137

Yeomanry regiments helped to suppress riots 123

York, growth in area and population 74
    Diocese, Exchequer and Chancery probate series 39, 101
    regional capital with corporate government 74
    Roman origin of 5

Yorkshire, gaps in Domesday coverage 52
    lay subsidy poorly assessed and collected in 1524–5 33
    West, probate records partly lost in C18 101

You, the reader, ? a novice, ? member of a Local History Society, ? with some historical knowledge 135

Young, Arthur, agriculturist, author of *Annals of Agriculture* 30–1